An Introduction to the Study of the Pentateuch

An Introduction to the Study of the Pentateuch

Bradford A. Anderson

First edition by Paula Gooder

Bloomsbury T&T Clark
An imprint of Bloomsbury Publishing Plc

B L O O M S B U R Y
LONDON · OXFORD · NEW YORK · NEW DELHI · SYDNEY

Bloomsbury T&T Clark

An imprint of Bloomsbury Publishing Plc

Imprint previously known as T&T Clark

50 Bedford Square
London
WC1B 3DP
UK

1385 Broadway
New York
NY 10018
USA

www.bloomsbury.com

BLOOMSBURY, T&T CLARK and the Diana logo are trademarks of Bloomsbury Publishing Plc

First published 2017

© Bradford A. Anderson and Paula Gooder, 2017

Bradford A. Anderson and Paula Gooder have asserted their right under the Copyright, Designs and Patents Act, 1988, to be identified as Authors of this work.

British Library Cataloguing-in-Publication Data
A catalogue record for this book is available from the British Library.

ISBN: HB: 978-0-5676-5638-4
       PB: 978-0-5676-5639-1
       ePDF: 978-0-5676-5637-7
       ePub: 978-0-5676-5640-7

Library of Congress Cataloging-in-Publication Data
A catalog record for this book is available from the Library of Congress

Cover image © The Church of Pater Noster, 1615. Photograph by Zev Radovan.

Typeset by Integra Software Services Pvt. Ltd.

Contents

List of Maps

List of Tables

Preface

This introduction to the study of the Pentateuch is designed for students who are new to the subject. With this in mind, the book is divided into two parts. The first part, 'Getting to Know the Pentateuch' (Chapters 1–6), offers a concise introduction to the Pentateuch as a collection, as well as to each of the five books, looking at issues such as structure and content, as well as significant themes and theological concerns. These chapters aim to orient the reader to the content, story, and themes of the Pentateuch. The second part, 'Thematic and Critical Explorations', explores a number of elements related to the academic study of these books and the collection as a whole. While not every text and topic can be covered, an attempt has been made to offer a broad range of relevant issues and interpretive approaches. This part begins by situating the study of the Pentateuch in an academic context with explorations of 'The Origins and Formation of the Pentateuch' (Chapter 7) and 'Academic Approaches to Reading and Studying the Pentateuch' (Chapter 8). It then moves to investigating the content, themes, and scholarship of smaller sections of the Pentateuch, looking at the primeval history of Genesis 1–11 (Chapter 9); the ancestral narratives of Genesis 12–50 (Chapter 10); Moses and the exodus as recounted in Exodus 1–15 (Chapter 11); the material known as 'the law' in the Pentateuch (Chapter 12); and the texts related to the wilderness wanderings (Chapter 13). In these chapters, various historical, literary, and theological issues related to these parts of the Pentateuch are explored, highlighting elements that are important for the study of these particular texts and traditions. Finally, Chapter 14 explores the reception of the Pentateuch – that is, how these texts have been used and understood in religious traditions, as well as their impact in broader social and cultural contexts.

Although the book can be read from front to back, it is not necessary to do so. Readers may wish, for example, to consult the chapter introducing Genesis (Chapter 2) before looking at those outlining issues in the primeval history (Chapter 9) and the ancestral narratives (Chapter 10), and so on.

Acknowledgements

First edition

Thanks are due to many people who, in their different ways, have contributed to the writing of this book. I first began thinking about issues surrounding the interpretation of the Pentateuch through my teaching at Ripon College Cuddesdon and would like to extend my thanks to all those students who have helped me to think and rethink my ideas.

Thanks are also due to John Davies for his tireless efforts in the library of Ripon College Cuddesdon, tracking down references and seeking out new publications when I needed them. I am also grateful for the help of Catherine Grylls and my husband, Peter Babington, who read drafts of this book and offered helpful comments for its improvement.

I dedicate this book to my daughter, Susannah Joy, whose own beginnings took place while I wrote it.

Second edition

A number of people have been instrumental in the development and completion of the second edition of this volume. The staff at Bloomsbury T&T Clark has been both encouraging and resourceful during the course of this project, and thanks are due to Dominic Mattos and Miriam Cantwell in particular for their patience and direction. Several friends and colleagues have offered insightful comments on elements of the volume, including Jonathan Kearney, Joel Lohr, Walter Moberly, Konrad Schmid, David Shepherd, and James Watts; their input is greatly appreciated, and the book is much stronger for their careful attention. Colleagues at Mater Dei Institute and Dublin City University have been very supportive in helping create space for the development of this book, and worthy of special thanks in this regard are Ethna Regan and Andrew McGrady. Finally, research for the volume included a visit to the École biblique et archéologique française de Jérusalem, and thanks are due for the hospitality which was shown there.

Abbreviations

AB	Anchor Bible
ABD	*Anchor Bible Dictionary*, New York: Doubleday
ANE	Ancient Near East
ANET	*Ancient Near Eastern Texts Relating to the Old Testament*
BBC	Blackwell Bible Commentaries
BETL	Bibliotheca Ephemeridum Theologicarum Lovaniensium
BZABR	Beihefte zur Zeitschrift für altorientalische und biblische Rechtsgeschichte
BZAW	Beihefte zur Zeitschrift für die alttestamentliche Wissenschaft
CBQ	*Catholic Biblical Quarterly*
CC	Continental Commentaries
EBR	*Encyclopedia of the Bible and Its Reception*, Berlin: de Gruyter
FAT	Forschungen zum Alten Testament
HTR	*Harvard Theological Review*
IBC	Interpretation: A Bible Commentary for Teaching and Preaching
JAJ	*Journal of Ancient Judaism*
JANES	*Journal of the Ancient Near Eastern Society*
JBL	*Journal of Biblical Literature*
JJS	*Journal of Jewish Studies*
JPSTC	Jewish Publication Society Torah Commentary
JSOT	*Journal for the Study of the Old Testament*
JSOTSup	*Journal for the Study of the Old Testament Supplement Series*
JSS	*Journal of Semitic Studies*
JTS	*Journal of Theological Studies*

LHBOTS	Library of Hebrew Bible/Old Testament Studies
NCBC	New Cambridge Bible Commentary
NRSV	New Revised Standard Version
OBO	Orbis Biblicus et Orientalis
OTG	Old Testament Guides
OTL	Old Testament Library
SBL	Society of Biblical Literature
SBLSymS	Society of Biblical Literature Symposium Series
VTSup	Vetus Testamentum Supplements
WBC	Word Biblical Commentary
WMANT	Wissenschaftliche Monographien zum Alten und Neuen Testament
ZAW	*Zeitschrift für die Alttestamentliche Wissenschaft*

Part One

Getting to Know the Pentateuch

1

The Pentateuch – Introductory Issues

The Pentateuch: What is it?

What is the Pentateuch? Broadly speaking, the Pentateuch is a collection of five books – Genesis, Exodus, Leviticus, Numbers, and Deuteronomy – that stands at the beginning of the Bible in both the Jewish and Christian traditions. However, when we begin to dig a bit deeper, we see that there are various ways in which this question can be answered.

In one sense, the Pentateuch is a collection of writings that are part of a larger 'library', the Bible, and because of this, the stories, laws, and other elements found in these pages are considered sacred for Jews and Christians. From this perspective, these texts are Scripture, which means that they have a privileged, authoritative place in these religious traditions (even if this can vary quite dramatically between these traditions, as we will see throughout this volume).

In another sense, the Pentateuch is a literary collection and can be read as a story. Indeed, the placement of these books at the beginning of the Bible suggests that this is a story of beginnings. Genesis famously begins by describing creation: the beginning of the whole world and of humanity. Yet, on reading further, it becomes clear that the whole of the Pentateuch is describing the beginnings of the people of God, from Abraham and his descendants to the people who follow Moses out of slavery in Egypt. These books, in a variety of ways, are interested in questions of origins: Where has the world come from, and why is it the way that it is? Who are the people of Israel, and what is their story? The Pentateuch, then, is a story that narrates multiple beginnings: the beginning of the world and the origins of Israel.

From yet another perspective, the Pentateuch is an object of critical enquiry. As we will see in subsequent chapters, questions ranging from the origins of this collection to those exploring issues of gender in these texts have fascinated readers for centuries, and such issues are still the subjects of intense scrutiny today. In fact, the Pentateuch has served as the starting point for many of the larger developments in critical biblical studies over the past several hundred years.

The Pentateuch, then, can mean different things to different people, and can be understood in several different (yet sometimes overlapping) modes: as sacred text, as story, and as an object of critical enquiry. While readers may naturally be drawn to one perspective more than another, it is important to recognize the multifaceted nature of the Pentateuch, and to be open to examining these texts from a variety of vantage points.

Naming the collection

The title of the present volume refers to the collection in question as the 'Pentateuch', a term which refers to a five-volume work. However, these books are referred to in a number of other ways that reflect their content and number.

In the Hebrew Bible, reference is made to 'the torah/law', 'the book of Moses', 'the law of the LORD', or some combination of these (see, e.g., Ezra 7.10; 10.3; Neh. 8.3; 8.18; Dan. 9.11; Mal. 4.4). In parts of the New Testament reference is also made to 'the law' and 'the law of Moses' (see, e.g., Mt. 12.5; Mk 12.26; Lk. 2.23-24; Jn 7.23; Gal. 3.10). Although these references seem to indicate material found in the first five books of the Bible, it is unclear exactly how these titles relate to what would become known as the Pentateuch. Nevertheless, the use of these titles is instructive as they reflect the nature of the material found in these books, as well as their association with Moses, who in many ways is the central character in this collection.

In Jewish tradition, these first five books are most often referred to as *Torah*, a term commonly translated as 'law', but which in fact has a much broader range of meaning (including 'instruction' or 'teaching'). This designation can be seen in the structure of the Hebrew Bible in the Jewish tradition, where the canon is divided into three sections with the Hebrew names of *Torah* (law, instruction), *Nebi'im* (prophets), and *Ketubim* (writings). The first letter of the name of each section gives the acronym *TaNaK*, by which many Jews refer to the Hebrew Scriptures. In Jewish tradition these five books can also be referred to as *ḥumash*. This term is related to the Hebrew word for 'five', and is probably an abbreviated form of the phrase *ḥamishah ḥumshe ha-Torah* ('the five fifths of the Torah'). It is possible that this Hebrew phrase is the basis for the term *Pentateuch*, a word that originated in Greek and which indicates a five-volume work (Ska 2006).

It should be kept in mind that the term 'Torah' is used in a number of ways in Judaism. For example, an idea that developed in rabbinic Judaism was that Moses received the whole Torah on Mount Sinai, but that this was made up of two parts: 'written Torah' and 'oral Torah'. Both were passed down from generation to generation: the 'written' in the form of what we have in the Bible and the 'oral' in the teachings of the Rabbis (see Mishnah *Pirke Avot* 1.1). While 'Torah' is a complex term and can be used to refer to many things, our focus in this volume is on the notion of the written Torah, the first five of the biblical books.

Unity and diversity in the Pentateuch

A unified collection

We noted above that the Pentateuch can be read as a story which recounts the origins of the world and the emergence of the people Israel. Indeed, each of the five books is explicitly linked with that which precedes it, so that there is a natural progression as one makes their way through the Pentateuch.

Within this, there are a number of recurring themes and theological concerns that also give a sense of unity to the Pentateuch. For example, the character Moses plays a vital role in all four of the books following Genesis. If there is a main character in the Pentateuch, it is Moses, and his role is a thread that holds these books together. One might also note the theme of creation; while this is of obvious importance in Genesis 1–2, chapters which outline the origins of the world and of humanity, creation is a recurring theme in the Pentateuch. We see resonances of this theme, for example, in the flood account (Genesis 6–9), as well as in Israel's exodus from Egypt (Exodus 14).

Another recurring idea is that of covenant. A covenant is a special contract or agreement, and we find this theme throughout the pentateuchal material. God first makes a covenant with Noah, promising never again to destroy the earth with a flood (Genesis 9). Later in Genesis, God chooses Abraham and his family to be his special people (Genesis 12), and makes a covenant with Abraham, which indicates a special relationship (Genesis 15). Later still, the whole of Israel is set apart as a chosen people, and a covenant is established between God and Israel (Exodus 20; Deuteronomy 6).

Thus, both in the literary flow of the collection as well as in the characters, themes, and concerns found within it, there is a unity to the Pentateuch that suggests purpose and continuity.

A diverse and complex collection

While the Pentateuch can be read as a unified whole, we also need to keep in mind that it is a large and diverse collection which took shape over a long period of time. This diversity can be seen in a number of ways, including the various genres and perspectives we encounter when reading these books.

The Pentateuch begins with Genesis, a book composed primarily of narrative material, which, along with some genealogies, outlines the beginning of the world and humanity, as well as stories of Israel's ancestors. The second book, Exodus, also contains narratives, in this case detailing Israel's escape from slavery under the leadership of Moses. However, Exodus also introduces us to another genre that will be important in the Pentateuch: law and legal material. It is here that we first encounter Israel's law, most famously the Ten Commandments, which were received at Mount Sinai. Leviticus, the third book of the Pentateuch, continues with a focus on law. However, in Leviticus the emphasis is largely on issues of holiness and ritual, related to religious practice and right living. The book of Numbers, meanwhile, is a diverse collection of genres, including stories, laws, and even censuses, all of which recount Israel's time in the wilderness. Finally, Deuteronomy, the final book in the Pentateuch, is presented as one long speech from Moses delivered to the Israelites before his death, but it too is diverse, containing stories and laws as well as ritual elements. Thus, in the Pentateuch we find narratives (with distinct styles), genealogies, diverse laws, along with other genres such as poems and hymns – and very often the pentateuchal material jumps from one to another with little warning. These diverse genres, and their relationships to one another, point to the complexity of the Pentateuch as a literary collection.

The Pentateuch is also diverse in the perspectives which it puts forward. Several of these issues will be outlined in greater detail in the following chapters, but a few examples are worth noting. It has long been noted that the first two chapters of Genesis appear to contain two creation accounts: the first account (1.1–2.4) offers a transcendent, 'God's-eye' view of creation, and is written in a more poetic and repetitive fashion. The second account (2.4-25), meanwhile, is more 'earthy': it takes place on the ground, is focused on God's engagement with his creation, and is written in a more flowing narrative style that continues into Genesis 3. It seems likely that two accounts were brought together, in part because they were understood to complement one another, even if offering differing perspectives on the creation story. Other examples abound: stories of the patriarchs are told more than once with details or characters changed in the various retellings, Deuteronomy seems to revise and rework laws that are found in Exodus 20–23, Numbers and Deuteronomy offer differing perspectives on Israel's time of wandering in the wilderness, and so on.

These issues are complex and have been the subject of much scholarly debate; indeed, the issues of diversity have been important elements in the search for the origins and formation of this collection, issues which are the focus of our attention in Chapter 7. However, for now it is worth noting that such examples highlight the fact that the Pentateuch exhibits a diversity of voices and perspectives. While the Pentateuch can be read as a unity, this does not imply a singularity of perspectives or viewpoints. Rather, this story is told through a rich multitude of voices, and in many ways gives witness to a living and dynamic tradition, with dialogue and interpretation built into the very fabric of these texts.

Why do we highlight these issues here? The fact that the Pentateuch exhibits both unity and diversity has implications for the ways in which this collection is read and interpreted, as different approaches focus on different aspects of the text. Throughout this book we will be exploring how both unity and diversity are important elements that need to be considered when studying the Pentateuch.

Further reading

There are a number of helpful introductions to the Pentateuch which approach the collection from varying perspectives, including Blenkinsopp (1992), Fretheim (1996), Ska (2006), and Kaminsky and Lohr (2011). On the various ways of approaching the Bible – including as sacred text and as object of enquiry – see Sommer (2015). Issues related to the unity and diversity of the Pentateuch are discussed in Ska (2006).

The Book of Genesis

Introductory issues

The Bible begins – in all branches of the Jewish and Christian traditions – with the book of Genesis. In the Jewish tradition, names for biblical books are often based on the first word of the Hebrew text or an important word that occurs early on. Thus, in the Jewish tradition this book is referred to as *Bereshit*, the first word in the Hebrew text and which translates as 'in the beginning'. The English title for this book, Genesis, comes from the Greek term *geneseos*, from which we get the word 'genealogy'. This word was probably chosen as the title because it is, in the Greek Septuagint, found throughout the book within the genealogical lists (see Gen. 5.1) and signals the idea of beginnings. Both are fitting titles for the book, yet they serve as another reminder of the different ways that Jews and Christians use these shared texts. Genesis is the longest of the books of the Pentateuch, and is fifty chapters in modern translations.

Structure and content

There are a number of ways in which the structure of Genesis can be understood. One such approach looks at the use of the Hebrew term *toledot*, meaning 'generations', which can be found throughout the book (Gen. 2.4, 5.1, 6.9, 10.1, 11.10, 11.27, 25.12, 25.19, 36.1, 36.9, 37.2). In light of this recurring term, the book of Genesis can be seen as a story of generations, from creation down through the family of Abraham. Another approach, which we will follow here and elsewhere in this volume, is to divide Genesis broadly into two sections (though not equal in length): chs 1–11, known as the primeval history, and chs 12–50, referred to as the ancestral narratives. In terms of genre, the book is almost exclusively composed of narratives, with genealogies punctuating these stories and serving to guide the reader. What follows is a brief overview of the book of Genesis; a number of the issues raised here are discussed in greater detail in Chapter 9 (Primeval History) and Chapter 10 (Ancestral Narratives).

Genesis 1–11 is often referred to as the Primeval History, and contains famous stories such as the creation narratives and the account of Noah and the flood. These chapters are quite distinct from the stories that we find later in Genesis, as these first chapters tend to be more universal in scope and more mythic in nature. The book begins with the story of creation (Genesis 1–2), which is told in two distinct accounts. The first account (1.1–2.4) gives a God's-eye perspective on the origins of the world, and is told in a very structured, poetic manner. The second account (2.4-25) offers a more intimate, 'on the ground' account, told in a more story-like fashion that focuses on the creation of humanity. The second of these stories is intimately connected to what follows: the temptation scene in the Garden of Eden (Genesis 3). This is the first in a series of stories that seems to be trying to explain why, if God created a good world, things so often seem to be so bad. Thus, we have the temptation of Adam and Eve in ch. 3, followed by the first murder in the Bible with the story of Cain and Abel in Genesis 4. In Gen. 5.1–6.8 we encounter the first of the genealogies that play an important role in Genesis; this particular account traces the human story from Adam to Noah. It is the story of Noah, his family, and the great flood that occupies Gen. 6.9–9.29. Following another genealogy in ch. 10, Genesis 11 begins with the story of the Tower of Babel and the confusion of languages. In 11.10 we find another genealogy, a significant one as it leads to the story of Abraham. What we find in these chapters, then, is a story of creation and subsequent corruption: what starts off with God's good creation is depicted as a world descending into increasing disobedience and chaos.

Genesis 12–50, meanwhile, contains what are known as the ancestral (or patriarchal) narratives. At this point, the story of Genesis narrows its focus to one family. Though there are other characters that play important roles in these chapters, for convenience we can note that there are basically three sections within Genesis 12–50 that revolve around three of Israel's ancestors: the stories of Abraham (chs 12–25), the stories of Jacob (chs 25–36), and the stories of Joseph (chs 37–50).

In Gen. 11.27, the story turns its attention to Abram and Sarai, later to become Abraham and Sarah. Chapter 12 begins with the call of Abram, and the family's subsequent move from Ur of the Chaldeans (Mesopotamia, or modern-day Iraq) to the land of Canaan. Abraham's call introduces several important elements in the story, including the promise which God makes to provide offspring for Abraham as well as the promise of the land. What follows are numerous stories that recount Abraham's trials and successes (Genesis 12–25). One key issue relates to the lack of offspring, as both Abraham and Sarah are advancing in age. Eventually a miracle child is born – Isaac – and the story will continue with him, though the story of the unchosen son Ishmael, born to the handmaiden Hagar, introduces an important (and difficult) theme of divine election that recurs throughout these stories. The final scene that showcases Abraham is found in Genesis 22, where he is asked to sacrifice Isaac, the child of promise. This complex scene highlights Abraham's status as the obedient and faithful patriarch, though as will be discussed in subsequent chapters, this story has provoked much conversation through the ages.

Although Isaac is the son of Abraham and Sarah, he is, in fact, given relatively little space in the story of Genesis. Rather, after he has found his wife Rebekah, the story moves quickly on to their sons, Jacob and Esau (Genesis 25–36). While it is clear that Abraham is a model of faith and obedience, Jacob is a more complex character. Born just after his elder twin Esau, Jacob's life is filled with competition and strife with his brother from the very beginning. Although he is the younger son, Jacob, through a series of events that show his cunning and perhaps lack of moral scruples, becomes the son who will continue the line of Abraham, and he is the one through whom the story will continue. An important element of Jacob's story is that he is renamed 'Israel', the name by which the people descended from Abraham will eventually become known.

The final portion of the book (Genesis 37–50) follows the story of Jacob's twelve sons, and in particular Joseph. Because Jacob favours Joseph, his brothers fake Joseph's death and he is sold into slavery; thus, the favoured son ends up far from his family, in Egypt. Following a series of trials and tribulations, Joseph is able to demonstrate his worth, and he works his way up to become a significant figure in the Egyptian hierarchy. A famine in Canaan leads to a serendipitous reunion, as Joseph's brothers come to Egypt for food, unaware of their brother's rise in this foreign land. After putting his brothers to a test, Joseph reveals his identity, and is reunited with his siblings and, eventually, his father. And this is where Genesis comes to an end: Abraham's family is indeed continuing to grow. However, they are in Egypt, outside of the land of promise, leaving a sense of unfinished business, even with the happy family reunion.

Taken together, we find in Genesis 1–11 a series of stories that are universal in scope, while chs 12–50 narrow the focus onto one family, that of Abraham, whose progeny will eventually become the people Israel. As such, Genesis is a story of *beginnings*, plural: the origins of the world and humanity, and the emergence of Israel's ancestors.

Themes and theological issues

Genesis is a fascinating book that introduces a number of very significant themes – issues which are not only important for understanding the book itself but also vital for making sense of the Pentateuch and indeed the broader Hebrew Bible.

The first issue worth noting is that Genesis introduces some important concepts about the nature of the world and of humanity. As is made clear in the creation narratives, the created world is inherently good (Gen. 1.4, 10, 31); the goodness of creation is foundational and was considered important enough to place it at the forefront of Israel's story. Along with this, the first two chapters speak of human nature as, in some sense, divinely imbued. Humanity is created in the image of God (1.26), and is God-breathed (2.7). However, this is not the whole story; the authors and compilers of these texts knew well that life is difficult, and that there is injustice, hardship, and death. And so the stories of Genesis 3–11 introduce concepts such as disobedience, chaos, and violence that might be seen as attempts to make sense of the world as it is experienced.

A second significant theme introduced in Genesis is that of the chosen people. As the story focuses in on Abraham and his descendants, it becomes clear that this family is set apart, chosen by God. God promises to bless (*barak*) Abraham and his progeny: they will become a nation, and will inherit the land of Canaan. We also find here the introduction of the notion of covenant (*berit*): God makes a special contract agreement with Abraham and his descendants that he will be their God and they will be his people. This idea of covenant will continue in the subsequent books of the Pentateuch in the story of Israel. However, this idea of a chosen or elect people also brings complications: if some are chosen, this implies that some are not chosen. And so the notion of 'insiders' and 'outsiders' introduces strife, conflict, and pain between siblings, parents, and various others (Kaminsky 2007).

Finally, Genesis introduces us to the God of the Bible. What is this God like? Well, we immediately encounter the complexity of these issues in the first two chapters of Genesis. In the first creation account, God (*elohim*) is transcendent: wholly apart from the created order, God simply speaks the world into being. In the second account of creation, the LORD God (*yhwh elohim*) is immanent: here God is on the ground, involved with his creation, walking and talking, getting his hands dirty (literally) in the creation of humanity. We also see various sides to God's character in the story of the flood (Genesis 6–9): Israel portrays its God as just and demanding holiness, and yet merciful and responsive. As we will see below, some of these different aspects of God's character may have emerged from diverse sources and traditions that have been brought together in these texts; however, it remains the case that these traditions were combined to form a coherent whole which holds these different dimensions together in a purposeful tension. The God of Genesis is completely other, yet intimately involved with his creation and his people; he is holy and demands holiness, yet is known for extending second chances.

You may have noticed that the names used for God in the creation accounts of Genesis 1 and 2 are slightly different. The first account uses the Hebrew term *elohim*, which is most often translated into English as 'God'. This was a standard term used elsewhere in the ancient Near East (ANE) to refer to a god or the gods (it is a noun that can be rendered as singular or plural). The second creation account uses *elohim* along with the personal name for Israel's God, YHWH, sometimes referred to as the *Tetragrammaton*. English translations most often translate this phrase as 'LORD God'. The name YHWH contains no vowels and so is, in a sense, unpronounceable. In the Jewish tradition this name is never pronounced, and it is common when reading the Hebrew text to replace this word with the term *adonay*, another word that means 'lord'. In Christian traditions it has become more acceptable to vocalize and pronounce this name, often as Yahweh. We will see in subsequent chapters that these differences in how God is named can be found throughout the Pentateuch, and this would become one of the primary issues that inspired early critical scholars of the Bible to posit different sources or traditions for these texts. In what follows we will most often make reference to 'God', unless a specific context calls for a differentiation between divine names. The question of pronouns in relation to God is another complex issue. For the sake of convenience we use 'him' and 'his' to refer to Israel's God, though this is not without problems.

Critical issues

Genesis brings to the fore a number of critical issues, some of which were touched on in the summary offered above. Indeed, Genesis has served as ground zero for a number of issues that have driven academic biblical studies over the past several centuries. These receive fuller treatment in Chapters 7–10, but we highlight them here briefly.

First, a key concern is the question of the authorship and origins of Genesis and, indeed, the other books of the Pentateuch. A number of issues – including recognition of two distinct creation accounts, stories which are told more than once, and the different names used for God – have led readers to enquire about the unity and authorship of Genesis. The book itself, of course, is anonymous. While early tradition associated Genesis (and the entire Pentateuch) with Moses, it is quite clear that there are elements in the text that suggest it contains multiple traditions brought together over time. We explore this in greater detail in Chapter 7.

The second issue relates to questions of history. What kind of stories are these? Are they history or historically accurate? Are they true? (And what do we mean by true?) These questions have been asked down through the centuries, but have become more prominent in the modern period. This has been exacerbated by social and cultural issues such as debates surrounding creation and evolution and supposed discoveries of Noah's ark, as well as discoveries from the ANE that have shed light on biblical material. These are complex but important issues, and we discuss them further in Chapters 9 and 10.

Further reading

There are numerous helpful commentaries on Genesis that give greater space to some of the above-mentioned themes and issues. The commentaries of Gunkel ([1910] 1997) and von Rad ([1956] 1972) are now dated but remain insightful. Other helpful commentaries include Brueggemann (1982), Wenham (1987, 1995), Westermann (1988), Sarna (1989), Fretheim (1994a), and Arnold (2008). A helpful starting point in relation to literary and historical issues is Sarna (1966). Critical and thematic issues are explored in the essays found in Wenin (2001) as well as Evans, Lohr, and Petersen (2012). Moberly (2009) and Briggs (2012) helpfully introduce some of the major theological concerns of Genesis.

The Book of Exodus

Introductory issues

Exodus is the second book in the Pentateuch, and, at forty chapters, is also the second longest. The Hebrew title for this book is *Shemoth*, a word meaning 'names'. This term occurs in the first verse of the book: 'These are the *names* of the sons of Israel who, accompanied by their households, entered into Egypt with Jacob' (Exod. 1.1). The English title of the book comes from the key event that takes place in the first part of the book: the parting of the Red Sea leading to the exodus of the Israelite slaves from Egypt.

Structure and content

The book of Exodus can be divided into four sections. The first part, Exod. 1.1–12.36, tells of the Israelites' life in Egypt. This is followed by the recounting of the exodus from Egypt, found in 12.37–15.21. Exodus 15.22–18.27 describes the first stages of the people's movement away from Egypt and their journey to Sinai. In the final part of the book, Exodus 19–40, we find the initial giving of the law at Sinai, followed by a description of the Tabernacle, the portable tent shrine used in the wilderness, along with instructions regarding its construction and use.

The prologue to the book connects the story of Exodus to that of Genesis. Genesis ends with Joseph, his father, his brothers, and their families settling in Egypt. Exodus commences by recounting those from Jacob's family who made this journey (1.1-5). Over time, we are told, the family multiplies and grows 'so that the land was filled with them' (1.7). The family is now becoming a people, called the Israelites (they're also referred to as the Hebrews). The narrative recounts that the goodwill shown towards Joseph and his family does not last, and the Egyptians, fearing a revolt, enslave the Israelites (1.8-14). To make matters worse, the Pharaoh issues an order that all sons born to the Israelites are to be killed to curb their growth (1.15-22).

It is at this point that Moses comes on the scene. Born to Israelite parents, Moses is hidden in an attempt to save his life from the royal decree

(2.1-10). When he can no longer be hidden, he is placed in a floating basket and put in the River Nile, where he is discovered by none other than the Pharaoh's daughter, who will raise him. The story quickly jumps forward to a grown Moses, who at some point has become aware of his roots. Seeing the severity of the oppression of the Israelites, Moses lashes out and kills one of the Egyptian taskmasters. Moses is forced to flee for his life, and he heads to Midian, where he settles and marries (2.11-22). It is at this point that Moses, while tending sheep in the wilderness, is called by God, who appears in the form of a burning bush, to deliver the Israelites from slavery. Moses is reluctant and unwilling, but eventually agrees after God makes several concessions, including that his brother Aaron will be his helper (3.1-4.17).

Moses returns to Egypt and, along with Aaron, confronts Pharaoh, telling him to let God's people go. Pharaoh is not convinced, and this first confrontation backfires, as the Israelite slaves are treated worse than before as punishment for this demand (5.1-21). This is followed in chs 7-13 with a series of ten escalating plagues that are brought on Egypt to convince Pharaoh to let the Israelites go. All of these plagues afflict the Egyptians, but not the Israelites. Pharaoh's magicians are able to mimic some of the plagues, casting doubt on Moses' god, and Pharaoh's heart is increasingly hardened. There is a lengthy interlude in chs 12-13 before the final plague occurs, the death of the firstborn sons. Moses instructs the people on how to avoid this plague: blood from a lamb is to be put on the doorpost, and the angel of the LORD will pass over houses bearing this mark. This becomes the first Passover celebration – commemorating Israel's deliverance from Egypt. All the firstborn sons in Egypt die, including the Pharaoh's son, and he finally relents and agrees to let the Israelites leave. It is at this point that the story reveals that the Israelites have been in Egypt for 430 years and 600,000 men (not including women and children) are departing from Egypt (12.37-41).

The Israelites hurry on their way, but Pharaoh again changes his mind and chases after the people. The Israelites are nearing a body of water – the Red Sea – and have Pharaoh's army pursuing them from behind. God tells Moses to stretch out his hands over the water, and it will be divided. The sea divides, and the people of Israel cross over to safety, as the waters return and Pharaoh's armies are drowned. The next several chapters (16–18) outline the Israelites' journey to Sinai, a place which, as we shall see, is significant in the story of the Pentateuch.

Much of the material in Exodus up to this point has been narrative and story-like. Beginning in ch. 19, however, there is a shift; the rest of the book outlines the divine revelation given to Moses, and is more legal in nature. The people encamp at the base of Mount Sinai, and God proposes to make a covenant with the people (19.3-8). It is on Mount Sinai that Moses receives the law from God and delivers it to the Israelites. The first part relayed is perhaps the most famous element of Israel's law: the Ten Commandments (Exodus 20). These give broad instructions regarding how Israel is to relate both to God and their fellow humans. The next several chapters (20–23) outline various other aspects of the law, including laws concerning crime, violence, respect of property, issues of justice, Sabbath, and annual festivals.

The final section of the book, chs 25–40, deals with the question of how God will dwell with his people while they are in the wilderness. The answer is that God will dwell in a Tabernacle, a portable tent shrine that will move with the people as they journey in the wilderness. These chapters give instructions on how this sanctuary is to be constructed and subsequently narrate the building of this tent shrine as well as the decorations, the altars and the consecration of the priests who will be needed to ensure it is properly run and maintained. (Further reflections on law and the Tabernacle can be found in Chapter 12.)

Themes and theological issues

Exodus introduces a number of issues that are significant in the story of the Pentateuch, and in the broader biblical tradition.

The first thing to note is the emergence of Moses. If there is a main character (besides God) in the Pentateuch, it is Moses, who arrives in Exodus 2 and remains a central figure until the end of Deuteronomy. With the exception of Genesis, Moses is the key character in each of the remaining four pentateuchal books. He is also the most revered leader in the biblical tradition, and is in many ways a paradigmatic leader who functions as prophet, priest, and king, all rolled into one. The importance of Moses can be seen in the fact that, like Abraham, he has become a central figure for not only Jews but for Christians and Muslims as well.

Another important issue raised in Exodus is the notion of deliverance, as God hears and responds to his people in their time of need. The foundational story of the escape from Egypt has loomed large in both religious and popular culture. It is the basis of the Passover celebration in Judaism and has also been key in Christian theology and practice. It has served as inspiration for spirituals in the slavery-era United States, as well as liberation theology's insistence that the God of the Bible has a preference for the poor and the oppressed. And it has captured the imagination of artists and filmmakers down through the ages and right into the twenty-first century. There are few stories that have had as significant an impact as that of the exodus, and this is tied, no doubt, to the strong focus on deliverance.

Finally, Exodus is where we first witness Israel's collective covenant with God and where we are introduced to the laws of the Torah. Most famous of these are, of course, the Ten Commandments. But the law is much more than this, and in the Pentateuch it will extend through Leviticus, Numbers, and Deuteronomy. We see already in Exodus that these laws are more than legalistic rules. Rather, they point to the fact that all human behaviour matters, whether in relation to God, fellow people, or the created world.

Critical issues

Like Genesis, the book of Exodus has also been the subject of much critical enquiry. Several of these are worth noting here, though some will be given further attention in Chapters 11–13.

A number of the critical issues one encounters in studying Exodus are broadly related to issues concerning the historicity of the accounts. One such issue that has interested readers from antiquity has to do with how, if at all, a large body of water could have parted for the Israelites to cross. There have been various reconstructions through the years to explain the phenomenon from a naturalistic perspective. It's worth noting that even the biblical text itself says that a strong wind played a part in the event (Exod. 14.21), but it also makes clear that it all takes place on divine initiative. A related question has to do with the route of the exodus. The text is unclear as to where the crossing happened, and the name 'Red Sea' is not helpful in narrowing this down, as it designates a large body of water, including tributaries. Again, these have led to various hypotheses as inquisitive minds – academic and amateur – have tried precisely to locate possible locations for the crossing.

Another critical issue raised in Exodus revolves around the number of Israelites said to have left Egypt. As mentioned earlier, this number is put at over 600,000 men in the biblical text. Adding in women and children, this would put the number of travellers at between 2 and 3 million, not to mention animals. This number seems improbably high; crossing a body of water with this number would be impossible, let alone surviving in the desert. This had led to a number of critical hypotheses, and we discuss these and related issues further in Chapter 11.

Further reading

Helpful commentaries on Exodus include those from Childs (1974), Fretheim (1988), Propp (1999), Meyers (2005), and Dozeman (2009). An engaging introduction to various historical and literary issues in Exodus can be found in Sarna (1986). The collection of essays in Dozeman, Evans, and Lohr (2014) is a useful introduction to various critical and interpretive issues in Exodus. Some of the issues related to the exodus and history are helpfully laid out in Hendel (2005).

The Book of Leviticus

Introductory issues

The book at the centre of the Pentateuch is Leviticus, and it is the shortest of the five books, consisting of twenty-seven chapters. The Hebrew title for the book is *Vayikra*, which is drawn from the first word of the book in the Hebrew text, often translated as 'and he called'. The English title goes back to the Greek phrase *leuitikon biblion*, which associated the book with the Levites, those who assisted the priests in Israel's religious duties. While not strictly concerned with Levitical or priestly duties, the book is very interested in religious and cultic matters.

Structure and content

The book of Leviticus is a book of law, instruction, and ritual, with occasional brief narrative interludes. One way in which the book can be divided is into two main blocks, though there are some texts that do not fit within this division: chs 1–16 contain much that is relevant for priests, including ritual instructions. Meanwhile, chs 17–26 are concerned with a variety of issues related to living a holy life, and so are called the 'Holiness Code', sometimes using the siglum 'H'.

It was noted earlier that Exodus picks up where the story of Genesis leaves off; in a similar manner, Leviticus follows on from Exodus. The book begins with the Israelites still encamped at Sinai, and continues the relaying of the divine instructions to Moses for the people (Lev. 1.1). In fact, the book wastes little time in jumping into its concerns, as the first seven chapters deal with various sacrifices and offerings the Israelites are to offer: burnt offerings (ch. 1), grain offerings (ch. 2), offerings of well-being (ch. 3), the sin or purification offering (4.1–5.13), and the guilt offering (5.14–6.7). In chs 8–10, the subject shifts to discussing the role of the priests, as well as how they are to be appointed for the task. The following chapters (11–15) outline issues relating to purity, or what is considered clean and unclean. Here issues of purity related to food, childbirth, and skin diseases are dealt with, along with regulations for how such impurity should be handled. Chapter 16 then discusses the annual Day of Atonement (*Yom Kippur*), a day set aside for spiritual cleansing of the sanctuary and the people.

Much of the rest of the book is primarily concerned with matters of holiness. Chapter 17 deals with the appropriate slaughtering of animals, as well as the prohibition on consuming blood. This is followed by guidelines regarding sexual relations (18) and various instructions for living a holy life (19). It needs to be remembered that law and ethics are inseparable in Leviticus, and indeed elsewhere in the Pentateuch. Thus, we find in Lev. 19.18 the famous passage that Jesus uses in the New Testament as part of his programmatic summation of the law: love your neighbor as yourself. This statement is found near a number of other laws relating to living an ethical life, and yet, these ethical instructions are situated in and among other legal and ritual matters. Hence, the next few chapters deal with guidelines for priestly duties (21–22), and further reflections on sacrifices as well as the liturgical calendar and annual festivals (22–23). In ch. 25 regulations regarding the Sabbatical and Jubilee years are outlined, and ch. 26 contains various blessings and curses related to Israel keeping (or not) the covenant being made with God. The final chapter, 27, is something of an appendix and recounts further assorted regulations related to offerings and gifts offered to God.

Themes and theological issues

Leviticus is vitally important in Judaism, containing many of the commands still followed by many Jews today – issues such as kosher food laws and regulations for liturgical calendars and celebrations are based on the decrees of Leviticus. On the other hand, the book is often overlooked in the Christian tradition, because it can be difficult reading, and also because, to many, it is deemed irrelevant. Nevertheless, the themes explored in the book of Leviticus are important for understanding the world of the Hebrew Bible, and can also help make sense of a number of issues raised in the New Testament. The issues discussed in Leviticus underlie a number of issues with which groups in the second temple period, including early Christians, grappled. For example, issues relating to purity seem to have been of primary concern for the Jewish community at Qumran (where the Dead Sea Scrolls were found), and we know from the Mishnah that rabbinic Judaism, which emerged in the early centuries of the common era, was greatly concerned with interpreting law and legal materials from the Torah. Further, purity issues recur in the Gospels as a point of contention between Jesus and some of the other Jewish groups of his day (Mark 7), while Peter and others in the early church found themselves facing difficult questions relating to clean and unclean foods (Acts 10). All of these find their impetus in the laws of the Torah, primarily Leviticus, pointing to the importance these texts and traditions had in the formative stages of both Judaism and Christianity.

An element of the Pentateuch that readers find difficult is the amount of space given over to law and legal matters. However, it's important to note that law and narrative (and, indeed, other genres) are all considered part of *torah*, the instruction from God. J.W. Watts (1999) has suggested that pentateuchal law and narrative have been shaped so as to be persuasive rhetoric when read together, convincing the hearers (and readers) of their relevance (we return to this in Chapter 12). With specific reference to Leviticus, work has also been done exploring how the narrative world of the text and its ritual elements work together in the book (Bibb 2009). Thus, however difficult the law elements of the Pentateuch may seem to contemporary readers, they remain an important and integral part of the Torah, and should not – indeed, cannot – be divorced from other genres and the larger collection.

Holiness, purity, and ritual

Several important and interrelated issues run throughout the book of Leviticus, but the most prominent of these are holiness, purity, and ritual. Leviticus is full of holiness-related language. A key feature of this worldview is the notion that God is holy and set apart, and requires that which is set apart for him to be holy as well, including Israel and individuals who are part of this community (Lev. 11.44-45; 19.1-3). This holiness relates to various aspects of Israel's life, and seems to function on a spectrum. Thus, people can be considered holy (priests and high priest), places exhibit different levels of holiness (outside the camp, in the camp, and near to and inside the Tabernacle), and times of the year are considered more hallowed than others (Sabbath and festivals are holy days, while the Day of Atonement is considered the most holy day of the year).

Related to notions of holiness are those of purity and impurity. If something is holy, it is pure or clean. And conversely, if something is impure or unclean, it is unholy. As with notions of holiness, the idea of purity is complex. Recent research has noted that there are different aspects of purity in Leviticus, notably ritual and moral purity. In some cases, things are unclean because they are morally wrong or sinful. However, this is not always the case in Leviticus; there are a number of issues, notably in chs 11-16, where natural occurrences such as childbirth or skin diseases make someone unclean. In these cases, a person is unclean in a ritual sense, though this does not seem to be related in any way to morality or sinfulness. Indeed, such persons can become ritually clean by taking part in rituals that lead to a renewed state of purity. Thus, while issues of purity are very important in Leviticus, they are actually quite complex, and readers need to be careful not to assume that uncleanness or impurity always equates with immorality or sinfulness.

This brings us to a final prevalent theme in Leviticus, and that is ritual. Rituals, particularly as found in Leviticus, provide a way for people to move from impurity to purity. Of particular importance in Leviticus are sacrifices and offerings. As with the notions of holiness and purity, however, the biblical text does not clarify the logic underlying rituals, in general, or sacrifice, in particular.

At their core these issues of holiness, purity, and ritual are about boundaries that help define social norms and identity. These concerns are broad in focus, dealing with issues such as food, clothing, sexual practices, bodily fluids, and significant times and places. And yet, as T.E. Fretheim notes, 'For Israel, these distinctions have been integrated into the religious sphere. They identify those matters that are pleasing or displeasing to God because they affect the wholeness and stability, indeed the holiness, of the community – with implications for the entire created order – positively or negatively' (1996: 132).

Critical issues

One of the key, critical questions surrounding Leviticus is how best to make sense of the purity-related language and worldview of Leviticus, along with the place and function of ritual. Are the rules regarding holiness, purity, and ritual simply superstitions? Do they relate to archaic notions of hygiene or ethics? Or is there an underlying structure that makes sense of these issues as a whole? Various theories and models have been put forward to explain the nature and function of these purity and ritual elements, and we discuss several such theories further in Chapter 12.

Further reading

Commentaries on Leviticus that are particularly useful include Milgrom (1998, 2000, 2001), Levine (2003), and Watts (2013). On the issues of purity and holiness, Fretheim (1996) and Watts (2007) offer helpful introductions. Critical issues relating to the book are discussed in the essays collected in Rendtorff and Kugler (2006) and Römer (2008). Theological aspects of the book are introduced helpfully in Lohr (2012).

The Book of Numbers

Introductory issues

The fourth book in the Pentateuch is called *Bemidbar* in the Jewish tradition. This is the fifth word in the Hebrew text, and means 'in the wilderness'. As will become clear, this is a very appropriate name for this book. The English name, Numbers, comes from the Greek title of the book, *Arithmoi*. This probably derives from the two detailed census lists which are found in chs 1 and 26.

Structure and content

One of the greatest difficulties in understanding the book of Numbers is the variety of genres it contains. The book moves, apparently at random, from lists which enumerate the people who followed Moses through the wilderness (chs 1–4) to purity regulations (chs 5–6), law codes (15; 19; 27–30; 33.50–36.13), lists of donations (7.12-83), and songs of victory (21.14-15; 21.27-30). There are various theories regarding the structure of the book, though none has gained consensus. One suggestion, and that which we will follow here, is a trifold division: chs 1–10 outline Israel's preparations to leave Mount Sinai; in chs 11–20, life after Sinai, in the wilderness, is recounted; finally, in chs 20–36, the story shifts to the new generation and Israel's journey to Moab, just outside the land of promise.

Like Exodus and Leviticus before it, Numbers is situated so as to continue the book preceding it, in this case Leviticus. In ch. 1 we see that the Israelites are still encamped at Sinai, and God tells Moses to take a census of the people in preparation for their departure. The following chapters outline instructions for how the Israelites, in their tribes and clans, are to encamp after leaving Sinai, as well as instructions for transporting the tabernacle (chs 2–4). Chapters 5–10 outline a number of issues related to the purity of the people, including special vows and offerings.

The Israelites are divided in Numbers (and elsewhere) according to their tribes. These tribes are said to come from the sons of Jacob, from where they get their names: Reuben, Simeon, Judah, Isaachar, Zebulun, Ephraim, Manasseh, Benjamin, Dan, Asher, Gad, and Naphtali. Two of Jacob's sons are not among the tribal divisions: Levi, whose ancestors would become a separate group, the Levites, from whence the priestly class would come; and Joseph, whose two sons – Ephraim and Mahasseh – are given tribes, ostensibly as an honour to their father, who was Jacob's favourite son. The historical basis of these tribal divisions is complex; nevertheless, these divisions are an important part of the identities of the Israelites throughout the Hebrew Bible.

In the second part of the book (10.11–20.13), Numbers returns to a more narrative style, and tells the story of Israel's departure from Sinai and their journey into the wilderness. These chapters highlight a change in the people, introducing rebellion and eventually death into the story of the wilderness. In ch. 11, the people begin to complain about the lack of food, and sustenance is provided. Following this, Moses' helpers Miriam and Aaron become jealous of his leadership, and challenge him (ch. 12). Then one of the critical scenes in the book is given: the story of the twelve spies (chs 13–14). Having made their way to the southern border of Canaan, God instructs the people to send one man from each of the twelve tribes to spy out the land which is to be given to them. The spies go out and return with a mixed message: on the one hand, the land is beautiful, as is its produce. On the other hand, the people there are strong and their cities are fortified. Two of the spies – Joshua and Caleb – urge the people to move forward and occupy the land. The people, however, decide it is too risky, and choose not to move forward (14.1-12).

Because of this lack of trust, Numbers relates that God wants to give up on the Israelites and destroy them. It is only the intercession of Moses that prevents this from happening. God relents and forgives the people, but the punishment is that the entire generation who left Egypt and saw God's mighty works but refused to have faith to enter Canaan would die in the wilderness (14.20-25). This, according to Numbers, is the reason that the Israelites will spend forty years wandering in the wilderness.

After several further attempts at rebellion and revolt, there is a marked shift beginning in ch. 20, signalling a change is under way as the old generation passes on and the new one takes precedence. First, Moses' sister Miriam dies (20.1). Following this, another episode is recounted that explains why Moses and Aaron, because of an act of disobedience, will not enter the Promised Land with the people (20.2-13).

In the following chapters the people make their way towards Canaan, encountering various peoples and leaders, and eventually ending up in Moab, just east of the land of promise (chs 21–25). Of special note here is Israel's encounter with Balaam in Numbers 22–24, a prophet whom the king of Moab employs to curse Israel. A series of setbacks stop Balaam from cursing Israel, and he eventually pronounces a blessing on them. Finally, in Numbers 26 the second census of the Israelites takes place, and in ch. 27 Moses passes on his leadership role to Joshua, setting the scene for the next stage in Israel's journey. The book ends with instructions for the people as to how they are to enter the land of Canaan and how the land will be divided among the tribes (Numbers 32–35).

Themes and theological issues

There are a variety of themes that run throughout the book of Numbers, and we focus here on three important and interrelated ideas: trust and rebellion, the wilderness wanderings, and generations.

There are a number of stories throughout the book that contrast trust and rebellion: the people of Israel complaining about their situation, Moses' leadership being questioned, and the story of the twelve spies and the different perspectives among them are just a few examples. Many (but not all) of these stories of faithlessness and rebellion are found in the first half of the book. In the second half, we begin to see how trust is restored and the relationship with God is rebuilt. This move from rebellion to trust brings us to the second theme: that of the wilderness wanderings.

After the episode with the twelve spies, Israel is said to have wandered in the wilderness for forty years as the old (faithless) generation dies off, and the new generation gets set to enter the Promised Land. Thus, on one level this time in the wilderness can be seen as punishment for the generation that left Egypt but did not have faith to enter Canaan. However, the time in the wilderness is more than punishment; it would come to be seen as a time of purification and refinement before Israel enters the land of promise. This idea of the desert or wilderness as a time of testing and purification would become foundational in both Judaism and Christianity: Jesus' time in the desert (forty days; Mt. 4.1-11), for example, is clearly modelled on Israel's time in the wilderness.

The final theme to mention here is that of the generations, marked out by the two large census lists in chs 1 and 26. Numbers is clear in juxtaposing the two generations as faithless and faithful, as rebellious and trusting. There are elements that indicate that this is recounted in a way to heighten its narrative effect: the split between the generations with the entire first dying off in forty years is a bit neat and clean, as is the comprehensive contrast between the faithless and faithful generations. Nevertheless, the point is clear: trials and difficulties will come, and each generation has the opportunity to be either rebellious or faithful – to follow in the footsteps of those who lacked faith or those who chose to trust (Kaminsky and Lohr 2011).

Critical issues

One critical issue is the question of the number of Israelites, an issue already raised with regard to Exodus. The account of Numbers puts the population of Israel moving through the wilderness at around two million people. As Kaminsky and Lohr note,

> Solutions do not come easily. Perhaps the numbers are hyperbolic or superlative in order to stress Israel's divine blessing, something texts such as Exodus 1:7 and Numbers 22:3 suggest. Alternatively, according to some scholars the Hebrew word *eleph*, used to indicate 1000, could instead represent military or family units, thus bringing the number down to approximately 6000 soldiers or 20,000 Israelites in total. Such numbers would be more in line with population estimates for the ANE at the time. (2011: 126)

There are other theories, including those that posit that Israel was indigenous to Canaan. In such readings, the wilderness wanderings are seen as a projection of the exile and the forced migration of the people away from the land of promise. We return to these questions in Chapter 13.

A second critical issue relates to the structure of the book of Numbers, as well as its composition. Scholars have long struggled with how best to make sense of both of these issues. One current line of thought suggests that Numbers emerged as a way to bridge Priestly traditions in Exodus and Leviticus with those found in Deuteronomy. This might help account for the lack of structure in the book, as its originating purpose may have been to bridge these other traditions. More on these matters can be found in Chapter 7.

Further reading

Helpful commentaries on Numbers include Wenham (1981), Milgrom (1990), Olson (1996), and Levine (2003). The structure of the book and the theme of generations are discussed in Olson (1985). Critical issues related to Numbers are explored in Römer (2008) as well as in Frevel, Schart, and Pola (2013).

The Book of Deuteronomy

Introductory issues

Deuteronomy is the fifth and final book of the Pentateuch, and consists of thirty-four chapters. The name for this book in the Jewish tradition is *Devarim*, after the second word in the Hebrew text, meaning 'words'. The English title comes from a phrase in the Greek version, *deuteros nomos*, which means 'second law', and which seems to be a mistranslation of the Hebrew phrase 'repetition of the law' (17.18).

Structure and content

The book of Deuteronomy is presented as a long, final farewell speech from Moses to the Israelites as they prepare to enter the land of Canaan without him. However, as in other books in the Pentateuch, within this there are multiple genres, including narrative, law, and legal materials, as well as songs and poems.

The book can broadly be divided into four sections: in chs 1–4, Moses recounts Israel's experiences during his lifetime; chs 5–26 return to the covenant relationship, and requirements for this, which includes a significant amount of legal material (12–26); chs 27–28 outline curses and blessings related to the covenant; and chs 29–34 conclude the book with final instructions from Moses, the transfer of leadership to Joshua, and Moses' death.

Deuteronomy begins where Numbers has left off: with the people 'beyond the Jordan', just outside Canaan in the land of Moab. In fact, the entire book takes place in this setting – in the plains of Moab. Here the book begins with Moses recounting Israel's story during his lifetime, though it is not presented in a linear, chronological manner. The account begins (Deuteronomy 1–3) with the journey from Horeb (the name Deuteronomy often uses for Sinai) to their present location in Moab, including the wilderness wanderings.

Beginning in ch. 4, the book returns to the covenant made between God and Israel, and the giving of the law. The Ten Commandments are given in ch. 5, with some minor differences from the Exodus version, and the special position of Israel as the chosen people is reiterated in ch. 7. In Deuteronomy 8–11 the text returns to the issues which Israel faced at Horeb and in the wilderness, with encouragement and warnings to be faithful to the covenant.

The middle of the book, chs 12–26, returns to the law. Some of these stipulations are similar to and reinforce what is found in Exodus, Leviticus, and Numbers, while others modify, challenge, or even overturn elements found in these other books, though the question of priority in relation to Deuteronomy and other parts of the Pentateuch is contested. Nevertheless, a noticeable example of this is found in the laws concerning slavery. In Exod. 21.1-6 we are told that male Hebrew slaves are to be released after six years. In Deut. 15.12-18, however, all slaves – male and female – are to be set free, and the text even gives ethical rationale for this generosity, namely that the Israelites themselves were once slaves in Egypt. Further examples of such changes can be found in the guidelines and stipulations concerning the festivals, in particular Passover (see Exodus 12 and 23 as well as Deut. 16.1-8), and in the shift of language relating to helping an 'enemy's' ox or donkey in Exod. 23.4-5 to that of a 'brother's' ox or sheep in Deut. 22.1-4.

Deuteronomy 27–28 contain a list of blessings and curses related to Israel's adherence to the covenant with God. Following God's ways leads to 'life' and blessing, while disregarding the covenant leads to a lack of blessing and 'death', an idea that is used metaphorically. This notion of blessings and curses bears resemblance to the enforcement of covenant treaties in the ANE, an issue to which we return in Chapter 12.

The book concludes in chs 29–34 with a renewal of the covenant (29); Moses turning over his position as leader to Joshua (31); the 'Song of Moses', a hymn that outlines God's history with Israel (32); and Moses' final blessings on the tribes of Israel, given in poetic fashion (33). The final chapter (34) outlines the end of Moses' life: he is taken to a mountaintop so as to see the Promised Land across the Jordan, but he will not enter with the people. Instead, the text says in 34.5-6, 'Moses, the servant of the LORD, died there in the land of Moab, at the LORD's command. He was buried in a valley in the land of Moab, opposite Beth-peor, but no one knows his burial place to this day.' Verse 10 famously notes, 'Never since has there arisen a prophet in Israel like Moses, whom the LORD knew face to face.'

Themes and theological issues

One of the resounding themes in Deuteronomy is the idea that Israel is the chosen people, and they are to serve the one God (Moberly 2013). This can be seen in two key texts which highlight these themes in memorable fashion. To begin, ch. 7 sets out Israel's special status as the chosen, elect people:

> For you are a people holy to the LORD your God; the LORD your God has chosen you out of all the peoples on earth to be his people, his treasured possession. It was not because you were more numerous than any other people that the LORD set his heart on you and chose you – for you were the fewest of all peoples. It was because the LORD loved you and kept the oath that he swore to your ancestors, that the LORD has brought you out with a mighty hand, and redeemed you from the house of slavery, from the hand of Pharaoh king of Egypt. (Deut. 7.6-8)

Here we see that Israel is God's chosen people. However, this chosenness is not based on anything Israel has done to earn this position, but rather stems from God's special interest in and love for the people, going back to their ancestors. Further, it's this special relationship that has led to God's deliverance of and care for the Israelites.

In the chapter just previous to this declaration of Israel's status we see the other side of this equation, as Israel is called to complete loyalty to YHWH.

> Hear, O Israel: The LORD is our God, the LORD alone. You shall love the LORD your God with all your heart, and with all your soul, and with all your might. Keep these words that I am commanding you today in your heart. Recite them to your children and talk about them when you are at home and when you are away, when you lie down and when you rise. Bind them as a sign on your hand, fix them as an emblem on your forehead, and write them on the doorposts of your house and on your gates. (Deut. 6.4-9)

Known as the *Shema*, after the first word in Hebrew, meaning 'hear' or 'listen', this is perhaps the most significant text in the Hebrew Scriptures in the Jewish tradition, outlining Israel's commitment to their one God (though whether this speaks of monotheism is debated). It is repeated every morning and evening in Jewish prayers, and is also the basis for the use of *tefillin* (or phylacteries, prayer boxes, and straps) that are used by Jews. While not as central, this text has played an important role in Christianity as well. When Jesus is asked what is the most important commandment, his response incorporates part of the *Shema* (Mk 12.28-31).

Taken together, Deuteronomy is clear in highlighting both Israel's special relationship with God as well as their responsibilities and duties. This, in short, is the nature of the covenant relationship.

A corollary to the previous theme is that Deuteronomy poses serious and difficult questions regarding Israel's relationship to other nations. As noted above, Israel is portrayed here as the chosen people, serving the one true God, on their way to the land of promise. And yet, they will encounter others along the way, including those already residing in Canaan, issues which continue into the books of Joshua and Judges. In Deut. 6.39, the Israelites are told that when they enter Canaan, they are to utterly destroy (or commit to the ban, *herem*) those living there. There are various ways this notion of *herem* has been understood, including that it never took place historically, or that it should be interpreted metaphorically (on various interpretations, see Lohr 2009 and Moberly 2013). However, it remains a difficult issue, particularly for those who wish to read these texts as Scripture. There are some elements of Deuteronomy that run counter to this theme and which are suggestive of God's interaction with other nations (Miller 2000), but this nevertheless remains a problematic subject.

One further theme that we find in Deuteronomy is that of endings and beginnings. As the end point of the Pentateuch, Deuteronomy brings a number of storylines to a close, most notably with the death of Moses. However, Deuteronomy also points forward, by introducing Joshua and leaving the people on the edge of the Promised Land. Indeed, the book of Joshua will pick up directly where Deuteronomy leaves off (Josh. 1.1-3), something which has led to speculation regarding the relationship of Deuteronomy to the books which follow it. Thus, some have argued for an original *Hexateuch* that includes Joshua with the first five books, while others have suggested that Deuteronomy bears closer resemblance with the books that follow it than it does with the first four books, and was originally part of a larger body of material that extends through much of the historical books (often called the Deuteronomistic History). We'll return to these issues in Chapter 7. Whatever the case, it is clear in the final shape of the Hebrew Bible that Deuteronomy both concludes the Pentateuch and prepares for the next phase of Israel's story.

Critical issues

The book of Deuteronomy, as noted above, has sparked critical enquiry into a number of important areas, three of which we note here.

First is the issue of authorship and origins. Tradition held that Moses was responsible for the book of Deuteronomy, along with the other books of the Pentateuch. However, Deuteronomy's distinctive language, its modification of other pentateuchal legal materials, and the fact that it recounts Moses' death all captured the attention of readers over time. (The fact that Deuteronomy recounts Moses' death was noted from antiquity in relation to the question of Mosaic authorship of the book, with some suggesting that his successor Joshua finished the book.) One influential theory that emerged with the rise of critical biblical scholarship was based on the many similarities that can be found between Deuteronomy and the reforms said to have been undertaken by King Josiah of Judah in the seventh century BCE, as recounted in 2 Kings 22–23. In light of this, many now hold that Deuteronomy, or parts of it, emerged in the seventh century as part of the major reforms that took place in this period.

A second issue has to do with Deuteronomy's relation to the other books of the Pentateuch. As noted earlier, Deuteronomy's materials on the law sometimes agree with and at other times modify other legal materials in the Pentateuch, pointing to the fact that even within the biblical corpus there is already interpretation taking place. Further, there are variances in the narrative portions of Deuteronomy that are not easily reconciled with counterparts in other books such as Numbers. Thus, the relationship of Deuteronomy to these other books and traditions has continued to be a source of much speculation.

Finally, discoveries from the ANE over the past several centuries have illuminated the study of Deuteronomy, particularly in relation to treaties and covenants. It has become clear that treaties between nations or peoples – oftentimes forged between a stronger and a weaker group – were quite common in the ancient world. Excavations have unearthed multiple examples of such treaties, and the recurring structure found in these documents is striking when compared with the structure of Deuteronomy. Such treaties often had a preamble, relayed the historical background or relationship between the parties, outlined stipulations and laws, recounted a public reading, invoked a divine witness, and listed blessings and curses; all of these elements can be found in Deuteronomy, roughly in this order, suggesting that Israel's understanding of covenant, and the book of Deuteronomy in particular, might have some relation to ancient political treaties. The question of which eras and cultures offer the best point for comparison remains a matter of debate, as such treaties have been found in eras and cultural groups ranging from Hittites in the second millennium BCE to Assyrians in the seventh century BCE.

Further reading

Helpful commentaries on Deuteronomy include Miller (1990), Weinfeld (1991), Tigay (1996), and Lundbom (2013). Discussions on Deuteronomy in relation to the Pentateuch and the Deuteronomistic History can be found in Römer (2000) and Person and Schmid (2012). The laws of Deuteronomy in relation to other legal traditions in the Pentateuch are discussed in Levinson (1997) and Stackert (2007). Barrett (2012) and Moberly (2013) helpfully unpack several theological elements within Deuteronomy.

Part Two

Thematic and Critical Explorations

The Origins and Formation of the Pentateuch

From the beginning of the academic study of the Bible, research on the Pentateuch has often been at the forefront of developments in biblical scholarship. The present chapter will focus on one such set of issues that has been particularly important in the academic study of the Bible, and that is research related to the origins and formation of the Pentateuch. We focus here on two relevant and interrelated issues: (1) the authorship and origins of these texts and traditions, and (2) the development of the Torah as an authoritative collection.

The authorship and origins of the Pentateuch

Mosaic authorship

The books of the Pentateuch, like much of the biblical material, are anonymous. The tradition of the Mosaic authorship of the Pentateuch seems to have arisen from a few statements which make reference to Moses writing, such as Deut. 31.9, where we read that 'Moses wrote down this law, and gave it to the priests, the sons of Levi, who carried the ark of the covenant of the LORD, and to all the elders of Israel' (see also Exod. 24.4). Over time 'this law' would come to be understood as the whole of the Pentateuch, not just the law spoken by Moses to the people in Deuteronomy. Consequently, by the time of Ezra, reference can be made to 'the book of the law of Moses' (Neh. 8.1). As time went on, this became the traditional view on the authorship of the entire Pentateuch, and this idea can be found in numerous Jewish and Christian texts (e.g. Ecclus 24.23; Josephus, *Ant.* 4.326; the Mishnah *Pirke Avot* 1.1; and various New Testament texts such as Mk 12.26).

A complicated text

Thus far, our consideration of the Pentateuch has assumed that the books Genesis to Deuteronomy can be understood as forming one continuous narrative from the creation of the world to the arrival of the Israelites at the borders of the Promised Land. While the Pentateuch does have an overarching structure, such a description oversimplifies the text we have before us. Even the most superficial reading indicates that the Pentateuch contains a variety of literary styles: flowing narratives are placed next to genealogical lists, and complex law codes appear alongside elaborate visions of God. The narrative of the Pentateuch does not flow seamlessly from beginning to end; rather, the story develops in leaps and bounds, told using a variety of different genres.

A closer examination reveals certain perplexing elements of the text, including the fact that some stories and laws appear to be told two or three times, in different ways. Table 7.1 gives some examples of this.

The difficulty with the tradition of Mosaic authorship is not just the repeated elements, however. Other factors also lead to questions about the likelihood of Mosaic authorship. One such issue is that Moses' death is reported in the Pentateuch itself, though this is not an insurmountable problem because it is recorded at the very end of the book of Deuteronomy

Table 7.1 Some examples of doublets and triplets in the Pentateuch

1.	Creation of humanity (Gen. 1.26)	Creation of Adam (Gen. 2.7)	
2.	Flood waters continue for 40 days (Gen. 7.17)	Flood waters continue for 150 days (Gen. 7.24)	
3.	Abraham passes off Sarah as his sister (Gen. 12.10-20)	Abraham passes off Sarah as his sister (Gen. 20.1-18)	Isaac passes off Rebekah as his sister (Gen. 26.1-11)
4.	Joseph's brothers agree to sell him to some Ishmaelites (Gen. 37.28)	Joseph's brothers sell him to some Midianites (Gen. 37.36)	
5.	Moses goes up the mountain at the command of the LORD (Exod. 24.1-2)	Moses goes up the mountain at the command of the LORD (Exod. 24.9-11)	Moses goes up the mountain at the command of the LORD (Exod. 24.15-18)
6.	Manumission of male slaves (Exod. 21.1-6)	Manumission of male and female slaves (Deut. 15.12-18)	
7.	Israelites travel around Edom (Num. 20.14-21)	Israelites travel through Edom (Deut. 2.1-8)	
8.	Joshua is appointed as leader of the people (Num. 27.18-23)	Joshua is appointed as leader of the people (Deut. 31.23)	

(Deut. 34.5). Rather more problematic is the list of Edomite kings in Gen. 36.31-39. As these kings lived a long time after the death of Moses, it seems unlikely that he could have written the list. A closer examination also indicates that narrative style and terminology also vary greatly within the five books. Weighing the cumulative evidence, the seventeenth-century philosopher Benedictus de Spinoza concluded that 'it is ... clearer than the sun at noonday that the Pentateuch was not written by Moses but by someone who lived long after Moses' (cited in Blenkinsopp 1992: 2). If Spinoza's observation is correct and Moses was not the sole author of the Pentateuch, then others must have been involved in writing and collecting it. Attempts to identify who the author or authors might have been have played an important part in scholarly examination of these five books.

Source criticism: Julius Wellhausen and the Documentary Hypothesis

From antiquity, readers of the Pentateuch had observed some of the issues noted above. And yet, while occasional misgivings did arise, the general idea of Mosaic authorship was upheld in both the Jewish and Christian traditions in the premodern period. It was in the modern period that questions concerning the origins and formation of the Pentateuch began to be addressed with more urgency. An important development in the early modern period was that scholars began to identify strands within the Pentateuch which use the same style and terminology, suggesting that the inconsistencies in the text are not random, but follow certain patterns. This, in its turn, raises the possibility that the text of the Pentateuch reached its present form as the result of the conflation of more than one original source, gathered together by an editor or redactor. The attempt to identify the different sources or traditions that lie behind the biblical text is known as 'source criticism'; the theory that identifies four separate sources behind the Pentateuch in particular is termed the 'Documentary Hypothesis'.

The notion that a number of sources lay behind the final text of the Pentateuch was raised as early as the seventeenth and eighteenth centuries in the work of scholars R. Simon (1678) and J. Astruc (1753), with criteria such as the use of divine names and unique literary styles and vocabularies being employed to distinguish between possible sources. However, the tradition of Mosaic authorship remained strong in these early stages; Astruc, for example, maintained that Moses was the redactor of these sources behind the Pentateuch. During the following two centuries, scholars would debate the number and dating of these possible sources. While there were numerous scholars who played important roles in these developments – including W.M.L. de Wette (1805), K.H. Graf (1866), and A. Kuenen (1869) – it is the German J. Wellhausen whose name is most often associated with this school of thought. Wellhausen set out the 'Documentary Hypothesis' in its classic formulation in his now famous *Die Composition des Hexateuchs* (The Composition of the Hexateuch, first published in 1876/7). The significance of Wellhausen's theory lay not in his enumeration of four sources, since that had been done before, but in the order he proposed for their composition. This proposal rapidly became accepted in scholarly circles.

The four sources of the Pentateuch proposed in this classic formulation are the Yahwist Source (abbreviated as 'J' from the German 'Jahvist'), the Elohist Source ('E'), the Deuteronomic Source ('D'), and the Priestly Source ('P'). Source critics identify each source according to certain characteristics laid out in Table 7.2. The principle which lies behind the division of the text into these sources is that the consistent use of terminology and literary style identifies and differentiates the writings of one source from the others. The application of these basic characteristics to the text allows the source critic to identify the source in which each unit of text originated. Indeed, tables which divide the Pentateuch verse by verse into the four sources have been produced (see Noth [1948] 1972; Campbell and O'Brien 1993; Friedman 2003).

Wellhausen used this technique to identify what he was certain were the different sources of the Pentateuch. Once he had done this, he examined the major characteristics of the sources in an attempt to date them. He maintained that 'J' and 'E' were written first and joined together by an editor after their composition. Interestingly, Wellhausen did not always differentiate between these two sources and often referred to them as 'JE'. Likewise, he did not attempt to date either source more precisely than 'in the monarchical period' (the dates given in Table 7.2 originate from the work of subsequent scholarship). He placed 'D' next, on the grounds that 'D' seemed to know 'JE' but not 'P', and maintained that 'P' was the last to be written. Wellhausen used source critical principles on the book of Joshua as well as on Genesis to Deuteronomy. As a result he identified the presence of a 'Hexateuch' (six books), not just a 'Pentateuch' (five books).

Biblical scholars rapidly accepted the 'Documentary Hypothesis', with JEDP written in that order. Indeed, this understanding of the history of the composition of the Pentateuch was one of the most influential theories

Table 7.2 The developed consensus concerning the major characteristics of the sources of the Documentary Hypothesis

Source	Yahwist source ('J')	Elohist source ('E')	Deuteronomic source ('D')	Priestly source ('P')
Name for God	Yahweh	God ('elohim or 'el)	Yahweh	God ('elohim or 'el)
Name for Sinai/Horeb	Sinai	Horeb	Horeb	Sinai
Concentration on particular part of Israel	Judah	Northern Israel (Ephraim)	Judah	Whole of Israel
Major characteristics	Primeval history	No primeval history	No primeval history	Primeval history
	Flowing narrative style with concentration on lives of Patriarchs	Epic style Strong moral tone	No narrative: collection of exhortatory and legal material	Interest in dates and order genealogies
	Etymology of words often given		Long speeches Stress on Jerusalem	Interest in cultic ritual and law
Characteristics of God	God described in human terms	God often speaks in dreams	God's covenant with Israel	God viewed as transcendent
		Frequent references to fear of God		
Possible date of composition	c.950–850 BCE	c.850–750 BCE	622 BCE onwards but before 'P'	Late exilic/early post exilic, before Ezra
Where found in Pentateuch	Parts of Genesis, Exodus, and Numbers	Parts of Genesis, Exodus, and Numbers	Deuteronomy	Parts of Exodus, Leviticus, and Numbers; end of Deuteronomy

in Hebrew Bible scholarship in the twentieth century. D.M. Carr helpfully summarizes the consensus which emerged:

> Up through the first three-quarters of the twentieth century, historical scholars of the Pentateuch could rely on a consensus about the broad

contours of the development of the Pentateuch that originated within Protestant European scholarship of the nineteenth century ... Most agreed that the first written sources of the Pentateuch were a tenth century Judean 'Yahwistic' document ... (J), and a somewhat later (probably early eighth century?) Northern 'Elohistic' document ... (E). These early sources, it was held, were united into a yet later 'Yehovist' [JE combination] in the South, perhaps around the time that the Northern kingdom was destroyed (late eighth century). Sometime in the eighth or early seventh century an early form of the book of Deuteronomy was composed, was revised and served as the basis of Josiah's reforms, and was eventually united with the Yehovistic composition to form a new whole: JED. Finally, during the exile or post-exile the Priestly document was written separately from these early compositions (built partly around yet another legal code, an exilic Holiness Code [H] found largely in Leviticus 17–26), before this Priestly Document too was integrated into the present Pentateuch (JEDP). This basic four source theory for the formation of the Pentateuch ... could be presupposed as given by most scholars writing on Pentateuchal topics for over a hundred years. (2015: 433–4)

The extent of the impact of the Documentary Hypothesis is hard to measure. Indeed, the wealth of proposals and counterproposals that developed out of the original theory are now so complex that the hypothesis struggles to survive, as we will see below.

The Documentary Hypothesis: Developments and difficulties

One important task for scholars interested in exploring the origins of the Pentateuch has been to understand more about the sources noted above and their respective roles in the composition of the Pentateuch as a whole. Such attempts have played an important part in recent studies on the Pentateuch, with many questioning long-held assumptions about these sources.

The Yahwist Source

In more popular formulations, 'J' was thought to contain a continuous story (now divided up in the Pentateuch) spanning from creation right through to the placement of the Israelites just outside the land of promise following the time in the wilderness (and, according to some, also including the conquest story found in Joshua). In the pentateuchal material, this would include parts of Genesis, Exodus, and Numbers. This source, containing primarily narratives, was presumed by many to be the earliest pentateuchal source, dating from the era of the united monarchy (c.950–850 BCE). This source was thought to have several defining characteristics, a prominent one (and the one from which the source derives its name) being that it employs God's personal name, YHWH.

While the content, nature, and extent of the Yahwist Source has always been contentious (see Römer 2006), this source has been the subject of considerable further discussion in recent decades. Various proposals have centred on four major areas: the identification of different strands within 'J', the consideration of 'J' as a creative theologian, the redating of 'J' to a much later period, and questions concerning the very existence of 'J' as a continuous source.

Many scholars – dating back to Wellhausen himself, and including other significant voices such as H. Gunkel – have suggested that the basic 'J' source is made up of more than one strand within the source, normally indicated by a number or letter in superscript or subscript (e.g. J^1 or J_b). Others maintain the presence of an earlier strand out of which the 'J' and 'E' sources emerged (M. Noth calls this 'G' from the German *Grundlage*, meaning 'foundation'). G. von Rad's theory moved in the opposite direction. Despite his interest in the pre-literary background to the Pentateuch, von Rad was convinced that the 'Yahwist' was a creative theologian who stamped his own personality on his writing. Indeed, von Rad believed that the 'Yahwist' was one of the greatest theologians ever to write:

> As regards the creative genius of the Yahwist's narrative there is only admiration. Someone has justly called the artistic mastery in this narrative one of the greatest accomplishments of all times in the history of thought. (von Rad [1956] 1972: 25)

A much more radical re-envisioning of the Documentary Hypothesis has been to redate 'J' (and indeed the whole of the Pentateuch) to the exilic period. Part of the reason for this redating stems from the lack of archaeological evidence regarding the patriarchs and ancient Israel, and subsequent questions about the feasibility of reconstructing any such history (Thompson 1974). J. Van Seters, noting similarities with concerns of exilic and post-exilic texts, has argued that 'J' was written as a prologue to the history of Israel to be found in the books of Joshua to 2 Kings and therefore should be dated much later than Wellhausen first proposed. He further proposed that it was 'J' and not 'P' that provided the unifying basis for the Pentateuch as a whole. Instead he regards 'P' as 'composed from the start as a supplementation to the earlier work' (1999: 211; these ideas are expanded on and clarified in Van Seters

1992, 2013). C. Levin (1993) agrees that the Yahwist is late, but argues that 'J' should be understood as an editor or a redactor, bringing the non-Priestly narrative materials together into coherent form. In both cases, however, the redating of 'J' to these later periods is a major shift in that it is no longer the earliest source for the pentateuchal materials.

T. Römer helpfully summarizes these various complexities regarding 'J':

> With von Rad the Yahwist has become not only an author but also above all a theologian. For Van Seters, J is also an author, but he lives five centuries later and is more a historian than a theologian. For Levin, J is a redactor: his Yahwist shares the exilic location with Van Seters's Yahwist, but Van Seters would never agree with the idea of J as a redactor. And in addition there continues to be a bewildering diversity in the historical location of J: today one may find proposals for virtually each century between the tenth and sixth centuries BCE. (2006: 22)

Finally, the whole existence of a 'J' source has been called into question over the past half century (see the essays collected in Dozeman and Schmid 2006, with the title *A Farewell to the Yahwist?*, which followed on from a German volume, *Abschied vom Jahwisten*, from Gertz, Schmid, and Witte 2002). It is worth noting here an important development related to the study of oral traditions in the Pentateuch. H. Gunkel ([1901] 1964), though never questioning the validity of the Documentary Hypothesis and source criticism, was more interested in the oral tradition that lay behind the sources than in the sources themselves. He imagined the early Israelites telling and retelling the stories of their earliest history many times before they came to be written down. Consequently, Gunkel hoped to be able to rediscover something about these stories before they were written down. Most importantly, he maintained that these stories were remembered and told for a specific reason and were therefore to be regarded as 'aetiologies' or legends told to explain why things are as they are. The method that Gunkel developed to enable him to achieve his goal is known as form criticism because of his insistence that the form or genre of a story can tell us much about its history. He applied his interest in form criticism to the Psalter as well as to Genesis, and this theory greatly influenced subsequent study of both of these biblical books. Gunkel's theories, in their turn, influenced two other great Hebrew Bible scholars: von Rad ([1938] 1966) and Noth ([1948] 1972). Both of them were convinced of the importance of a 'pre-literary' stage in the composition of the Pentateuch and sought to reconstruct it. Like Gunkel they believed that the stories were remembered for specific reasons, though unlike him they identified the worship of ancient Israel as the reason for their retelling. Thus they maintained that the stories of the Pentateuch were preserved because of their use in the 'cultic life' or worship of Israel.

Later scholars would note a point of tension in this alliance of oral traditions and documentary sources. R. Rendtorff (1990), amongst others, suggested that the work of von Rad and Noth actually points to a vulnerability in the Documentary Hypothesis. As Blenkinsopp explains, 'in proceeding from the smallest units to the larger complexes of tradition and thence to the final form of the work, there is no place for hypothetical literary sources, sources which in any cases are nowhere referred to in the biblical corpus itself' (Blenkinsopp 1992: 23). Consequently, Rendtorff turned his attention to smaller units of tradition, and suggested that these were edited together at a later time. Further, T. Römer (1990) and K. Schmid ([1999] 2010), among others, have questioned the antiquity of the points of contact between traditions found in the Pentateuch, such as the patriarchal narratives and the exodus traditions. Together such developments cast serious doubt on a continuous narrative such as 'J' that spans the various books of the Pentateuch. As we will see, this has led to renewed interest in investigating the gradual growth of smaller traditions rather than larger documents, and has had significant implications for emerging theories regarding pentateuchal origins.

The Elohist Source

The 'E' source, in standard documentary theories, was thought to contain a story that ran parallel to what is found in 'J', offering stories that complement those in 'J', or which were variations on the same. This source was also thought to contain primarily narratives, and to have taken shape in the northern kingdom of Israel c.850–750 BCE. This source also derives its names from one of its characteristics, as it was thought to employ the more general name for God, *elohim*, as opposed to the personal name YHWH.

The 'E' source has from the beginning been the most commonly questioned source of the Documentary Hypothesis. There are a number of reasons for this. To begin with, the materials traditionally ascribed to 'E' are quite fragmentary in nature, and the various episodes do not add up to a cohesive narrative that one would expect from a source text. A further issue is the difficulty in differentiating it from 'J', and even Wellhausen himself often referred to 'JE' as a source. We have seen already that scholars such as Noth explain this as due to their basis in a common source. However, through the years scholars began to suggest that the source 'E' should be understood as smaller fragments that were added to 'J', or, increasingly, abandoned altogether.

There have been some attempts in recent years to rehabilitate the notion of 'E' as a viable source relying less heavily on the criteria of terminology or theology of the source and focusing more on narrative coherence (Baden 2012). Nevertheless, 'E' remains problematic in the eyes of many. Fuller discussion on the 'E' source can be found in J.C. Gertz (2014).

The Deuteronomic Source

From the beginning, 'D' has always had a slightly unusual position in the Documentary Hypothesis. While the other sources are seen as being spread relatively evenly throughout the first four books of the Pentateuch, the vast majority of 'D' traditionally was thought to be contained in the book of Deuteronomy. The content of the book has a number of parallels with the reforms of Josiah, the seventh-century BCE king of Judah, and many have suggested that the 'book of the law' discovered in 2 Kings 22 refers in fact to (at least parts of) Deuteronomy. While many still hold some connection between Deuteronomy and the Josianic reforms, it is common to presume that the book contains elements of both earlier material and later redactions (Römer 2005).

A crucial question for source critics is how much of 'D' can be found in Genesis to Numbers (sometimes called the Tetrateuch). If the answer is none, the Deuteronomic Source has little part to play in the Documentary Hypothesis as a whole. As we have noted elsewhere, because of continuity with the books of Joshua–Kings, Deuteronomy has been thought to be part of a so-called 'Deuteronomistic History' that extended through the historical books of the Hebrew Bible, and much attention has been given to this connection (Noth [1943] 1967). However, this notion, too, has become problematic, and has led to various proposals regarding the relationship of Deuteronomy and subsequent books in the Hebrew canon (Schearing and McKenzie 1999; Römer 2005; Schmid and Person 2012).

Meanwhile, scholars such as J. Blenkinsopp have argued for 'a more extensive D editing of the history from Abraham to Moses than the classical Documentary Hypothesis contemplated' (1992: 236). This idea resonates with that of Blum (1990), who suggests that there is a 'D' redactional layer to the whole Pentateuch, moving 'D' into a more central position regarding the formation of the Pentateuch, assuming prominence with 'P'.

The Priestly Source

The Priestly Source has traditionally been envisaged as the final source of the Pentateuch, containing both narrative and legal materials, and coming from the hands of priestly leaders in the exilic and post-exilic periods. This material, with its distinctive terminology and theology, has traditionally been recognized in parts of Genesis, Exodus, Leviticus, Numbers, as well as the end of Deuteronomy.

Advances in studies on the Priestly Source mirror the major areas of development identified for the Yahwist Source. The focus has been on locating more than one strand in the source, understanding the creative (or editorial) impulse of the writer or school of writers/editors, reconsidering the extent of the 'P' materials, and attempting to redate the source. What differentiates 'P' and 'J' is that the existence of the Priestly element of the Pentateuch has never been questioned, even if debate continues over the nature and extent of this tradition.

Wellhausen himself noted that there was a distinction between the narrative material of the Priestly Source and the legal material. Many subsequent scholars have supported this position, though there is not entire agreement as to what should count as narrative and what as legal material. Noth's abbreviation of P^g to refer to narrative material and P^s to refer to legal material is the most common, though not the only, way of referring to possible different strands within the source.

In addition, many regard the Priestly Source as comprising a number of pre-existing sources, two of the best known being the 'book of generations' (or *toledot*, from the Hebrew word for generations), as well as some of the legislative material concerning sacrifices in Leviticus 1–7. The theory about the 'book of generations' arises from the fact that the Pentateuch is punctuated in various places with long lists of genealogies. These begin with the Hebrew phrase *sepher toledot*, literally the 'book of generations' (though translated in the NRSV as 'the list of the descendants' – see, for example, Gen. 5.1). It is at least possible that these genealogies formed an original source, later incorporated into the Priestly Source.

This use of pre-existing sources raises questions about the Priestly Source's creative role in the formation of the Pentateuch. Since Wellhausen, most scholars have regarded 'P' as the last source to be written and often as responsible for redacting the Pentateuch into its current form. F.M. Cross went even further and suggested that 'P' was much more important as a redactor than as a source. He argues that the 'P' material present in the Pentateuch is so scanty that at best it can only be regarded as the 'précis of P' (1973: 294), not the whole narrative. 'P' was responsible for structuring the Pentateuch into its current form but contains little material from an original Priestly Source. In contrast to this minimal view of the Priestly Source, other scholars have a higher view of the source. N. Lohfink (1994) believes that it is possible to identify a Priestly historical narrative, and Carr (1996) and J.-L. Ska (2006) have offered similar proposals.

Another issue relates to the extent of an original 'P' narrative. The Priestly narrative materials traditionally were understood to run from Genesis 1 right through Numbers and, indeed, parts of Deuteronomy 34. However, a number of studies have suggested that an original 'P' source ends well before Numbers, with proposals of the reconceived ending ranging from Exodus 40 (Pola 1995) to Leviticus 16 (Nihan 2007).

A final concern relates to the dating of 'P' and stands in opposition to Wellhausen's theory of the development of the religion of Israel. One motivation behind Wellhausen's dating of the different sources was his belief that Israel's religious history developed over a period of time and that it is possible to trace this development in the different sources of the Pentateuch. Wellhausen believed that religions began as a spontaneous expression arising from the events of everyday life. Then, as it developed, it became more institutional and eventually lost all spontaneity. Consequently, he regarded 'JE' as the earliest sources, containing evidence of spontaneous worship, followed by 'D' with its interest in centralizing the worship of Israel, and, last of all, 'P' and its insistence on correct legal and ritual observance. Wellhausen's dislike of Judaism as a religious system is well known. His theory that Judaism developed from spontaneous worship to an institutionalized religion dominated by priests arises from this bias. This has led various scholars to question the basis of his judgement on the dating of the sources which lie behind the Pentateuch. A. Hurwitz (1982) and others have argued in favour of a pre-exilic date for the Priestly Source on linguistic and theological grounds, comparing the language of the Priestly Source with that of Ezekiel and post-exilic texts and maintaining that the language of the Priestly writer was earlier. Nevertheless, the majority of scholars still hold that 'P' – whether as source or redaction – is better situated in an exilic or post-exilic setting, even if eschewing Wellhausen's reasoning for dating as such (Ska 2006).

In summary: for a long time, a broad consensus existed among scholars about the nature and dating of the Pentateuch's sources. The brief survey given above demonstrates that this consensus no longer exists. Various factors have led people to question the hypothesis, ranging from the existence of 'J' and 'E', to the extent of 'D' and 'P' and their editorial influence, to the relative dating of each source. These developments have led to the flowering of different proposals and approaches, to which we now turn.

Current developments in the search for pentateuchal origins

Although there is no new assured consensus to replace that of the traditional Documentary Hypothesis, other proposals to explain the origins of the Pentateuch have emerged in recent decades. A number of broad developments are worth noting, namely the advancement of theories based on smaller traditions and units rather than sources, and approaches that rework elements of the traditional Documentary Hypothesis.

Fragmentary and supplementary approaches

One of the most significant shifts in recent decades has been the move away from examining continuous narratives in the Pentateuch and instead exploring smaller units or traditions. As noted above, Rendtorff was influenced by the scholarship of von Rad and Noth but, unlike them, considered that their theories concerning oral tradition placed the Documentary Hypothesis in question. He turned his attention to what he saw as discrete units of tradition such as primeval history, patriarchal narratives, the exodus, the giving of the law at Sinai, and the wandering in the wilderness (though there were others who had begun to suggest this prior to and simultaneous with Rendtorff; see Carr 2015). Rendtorff maintained that these units of tradition were not part of continuous strands (such as 'J' or 'E') but were independent units that had developed separately and had been joined together by a later redactor. This theory questions the basis of the Documentary Hypothesis that the Pentateuch contains continuous sources that stretch from beginning to end, in favour of numerous smaller units originally unrelated to one another. In this vein of thought, the notion of large documents being brought together is replaced by a focus on fragmentary and supplementary development of the text, along with significant redaction and editing of these materials.

Three related developments are worth noting. A number of these have been touched on in the above discussion, as they relate to research that has been undertaken on the various sources and new theories that have arisen from such investigations.

First, a growing number of scholars have expanded on or reworked elements of Rendtorff's hypothesis that greater attention should be paid to smaller units of tradition. Rendtorff's student, E. Blum, published two major volumes (1984, 1990) employing this tradition-based supplementary approach. In these studies, Blum highlighted the bringing together of smaller units of tradition, first in Genesis, and then in the wider Pentateuch, dismissing the need for notions of 'J' and 'E' (see also Carr 1996). Here a major development was the idea that Israel's stories of origins, as seen in the patriarchs and the Moses story, were not originally connected as had long been assumed. Furthering this idea, Gertz (2000) and Schmid ([1999] 2010) investigated Exodus and the connections with the ancestral traditions of Genesis, noting the distinct provenance of these traditions and suggesting in fact that such connections were quite late. These distinct stories of origins, in this reading, were brought together most likely in the post-exilic period, to form a cohesive whole. It is quite possible that elements of these stories of origins are quite ancient, and it is also plausible that the writers of the original traditions were aware of the different stories of Israel's origins. Nevertheless, an increasing number of scholars suggest that it was the Priestly tradition that first brought these stories of origins together, much later than has traditionally been assumed.

A second development has been a substantial revisiting of the 'P' and 'D' traditions, which have become increasingly important in such reconstructions. A number of scholars now suggest that the Pentateuch emerged from two centres: a Deuteronomic core, and a Priestly strand (Otto 2000, 2013; MacDonald 2012a). Here, with the bringing together of these two centres and their respective texts and traditions, lies the beginning of the Pentateuch as we know it. Most who follow this view tend to see these collections as having taken shape in the exilic and post-exilic eras. There is also some consensus that there are both 'P' and 'D' redactions in the final shaping of the Pentateuch; however, there is less agreement as to how many Priestly and Deuteronomic revisions took place, and in what order they might have occurred.

Third, a related trend in recent years has been the recognition of what are referred to as 'post-Priestly' additions to the Pentateuch; that is, there is evidence of yet further additions and editing that seem to have come after the larger blocks of traditional 'P' (and 'D') material had taken shape (Giuntoli and Schmid 2015). Examples of this include elements of the non-Priestly primeval history in Genesis 1–11 (Blenkinsopp 1992), links between Moses and the patriarchal traditions in Exodus and Genesis (Schmid 2010), and the more radical notion that the book of Numbers, in its entirety, might be a 'post-Priestly bridge' that brings together the Priestly traditions with Deuteronomy (Achenbach 2003).

Taken together, there are a number of points of convergence that can be seen in these recent approaches which focus on smaller units and the supplementing of these traditions. There is agreement that (1) there were diverse stories of origins based around the ancestors and Moses which emerged separately; (2) there was development of legal and narrative traditions from Priestly and Deuteronomic traditions that also developed separately, though there may have been awareness of and reworking of older, received traditions within both; (3) the Pentateuch exhibits both Deuteronomic and Priestly redactions; and (4) there are post-Priestly additions and redactions of the material that continued on for some time.

How does this relate to the dating of the pentateuchal material? Differences of opinion remain on these matters, even among those supporting a supplementary model. Some hold that all of these materials took shape and were written down in the exilic, post-exilic, or even the Hellenistic eras. Others are more confident that some of these writings can be traced back to the early monarchy, though they were likely revised in the exilic and post-exilic eras (Carr 2011). In all of these reconstructions, however, the exile and its aftermath are understood to have been significant in the formation and development of the traditions as we now have them, even if some of the traditions – both narrative and legal – are quite ancient.

A further ramification of these developments has been the question of nomenclature for the various traditions and sources. Many of the scholars who have followed in Rendtorff's footsteps have abandoned any reference to 'J' and 'E' and instead tend to speak of Priestly ('P'), non-Priestly ('non-P'), and post-Priestly ('post-P', or Rp, for 'post-P redaction') materials. Some, including Carr (2010), have begun to refer to 'P' and 'L', for 'Priestly' and 'lay' traditions, reflecting the diverse contexts out of which these traditions seem to have emerged.

The Documentary Hypothesis, revisited

Meanwhile, work has continued in various directions that carry on elements of the Documentary Hypothesis. As noted above, scholars such as J. Van Seters (1999) and C. Levin (1993) have retained elements of the hypothesis such as the 'J' source, though reworking this and other elements in significant ways and moving them to the exilic period. These theories are in reality quite distinct from the original Documentary Hypothesis, even if retaining some of the nomenclature.

Another development in recent years, and one which bears a much stronger resemblance to traditional Documentary models, can be referred to as the Neo-Documentary Hypothesis (Baden 2009, 2012; Schwartz 2011; Stackert 2014). Here we find a renewed interest in the idea of documentary sources and the notion of four distinct sources (even the much maligned 'E' source). Nevertheless, these studies advocate for using different criteria than that which was employed by Wellhausen and others, focusing more on narrative threads than on distinctive terminology or theological frameworks. J.S. Baden (2012) suggests that the European-based supplementary approaches outlined above are circular: they argue for a lack of unity by positing that those parts which are suggestive of unity are later additions. Hence, a key element of these revised forms of the Documentary Hypothesis is the belief that the sources in question have been brought together with very little editing.

Dialogue in recent years between neo-Documentarian approaches and supplementary models has reinforced that there are significant differences in these approaches (see the essays in Dozeman, Schmid, and Schwartz 2011). Nevertheless, it is worth bearing in mind that, while we speak of 'source' and 'supplementary' models, advocates of the latter would say that the process very likely included both documentary sources and the supplementing of traditions (Römer 2013). As such, some caution is needed in drawing distinctions which are too sharp, particularly as this is an active and ongoing area of research.

There is also some common ground that cuts across the various approaches, and these issues are also important to keep in mind. To begin with, critical scholarship today agrees that there is not a simple, unified pentateuchal text. Literary and other approaches that focus on the text as a whole have become increasingly important in recent years, as will be discussed in Chapter 8. However, this does not imply any sort of return to pre-critical notions of a single author. Further, while there is disagreement about the extent and dating of 'P', there is nonetheless a general consensus that 'P' materials can be identified in the Pentateuch. Finally, most agree that the exilic and post-exilic periods were formative in leading to the present form of the Pentateuch. There are, then, several critical elements where agreement can be found from those across the spectrum of approaches (Kratz 2011).

The issues outlined thus far regarding the origins of these texts and traditions are closely related to questions concerning their emergence as an authoritative collection, and we turn next to explore some of the issues related to when and why this might have taken place.

The Pentateuch as an authoritative collection

The origin of these texts and traditions does not necessarily explain their emergence as an authoritative collection, though the two are intimately related. We offer here an examination of the evidence which points to the existence of the Torah as an authoritative collection before exploring reasons proffered for its emergence.

Evidence for the collection

The evidence for when these traditions emerged as *authoritative*, and later as an *authoritative collection*, begins in the Hebrew Bible itself. The narratives of the Pentateuch are echoed elsewhere in the Hebrew Bible, and certain themes found in the Pentateuch can be found in varying forms in many other biblical books, though establishing the direction of dependence (if any) is a complex task. Examples of this include creation (Ps. 148.5), God's covenant with the patriarchs (2 Kgs 13.23), the exodus (Jer. 2.6), and the giving of the law to Moses on Sinai (Neh. 9.13). It also seems at least possible that later biblical writers knew portions of the actual Pentateuch itself, as well as the stories it contains. An example of this is the book of Nehemiah, which describes Ezra reading to the people from the 'book of the law of Moses' after they had returned from exile (Neh. 8.1-3). The book of Nehemiah does not record the words that were read but it does record what the people did as a result of hearing the law read by Ezra. The reforms that the people undertook as a result of hearing the book's contents seem to be inspired by commandments found in both Leviticus and Deuteronomy. Consequently many scholars regard the book of the law from which Ezra read as being a part of the Pentateuch, though there is disagreement as to whether this should be understood as the whole Pentateuch as we know it (Blenkinsopp 1988; Pakkala 2011).

In addition to this, certain verses from the Pentateuch are found again and again in different contexts, though determining priority of these is again challenging. An example of this is Exod. 34.6: 'The LORD, the LORD, a God merciful and gracious, slow to anger, and abounding in steadfast love and faithfulness.' This verse became a standard description of God and is used in numerous other passages, though its source is never identified (see, for example, Neh. 9.17; Pss. 86.15; 103.8; 145.8; Joel 2.13; and Jon. 4.2). Thus, there are pentateuchal texts and themes found elsewhere in the Hebrew Bible, but it is difficult to draw any conclusions from these as to when the five books were understood as a distinct, authoritative collection.

Moving towards the Common Era we find further evidence. Ben Sira, from the second century BCE, makes reference to the law of Moses, but also retells much of the pentateuchal narrative, along with the rest of the story of Israel. Meanwhile, the Qumran materials, the earliest documentary evidence we have, point to the fact that they had some form of authoritative status for the community there (White Crawford 2007). Finally, in the New Testament, we find reference made to 'the law', 'the law of Moses', and 'the book of Moses', as well as reference to key characters and events from the Torah, together pointing to the fact that the five scrolls were a collection and had authority as well as a place of privilege in first-century CE Judaism (see, for example, Mt. 12.5; Mk 12.26; Lk. 2.23-24; Jn 7.23; Gal. 3.10).

Of relevance to this discussion on the authoritative status of the Pentateuch are the Samaritans, a group with ancient roots in Palestine and who still exist today in small numbers (on the historical emergence of the Samaritans, see Kartveit 2009 and Knoppers 2013). While many of the details are lost to history, it is clear that by the final few centuries before the Common Era, the Samaritan and Jewish communities in post-exilic Judea were forging distinct identities, in spite of holding much in common. One of the more interesting aspects of the Samaritan tradition is that the Samaritans use the Pentateuch as their Scriptures, and these five books constitute the entirety of their canon (Anderson and Giles 2012).

There are differences between the Jewish and Samaritan Pentateuchs, including the injunction in the Samaritan tradition to worship at Mount Gerizim, the location at which the Samaritans built their own temple. Nonetheless, the commonalities between the two Pentateuchs far outnumber the differences. Indeed, the Samaritan version of the Pentateuch is quite ancient, and seems to pre-date the Common Era. In this respect, the two traditions share textual traditions that may pre-date those which would become the received texts in both traditions (Knoppers 2011). In light of this, it is worth noting that the two traditions share the Pentateuch, not a collection of four or six books (Tetrateuch or Hexateuch, discussed below). This again points to the fact that in the centuries leading up to the Common Era, the material found in the Pentateuch seems to have been set apart as a unique collection with special authority in the Jewish (and Samaritan) tradition.

Thus, while some traditions and elements of the Torah no doubt are much older, the sum of the evidence – from the Hebrew Bible, the Samaritans, Qumran, and other ancient Jewish texts – suggests that by at least the fourth century BCE, and maybe earlier in the fifth century, the Pentateuch was recognized as a collection with some authoritative status.

When and how these texts and traditions became the five separate texts of Genesis to Deuteronomy is unclear. Both Philo (*Aet. Mund.*) and Josephus (*Apion*) make specific reference to five books, which suggests that by the time of these Jewish writers, the five works of the Pentateuch were well established as a collection with individual parts. It could be that there were physical reasons for such a division, related to how much material could practically be included on a scroll. However, there are obvious thematic and narrative breaks in the division of the books as we have them, and the lengths of the books are far from uniform, which suggests that length was not the only criteria when the division into five books was made (Blenkinsopp 1992). Recent work, particularly that on Numbers and Deuteronomy, has suggested that the combining of these larger works was instrumental in the formation of the Pentateuch, which would indicate that there were divisions between these 'books' from an early stage.

Issues related to authorization

What led to the authoritative status of this collection? A number of issues have been considered in relation to this question, including external pressure, internal factors, and the question of textual collections.

External pressure: Persian imperial authorization

One idea is known as the 'Persian Imperial Authorization' theory, suggesting that the Pentateuch emerged as a local legislation for post-exilic Yehud (Judea) authorized by Persian authorities (Frei 1984; see further discussion in the essays in Watts 2001). Some have attempted to explain the diverse redactional layers that are found in the Pentateuch, notably between 'P' and 'non-P' traditions, in light of such Persian authorization. An example of this is offered by E. Blum (1990), who posits that there are two compositional layers that can be detected in the Pentateuch: a 'D' layer (*D-Kompsition*) and a 'P' layer (*P-Komposition*). In Blum's view, both of these were post-exilic redactions, and these strands may be seen as a compromise between different voices in post-exilic Yehud, brought together because the Persians would allow only one authoritative document. This theory has come in for criticism in recent decades, as doubt has been cast on the involvement of the Persians in local affairs of this kind. However, other scholars have recently noted that Persian concerns and influence should not be completely disregarded, as it seems probable that the Persians may have responded to ad-hoc requests concerning authorization of local laws (Schmid 2007).

Internal developments

The suggestion of compromise within Yehud points to the fact that internal issues also played a role in terms of how and why the Pentateuch acquired its authoritative status, and some feel that these 'native concerns' should receive more consideration regarding the collecting of these texts and traditions. A number of theories highlight such issues.

Several of these theories note developments related to social formation, including the religious community and its leaders. Ska (2006), for example, points to the idea of citizens connected to the temple. Noting that temples functioned as cultural and social centres in the ancient world, Ska posits that the Torah would serve to provide criteria for membership and authorize the structures of leadership as the community organized itself around the rebuilt temple. J.W. Watts, meanwhile, suggests that the Torah emerged as authoritative because of its ritual authority, noting that 'more than any other factor, it was the authority of the temple's ritual traditions that established the Pentateuch's prestige' (2007: 214).

Others have argued that diversity within Judaism in this period is the most plausible explanation for the emergence of the Torah as an authoritative collection, with all of its complexity. For example, D. Edelman et al. outline a number of possible factors that led to 'the Pentateuch as a document of compromise between different scribal schools in Jerusalem in the late fifth or early fourth century BCE' (2012: 105). They note as follows:

> The schools agreed to bring the different traditions they regarded as authoritative – for example, the Priestly writing – and to combine them to create a normative account or, if one prefers, a 'founding legend' of the origins of 'Israel'. That normative account, while it preserved conflicting views, was nevertheless unified by a comprehensive narrative framework stretching from the origins of the world (Genesis 1) to the death of the lawgiver, Moses (Deuteronomy 34). (2012: 105–6)

The authors outline a number of such 'unresolved conflicts', including the discussion of altars in Exod. 20.24-26 and Deuteronomy 12. They go on to note,

> Even though the Torah was probably composed in Jerusalem, concessions were made to Yahwistic communities outside Yehud in order to make it acceptable to them. The decision to end the Torah with Moses' death outside of the land (Deuteronomy 34) rather than with Joshua's conquest is significant … This ending is best explained as a concession to the diaspora. It is not necessary to live inside the Promised Land to live in accordance with the Torah. (2012: 106)

They conclude that 'the relative openness of the Pentateuch was an attempt to cope with the complexity of the religious, ethnic and political situation during the Persian period, when several different groups could claim to be the true heirs to the former kingdom of Israel' (2012: 109).

Textual developments: Tetrateuch, Pentateuch, Hexateuch, or Enneateuch?

The previous issue is closely tied to how these first five books relate to others in the Hebrew Bible, notably those which continue the story of Israel after that found in the Pentateuch. The issues introduced here remain at the forefront of work on the Pentateuch (various proposals are discussed in the essays collected in Dozeman, Römer, and Schmid 2011).

Various scholars have regarded this collection not as a five-volume work but as a six-volume work ('Hexateuch') or as a four-volume work ('Tetrateuch'). Although he was not the first to propose it, J. Wellhausen made the idea of a Hexateuch popular at the end of the nineteenth century. In addition to the five books, Genesis to Deuteronomy, the Hexateuch also included the book of Joshua. The effect of this theory is to end the sweep of the narrative in the Promised Land itself, rather than on the brink of it as with the 'Pentateuch'. The difficulty with this idea is that we have no textual witnesses of a 'Hexateuch', and the special status given to the Pentateuch as a collection seems to be quite an ancient one.

In contrast, Noth proposed not a Hexateuch but a Tetrateuch. In his seminal work, published in English under the title of *The Deuteronomistic History* ([1943] 1981), he argued that the book of Deuteronomy did not form the conclusion to the books of Genesis to Numbers but instead acted as a prologue to what the Hebrew Bible terms the 'Former prophets' (Joshua to 2 Kings). Without its fifth book, the books of Genesis to Numbers become a Tetrateuch instead of a Pentateuch. Again, this proposal provided some important insights into the initial books of the Hebrew Bible, notably the significant stylistic and terminological differences between Deuteronomy and Genesis–Numbers. However, this theory, too, has come in for criticism in recent years, particularly as more and more Deuteronomic elements have been identified in the other pentateuchal books, along with discontinuity between Deuteronomy and some of the historical books (Dozeman 2009; Otto 2013).

A further proposal suggests that the books of Genesis–Kings form a coherent story of Israel from creation to the exile. This collection, the idea of which goes back to Spinoza, is sometimes referred to as the Enneateuch (the nine books), or the Primary History (Freedman 1962). Here the broad sweep of Israel's story is highlighted, but this theory on its own again struggles to explain why such a collection was ever narrowed down in such a way as to give special authoritative status to the Pentateuch.

Recent work on the origins of the Pentateuch has led to a renewed interest in these issues, although nuanced in approach. R.G. Kratz (2005), for example, has followed the notion of a Hexateuch, suggesting that the first complete account of Israel's origins actually extended through Joshua to include the conquest, but that Joshua was eventually excluded from this specific collection. T. Römer (2011a), meanwhile, presents an option focused on the place of Deuteronomy, positing that there were competing redactional camps in the post-exilic period which had differing views on the placement of Deuteronomy. He suggests that a collection had developed which included Deuteronomy with Joshua–Kings, along with other related texts (what he calls a Deuteronomistic Library). However, voices in the Holiness School wanted to bring together the Priestly and Deuteronomistic traditions, which instigated the development of the Pentateuch as a discrete collection. Thus, Deuteronomy comes to be associated with Genesis–Numbers, more so than Joshua and the books which follow:

> The removal of Deuteronomy from the Deuteronomistic Library is due to the fact that the coherence of the Torah as a compromise or consensus between the Priestly and the lay party was found in the figure of Moses. When Deuteronomy became the conclusion of the Torah, it acquired a new status; it was now considered to provide an explanation for the Sinai revelation. The origin of the Pentateuch was, according to this model, the partition of Deuteronomy from the following books. (Römer 2011a: 39)

While not the only factor to consider in relation to how this collection might have taken shape, the role of Deuteronomy in this process continues to be an important point in research (Schmid and Person 2012).

There are, then, both external factors (such as possible Persian influence) as well as internal and textual factors (related to literary collections of texts as well as compromise between various groups) that may have led to the consolidation and authoritative status of the Pentateuch in the post-exilic period. Indeed, a number of scholars would posit that some combination of these factors should be considered in relation to the development of the Pentateuch as authoritative (Schmid 2007).

Formation, authorization, and textual stability

Finally, it is also worth bearing in mind that the collection and authorization of these texts and traditions does not mean that we should assume corresponding textual stability. This is quite a substantial change from previous generations, where textual stability and authorization were thought to go hand in hand in a relatively straightforward process. However, along with the Samaritan Pentateuch, the texts from Qumran point to the existence of a good deal of textual fluidity and instability in 'biblical' texts right through to the beginning of the Common Era (Ulrich 2010). Even as these texts were undergoing the process of scripturalization and coming to have greater authority within the Jewish community, there were significant textual variants, a reality which indicates that authorization and textual stabilization were not one and the same process.

Concluding remarks

This chapter has explored questions relating to the origins and formation of the Pentateuch, and has focused on two interrelated issues: the question of the authorship and origins of these texts, and questions concerning the formation of these texts as an authoritative collection. The brief survey offered above highlights the complex nature of these discussions; the arguments put forward can be dense and difficult to navigate, and they are ever evolving. Indeed, as J.J. Collins notes, all of these developments demonstrate that 'the reconstruction of earlier forms of the biblical text is a highly speculative enterprise' (2014: 66). And yet, such questions remain central to pentateuchal scholarship, pointing to the continued importance of these texts in scholarship as well as in the religious traditions for which they are Scripture.

While the search for the origins of the Pentateuch has long captured the attention of scholars, recent decades have witnessed the rise of a variety of other approaches to studying and interpreting these five books. We turn to these other approaches in our next chapter.

Further reading

For helpful discussions on the historical development of pentateuchal criticism, including the Documentary Hypothesis, see Whybray (1987), Nicholson (1998), and Ska (2006). The various difficulties of the documentary sources, challenges to the hypothesis, and new directions in pentateuchal studies are noted in Blenkinsopp (1992), Kratz (2005), Ska (2006), and Carr (2015). Collections of essays that point to the state of the conversation on various issues outlined above include Dozeman and Schmid (2006), as well as Dozeman, Schmid, and Schwartz (2011). The various issues at work in discussions of the Tetrateuch, Pentateuch, Hexateuch, and Enneateuch are outlined in Dozeman, Römer, and Schmid (2011), as well as Person and Schmid (2012). The question of how and when these five books became authoritative is explored in the volume of essays edited by Knoppers and Levinson (2007).

Academic Approaches to Reading and Studying the Pentateuch

As outlined in Chapter 7, the issue of the origins and formation of the Pentateuch has been at the forefront of pentateuchal scholarship for much of the modern period, and continues to play an important role. However, recent decades have witnessed a general movement in biblical studies away from merely historical approaches to a host of other considerations, such as how the text functions as a piece of literature, and how these books might be understood from the vantage point of different readers and perspectives. Allowing for these various types of questions has opened up a range of ways in which these texts can be studied and understood.

With these developments in mind, the present chapter will concentrate on the variety of methods and approaches that are used in the contemporary academic study of the Pentateuch, using four broad categories: historical approaches, literary methods, reader-centred and theoretical approaches, and theological perspectives (Moyise 2013). What follows is a brief introduction to some of these approaches, though there is an ever-expanding range of options available to readers who wish to engage with the Pentateuch in a critical fashion.

Historical approaches

There are a number of methods and approaches in pentateuchal research that are historically focused. Indeed, a widely used phrase in biblical studies is 'historical criticism', or the 'historical-critical' method. This designation does not indicate one specific method or approach, but is something of an umbrella term that incorporates a number of methods and approaches that are oriented to historical concerns and a critical framework of interpretation. These tools are used by scholars to explore the world *behind the text*, and include questions such as where the text has come from, what led to its development and place in the canon, and how understanding the ancient world can help us better understand the biblical material.

Chapter 7 illustrated that a good deal of scholarly energy has been expended on the search for the origins of the Pentateuch, as well as its formation. Indeed, the roots of the academic study of the Bible were closely tied to these types of questions, from B. Spinoza to J. Wellhausen. Although the search for origins is a multifaceted field that contains a variety of approaches, that which is most commonly associated with these concerns is source criticism – the attempt to isolate particular sources in the Pentateuch as well as distinctive elements of these sources. The search for the origins of the Pentateuch continues to develop in new directions, as R. Rendtorff (1990) and others have turned their attention to fragmentary or supplementary models in the quest for origins – that is, the idea that there were smaller blocks of tradition which were brought together and supplemented over time.

Another key component of historical-critical research is textual criticism (Tov 2011). This method compares textual witnesses (such as those from Qumran and other ancient Hebrew, Greek, and Aramaic manuscripts) for similarities, differences, and adaptations that might shed light on the text and its history of development. As we have no 'original' autographs of biblical texts, textual criticism is used to compare available resources to produce the most authentic version of the text, as much as this is possible (on some of the difficulties in trying to re-produce an 'original' text, see Breed 2014).

A further set of historically based approaches revolves around what S. Moyise calls the 'search for context' (2013: 43–60). These approaches try to better understand the Bible by understanding the context in which it took shape. An example of this search for context can be seen in social-scientific research (Simkins and Cook 1999). Drawing on sociological and anthropological approaches, social-scientific research focuses on the social and cultural dimensions of the biblical text and the world behind the text. This includes exploring the cultures and traditions of the biblical world, focusing on issues such as family life in the ancient world, institutional structures, notions of prophets and prophecy, the impact and extent of movement and migration, and the Bible itself as a cultural artefact. Here attempts are made to better understand the historical context of the biblical material, and the world out of which these texts and traditions emerged.

Another important part of exploring the world behind the text is archaeology, a field which involves investigating the material culture of the ancient world. There is little archaeological evidence directly relating to the events portrayed in the Pentateuch, and this has led some to rethink the historicity of events such as the exodus or the wilderness wanderings. Nevertheless, archaeological discoveries from other ancient Near Eastern cultures have shed significant light on the world of the Bible and the first five books in particular, from discoveries that illuminate ancient religious practices to texts from other cultures that help contextualize what we find in the Bible. In this sense, archaeology is an important element of comparative research on the Pentateuch. These points of contact will be discussed in greater detail in subsequent chapters.

Literary approaches

An important development in biblical studies in the latter half of the twentieth century was the recognition that there are valid questions worth asking of the biblical text beyond those that are historically oriented. That is to say, there is more to the Bible than the world behind the text; there is also the *world of the text*. Influenced by developments in other fields and disciplines such as literary studies, there emerged a renewed interest in the text of the Bible as we have it.

Literary studies on the Pentateuch have been utilized most prominently on narrative materials; such approaches take special notice of issues such as plot, characterization, and wordplay. A significant development in this appreciation of literary and narrative issues was R. Alter's book *The Art of Biblical Narrative* (1981). Alter – a Jewish literary critic with knowledge of the Hebrew Bible and its language – highlighted the literary artistry that is found throughout the Hebrew Bible, most notably in the narrative texts. While aware of the various historical-critical issues relating to the Bible and its origins, Alter argued that there is a purposeful shaping of these texts that is suggestive of creative literary minds. Alter engaged with a number of texts from the Pentateuch in this book, which became influential in the field. His later annotated translation of the Pentateuch (2004) also highlighted many of these literary and narrative dimensions of the first five books.

Scholars have increasingly brought this type of literary focus to their explorations of the diverse materials found with the Pentateuch, sometimes as a whole, but most often in its parts. One might first note D.J.A. Clines, who offers a literary reading of the entire Pentateuch and locates an overarching theme for the whole of the collection. Rather than examining the theme of one source or book within the Pentateuch, Clines chooses to examine the theme of the 'final form' of the Pentateuch, that is, what we have now. The motivation behind this is a recognition of the importance of the Pentateuch as a collection within both the Jewish and Christian traditions. Clines identifies the theme of the Pentateuch as 'the partial fulfilment – which implies also the partial non-fulfilment – of the promise to or blessing of the patriarchs' (1997: 30). He maintains that this promise has three elements: posterity, divine–human relationship, and land. These, he maintains, are interdependent: a promise from YHWH must involve a divine–human relationship, which gains value by being for posterity and including land. He identifies that what he regards as the three major sections of the Pentateuch – Genesis 12–50, Exodus and Leviticus, and Numbers and Deuteronomy – each contain one element of this triple promise. Genesis 12–50 is concerned with posterity through the promise to Abraham, Exodus and Leviticus focus on the divine–human relationship, and Numbers and Deuteronomy explore the concept of land.

The majority of literary studies on the Pentateuch, meanwhile, have focused on smaller units of text, as well as characters and themes found within the five books. Some examples include studies on narrative issues in Genesis (Fokkelman 1975), explorations of the literary character of God in Genesis (Humphreys 2001), and the study of Leviticus as literature (Douglas 1999). All of these, in various ways, have shifted the focus to the world of the text and the literary elements that are found there.

Reader-centred and theoretical approaches

The value of literary approaches such as those mentioned above is that they examine and engage seriously with the content of the text. However, the factors that lead someone to identify a theme as the central message of a book or collection can often be open to individual interpretation. In fact, Clines, in the 1997 'Afterword' to his original 1978 book, recognizes this very point. Whereas he formerly considered the theme that he identified to be the meaning intended by the author, he would now regard it simply as the meaning that he himself encountered in the text and not necessarily what was originally intended. Clines is not alone in this shift in understanding. The trend in biblical studies over the past several decades has been to recognize that subjectivity should not be condemned, and that supposed objective approaches are themselves plagued with subjectivity. Indeed, in the current climate of biblical studies, the value of a multiplicity of readings is recognized, and the subjective role of the reader is appreciated. Such a realization plays an important role in reader-centred and theoretical approaches, what we might think of as exploring the *world in front of the text*. These approaches draw on the concerns and perspectives of the person reading, and include approaches that investigate the text from a variety of social, cultural and theoretical perspectives.

Feminist readings are, perhaps, the best-known interpretations of this type, and have made significant contributions to biblical and pentateuchal scholarship. Feminist readings can take on several forms, including reclaiming and recovering often-ignored stories of women, as well as re-reading texts to highlight issues of patriarchy and to challenge the text and its assumptions. As A. Brenner writes in her introduction to *A Feminist Companion to Genesis*, feminist approaches 'can expose the anti-woman bias, or reclaim the text by reading it afresh, or reform it by revisionist approaches'. And yet, she notes, in all of these readings, 'some form of counter-reading is unavoidable' (1993: 1). The feminist companions to Genesis (1993) and Exodus-Deuteronomy (2000), both edited by A. Brenner, are helpful in that they present the range of ways in which feminist interpretation engages with the biblical text. Other works that offer readings of the pentateuchal materials reflecting this diversity of perspectives include those of I. Fischer ([1995] 2005), P. Trible (1984), and J.C. Exum (2016).

Further approaches that intentionally focus on readers and their social location include liberationist and postcolonial readings. Drawing inspiration from liberation theology, liberationist readings focus on how the text can be a force for liberation, particularly for those on the margins of society. G.V. Pixley's commentary on Exodus (1987) focuses on how the exodus and related events can be read in light of liberation motifs. Meanwhile, A. Laffey (1998) has produced a study on the Pentateuch which she calls a 'liberation-critical reading', drawing inspiration from both feminist and liberationist readings of the text to again focus on constructive ways in which the text can be used as a source of liberation.

A related, yet distinct, approach is postcolonial biblical criticism, which is concerned with the effects of colonialism on the emergence of biblical texts, but also in terms of how the Bible has been and continues to be interpreted in light of these dynamics (Sugirtharajah 2006). Thus, postcolonial criticism asks what it might mean that Israel's Scriptures emerged primarily when this people group was under the reign of vast empires of the ANE. However, it also explores the implications of Israel's complex relationship with its neighbours, and its relation to (or colonization of) the land of Israel. Finally, postcolonial criticism looks at the various ways in which the Bible has been used to subjugate peoples and societies throughout history, and how reading the text from the perspectives of the colonizer and the colonized can be both illuminating and challenging. In relation to the Pentateuch, attention has primarily been given to how the development and formation of these books might relate to the empires of the time (from the Egyptians to the Persians), as well as how these texts have been used in various contexts to further imperial aims (such as a divine right to lands; see Yee 2010).

We have noted that both feminist and postcolonial readings can challenge the perspective of the text. Such readings are often called ideological critiques of the Bible, or ideological criticism. These readings attempt to unmask the ideologies or systems of ideas that undergird the Bible. Many of these readings push back against the systems of power within the text, highlighting the ways in which the Bible continues to be used as a tool of oppression. As R. Reed says, 'The focus on the text *as* ideology ... changes the locus of interrogation. The problem is no longer that the text through source manipulation or a history of tradition has had its message convoluted; the problem is the message of the text itself' (2010: 116). An example of this sort of ideological critique of the pentateuchal material includes R. Schwartz's (1997) study on biblical monotheism and its implications, where she suggests that the concepts of monotheism and election as presented in the Hebrew Bible are dangerous ideas that have led to violence and oppression in the name of God and religious identity.

The rise in readings such as feminist and postcolonial perspectives has allowed for other theoretical approaches to come to the fore in biblical studies. Here the biblical text is read in light of particular perspectives or concerns with the goal of interpreting and engaging with the biblical material in new ways. Examples include the following:

1. the employment of spatial theory to look at how space and place are conceived of and used in biblical texts (Berquist and Camp 2008);
2. the use of trauma theory to explore how traumatic events shaped the formation of the biblical text (Carr 2014);
3. studies that employ ritual theory to better understand the ritual aspects of texts (Watts 2005);
4. and environmental and ecological readings, responding to the emergence of environmental concerns in recent decades (Habel 2011).

Finally, it is worth noting the growing interest in reception history, a broad field which explores the use and impact of the Bible down through the centuries (Lyons and England 2015). Here the focus is not so much on the biblical text, but on how it has been read, understood, and used by different people in different places throughout history. As the focus is on how these texts have been used and understood by readers and hearers through the years, reception history again puts emphasis on the role of readers and the world in front of the text. With regard to the Pentateuch, such research has included studies ranging from explorations of the reception of the character Moses in different religious traditions (Beal 2014), to investigations of the varied use of Genesis (Hendel 2013), to studies on how the stories of the Pentateuch have been received in film (Shepherd 2008). Because of its relation to other fields and disciplines such as music, history, politics, and art, reception history has also helped to bring interdisciplinary research front and centre within biblical studies. We return to the reception of the Pentateuch in Chapter 14.

Theological approaches

As the biblical books here under discussion are sacred texts that are central for Judaism and Christianity, it is not surprising that readers have long been concerned with the theological dimensions of these writings. Indeed, as we discuss in Chapter 14, these first five books have been central to Christianity and, in particular, Judaism from the very emergence of these traditions. However, it is also worth noting that those interested in academic study of the Bible have pursued theological questions and concerns, and such studies often utilize many of the methods and approaches noted above. Indeed, there are theological approaches that draw on the world behind the text (historical concerns), the world of the text (literary concerns), and the world in front of the text (reader-centred perspectives).

To begin with, there are those that hold that theological reflection on the Bible needs to draw on, and perhaps even be wedded to, historical research. An example of this can be seen in the fact that the search for the origins and formation of the Pentateuch did not eliminate theological reflection on these texts. N. Lohfink, for example, accepted the basic premise of sources that lie behind the Pentateuch and from here examines some of the major themes that he identifies within 'P' and 'D'. This takes the form of looking in detail at certain individual passages but also of examining certain themes within the sources. An interesting example is his article 'The Priestly Narrative and History', which, as its title suggests, explores the understanding of history to be found in the writings of the Priestly tradition. Lohfink maintains that the Priestly narrative was written with a specific audience and purpose in mind. He argues that it was written for the people in exile to encourage them and give them hope for the future. Lohfink regards the priestly stories as 'paradigmatic'; that is, they present an example of how Israel could be. Within the narrative, the world falls 'repeatedly from its perfect form into the imperfection of becoming' (1994: 172). This challenges the readers in exile to re-enter the process and to return to the pattern of things intended by God.

Exploring theology through a historical lens is not the only approach that scholars have taken. Indeed, the broader shifts outlined above – towards an appreciation for literary elements of the biblical text in its final form, as well as a recognition of various perspectives and theoretical frameworks that impact biblical interpretation – have had significant implications for those interested in exploring theological dimensions of the Bible. A key figure in this regard was B.S. Childs (1985), whose work explored the theological aspects of the final form of these texts. Childs called this the canonical approach, as he located the texts in their canonical form – that is, as Jews and Christians have received them – as the locus for interpretive endeavours. Childs work served as inspiration for a host of scholars who were interested in exploring literary and theological dimensions of the biblical text, while remaining cognizant of critical historical issues related to these texts and their origins.

In relation to the Pentateuch, a number of studies have been put forward that bring together these literary and theological concerns in relation to the entirety of the five books. T.E. Fretheim examines the Pentateuch in its present form and, like Clines, opts to identify an overarching theme which he defines as an intention within the text to 'shape the life and faith of its readers' (1996: 62). T.D. Alexander (2012) concentrates his attention on a number of themes that he finds within the Pentateuch. His understanding of the Pentateuch is that it consists of numerous diverse themes brought together to form the unifying theme of God's relationship with the descendants of Abraham, Isaac, and Jacob. While such holistic studies on the theology of the Pentateuch can be found, more common are those which investigate smaller units, themes, and characters in order to better understand theological elements within parts of the Pentateuch. Investigations of the theology of individual books within the Pentateuch include R.W.L. Moberly's unpacking of the theology of Genesis (2009), as well as the collection of essays exploring each book of the Torah in R.S. Briggs and J.N. Lohr (2012). Others have considered theological motifs in the Pentateuch, such as the idea of Israel as the chosen people (Lohr 2009), or have focused on particular units of text within the Pentateuch, such as P.D. Miller's (2009) exploration of the Ten Commandments.

Finally, there have been numerous studies which have brought together reader-centred approaches and theological concerns. Hence, there are readings that are sensitive to both feminist and theological concerns (Trible 1984), as well as theologically informed readings that attempt to take into account ideological dimensions of the biblical text (Brueggemann 1997). In the case of the readings noted here, questioning the assumptions of the text when warranted – such as with the marginalization of women – is seen as part of the theological task, precisely because of the Bible's continued importance in the life of faith communities.

Thus, as with other perspectives and approaches, theological interpretation has received renewed interest and attention in recent years. Such research can utilize historical, literary, or reader-centred research, and can be seen in studies that cover the entire Pentateuch, as well as in those that focus on particular texts, themes, and characters within this collection.

Example: Genesis 22

It may be useful to illustrate how the various perspectives outlined above might be employed with regard to one particular pentateuchal text. We focus here on Genesis 22, the story of Abraham's near sacrifice of Isaac (sometimes called the *Akedah*, or 'the binding' of Isaac).

There are, to begin with, historically oriented questions that one might ask about this text. For example, scholars have explored the origins and formation of Genesis 22, suggesting that the final verses (vv. 15–18) are a later addition to the story from a different source or tradition (Westermann 1995). Others have investigated the social and cultural aspects of this text, arguing that this story is a narrative explanation of the abolition of child sacrifice in ancient Judaism, a practice known from the ancient world (Green 1975). In both cases, the reader is trying to get behind the text to better understand its origins, message, and context.

Readers have also noted literary and text-related issues in Genesis 22, focusing on narrative elements as well as the story's place in the larger canon of the Bible. The ancient rabbis focused on the location of Mount Moriah, the setting of the near-sacrifice, suggesting, based on other references to this geographic location in the Bible, that this event, in fact, takes place on the holy mountain of Jerusalem (Moberly 2000). The literary critic E. Auerbach (1953), meanwhile, noted the terse language and various gaps in the story, commenting that the text is 'fraught with background' which has the effect of pulling the reader into the story.

Reader-centred and theoretical approaches tend to highlight other issues in reading this account. Feminist critiques, for example, have noted that Sarah is absent from this narrative, and have questioned why, as Isaac's mother, she is not given voice in this harrowing scene (Trible 1991). Ideological critiques, meanwhile, have pointed out the ethical challenges raised by the fact that God asks Abraham to kill his son, a reality that remains even if he is not forced to follow through on the act (Gunn and Fewell 1993). Those interested in reception history have focused on an array of issues, from musical representations of this scene (Dowling Long 2013), to the retelling of this episode in the Islamic tradition (Firestone 1989).

Finally, this episode has provided much inspiration for theological interpretation. As one might expect, through the centuries Abraham has been seen as a model of piety, faith, and obedience in both the Jewish and Christian traditions (see, e.g., Heb. 11.17-19). In contemporary scholarship, J.D. Levenson (1993a) has explored the historical and theological contribution of this story to the broader biblical motif of the beloved son who symbolically dies but who is then given new life. From a Christian perspective, Moberly

(2000) has highlighted how Abraham – in ways analogous to Jesus in the New Testament – is a model of those who overcome testing and show true fear of God.

There are, then, a variety of methods and approaches which readers have employed when reading and interpreting just this one chapter of Genesis. Of course, these approaches are not mutually exclusive, as scholars very often utilize historical and literary approaches, along with reader-centred or theological concerns, when attempting to make sense of this account.

Concluding remarks

As noted at the outset of this chapter, there are more and more ways in which readers can engage with biblical texts, including the Pentateuch. Whatever your specific interests or concerns, we suggest that being aware of historical, literary, reader-centred, and theological concerns is a good place to begin when undertaking biblical study. It is also worth reiterating that an increasing number of scholars are employing a variety of methods and approaches in their research, many of which cross over the various boundaries outlined above (Roskop Erisman 2014). It is not uncommon to find a biblical scholar using several historical-critical tools, as well as drawing from literary and reader-centred approaches in her research. In this sense, it is important to bear in mind that methods and approaches are tools that scholars employ, and different tools are suited for different, yet sometimes complementary, purposes.

In the following chapters we explore a number of sections and themes within the Pentateuch. In doing so we bring to bear on these texts the various methods and approaches outlined above, using historical, literary, reader-centred, and theological approaches to illustrate the various ways in which these texts can be read and interpreted.

Further reading

A helpful and accessible introduction to the various methods and approaches used in biblical studies is Moyise (2013). Other works that focus specifically on the study of the Hebrew Bible (and the Pentateuch within this) include Barton (1996), Gillingham (1998), and Baker and Arnold (1999). On more recent developments and approaches in the study of the Bible, consult Clines (2015). There are also helpful resources that focus on approaches to specific books within the Pentateuch, such as the collected essays on approaches to

Genesis (Hendel 2010) and Exodus (Dozeman 2010). For those interested in the history of biblical interpretation, Soulen (2009) offers an accessible introduction, while the multivolume series from Hauser and Watson (2003, 2009) provides more comprehensive explorations.

The Primeval History (Genesis 1–11)

The first chapters of Genesis contain some of the most well-known stories in the Bible. The creation of the world, Adam and Eve, the Garden of Eden, Cain and Abel, Noah and the flood: these are stories that not only have influenced the Jewish and Christian traditions but have also had an immeasurable impact on the world in which we live. And while these are important and iconic stories, they are also complex and offer much food for thought; questions of history, anthropology, gender, and ecology all play a part in how these stories are read and understood. In this chapter we explore these and other issues which emerge in the study of Genesis 1–11.

Composition and formation of Genesis 1–11

As will be demonstrated below, it is clear that there are different sources or traditions at work in these first chapters of Genesis. How best to understand the relationship of these traditions, however, is another matter. Traditional source criticism held that the Primeval History consisted of material from the 'J' and 'E' sources (or 'JE') as well as from the 'P' source. The dominant 'Yahwist' material was held to be from the early monarchical period, and was related to the subsequent 'J' materials in the Pentateuch. The 'Priestly' material, meanwhile, was considered to be from the exilic or post-exilic periods, supplementing the 'JE' material in these chapters.

Some continue to argue for a theory of development broadly in line with the Documentary Hypothesis, and in particular for a 'J' source in Genesis 1–11 that pre-dates 'P' and has continuity with Genesis 12–50 (Hendel 2011). However, we noted in Chapter 7 that several major developments in pentateuchal studies in recent decades have called into question the 'J' and 'E' sources. These developments have had implications for the study of the Primeval History, as a growing number of scholars prefer to speak of 'P' and 'non-P' traditions in these chapters. Questions concerning dating have also been raised. Thus, recent studies have suggested that 'P' materials, though exilic or post-exilic in setting, are actually the earliest in the Primeval History, while the 'non-P' materials are in fact post-Priestly additions

(Blenkinsopp 2002). There continues to be debate as to whether the 'non-P' materials are additions which supplement the 'P' source or that these 'non-P' materials form a coherent unit, yet one unrelated to other traditions in the Pentateuch such as the stories of the ancestors (see discussion in Gertz 2011, 2012). Consequently, while scholars generally agree there are at least two identifiable layers which have been brought together in the Primeval History, there is disagreement as to which source or tradition is earliest, as well as on the question of whether the 'non-P' materials stand on their own as an independent unit or if they are connected to other pentateuchal traditions.

Genre and setting of Genesis 1–11

Jews, Christians, and other interested readers have long been both fascinated and perplexed by Genesis 1–11. For contemporary readers, these chapters can seem particularly bewildering because there is an implicit assumption on the part of many that the Bible is, in some sense, historical. A related issue, especially prominent since the rise of the modern period, concerns how one might best read these chapters in light of scientific developments. Even a cursory look at the news, principally in North America, will show that questions related to creation and evolution remain significant for many people.

There is, of course, a good deal of history in the Bible, and there are very real historical concerns in its pages. However, the primeval history is decidedly not history in any contemporary understanding. And while these texts are concerned with existential and cosmological questions, they are not scientific in a modern sense (on questions related to Genesis and science, see the essays collected in Barton and Wilkinson 2009, as well as Harris 2013). How, then, should readers think about these chapters? Two issues that need to be considered are (1) the genre of these chapters and (2) the historical setting out of which such stories emerged.

Previously we have referred to Genesis 1–11 as 'primeval history', a phrase often used by scholars to refer to the events described in Genesis 1–11 and the term used generally by ancient historians to refer to a time that precedes recorded history. Accounts of primeval history exist in many cultures and are often concerned with the origins of the world. Scholars regularly refer to the accounts contained within these 'primeval histories' as myths. This terminology can be problematic, not least because in modern parlance myth is used increasingly to mean something that is untrue. For some, the word 'myth' evokes a fairy tale, that is, a story which is largely fictitious and not based upon fact. For others it is equated with 'urban myths', stories said to have happened to the 'friend of a friend' but never actually verified. When the biblical stories are referred to as 'myth', this is not what is meant. Rather, accounts like those found in Genesis 1–11 were important in the ancient world because they reflected the worldview of those who told and passed on these narratives, even if set in a primeval past (Gertz 2012). Because of these and other issues, there are many who continue to find the language of myth insufficient (Fretheim 1994b; Moberly 2009).

Modern scholarship has offered numerous alternative definitions of 'myth', and difficulties in the use of the term remain (Rogerson 1974; Fishbane 2003). Nevertheless, despite the problems that arise from its use, the word 'myth' is useful because it signals the unusual nature of the stories in Genesis 1–11. In these stories, serpents speak, heavenly beings take human wives, animals live together peacefully on a boat for many days, and humans attempt to build a tower that reaches to the heavens. Whatever one thinks of these narratives, one cannot deny their unusual nature. The characters featured in the story inhabit a world very different from our own. The word 'myth' signals this difference to us and prepares us for the type of stories contained in Genesis 1–11. The essays in D.E. Callender (2014) offer helpful explorations of the relationship of myth and Scripture, and several of the chapters touch on aspects of Genesis 1–11.

Along with the question of genre, another important issue to be considered is that of the ancient historical setting of these texts. These are stories that emerged in the ANE, and it is clear that the writers of the Bible drew from concepts, stories, and motifs from the world in which they were situated. Archaeological discoveries of the nineteenth and twentieth centuries brought to light the existence of numerous myths from elsewhere in the ancient world. The existence of other stories which attempt to describe the origins of the world is not surprising, as most cultures attempt to describe their origins in some way. What is remarkable about these texts is that they originate from a similar area and culture to the biblical accounts and, in certain respects, reflect a similar view of the world.

The 'ancient Near East' (ANE; Map 9.1) is a loose term used to describe various groups of peoples who lived in the area of land which stretches from the Mediterranean coast (modern Egypt in the south to modern Turkey in the north) to the east (modern Iran and Iraq). While parallels have been discovered in texts from all over the ANE and beyond, the most striking are Sumerian, Akkadian, Babylonian, Egyptian, and Ugaritic in origin. Sumerian, Akkadian, and Babylonian texts all originate, at different times, from Mesopotamia, a region bounded by the river Euphrates and the river Tigris. Sumerian civilization was at its peak from the third to the early second millennium BCE. The Sumerians were not Semitic and spoke 'Sumer',

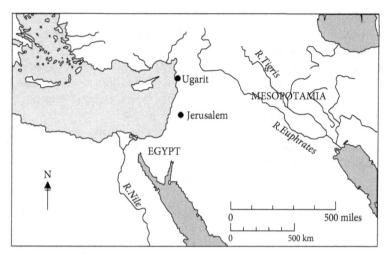

Map 9.1 The ancient Near Eastern world

a language that died out in the second millennium BCE, although it continued as a written language for much longer. The Akkadians were a Semitic people whose power began to increase towards the end of the third millennium BCE. Their influence was replaced during the second millennium BCE by that of the Assyrians in northern Mesopotamia and the Babylonians in southern Mesopotamia. To the south, the empire of Egypt produced various important texts over a long period of time. Texts from these major, well-known empires have long been recognized as containing material parallel to the narratives of Genesis. Meanwhile, the material of the ancient kingdom of Ugarit, discovered in the twentieth century, also contains parallels with the biblical material. Ugarit is on the Mediterranean coast of modern-day Syria and was the capital of the kingdom of Ugarit, whose power was at its peak in the second millennium BCE. Thus, this material seems to have originated geographically closer to the land of Israel/Judah than the Mesopotamian texts.

While many of the myths from other ancient Near Eastern cultures are quite different from the accounts in Genesis 1–11, some of them seem remarkably similar, including creation stories and flood accounts. This has led scholars to reflect upon the connection between the biblical accounts and other ancient texts. Some have suggested that, when read as a whole, Genesis 1–11 is a subversive critique of the ideologies and myths of the ancient world, presenting Israel's perspective on God, the world, and humanity (Middleton 2005). We return to several such examples in what follows (further discussion, with examples, can be found in Hays 2014).

Taken together, genre and historical setting are both vitally important elements of understanding these early chapters in Genesis. However one chooses to approach these chapters, questions concerning their genre as well as the historical setting out of which they emerged need to be considered.

Structural and thematic elements of Genesis 1–11

While these first chapters of Genesis seem to have been brought together from diverse traditions, it is possible to identify structural and thematic links. One such approach sees Genesis 1–11 as narrating a world finely balanced between good and evil. The cycle of good followed by imperfection followed by punishment is one which rolls repeatedly throughout Genesis 1–11 and on into the rest of the narrative of the Pentateuch.

The first two chapters of Genesis are taken up with a description of the process of creation, and the 'goodness' of this creation. The imperfection begins in Genesis 3 as Adam and Eve break the bounds placed upon them by God which prevents their eating from one of the trees in the garden. Their punishment is banishment from the garden and increased toil in the life God has given them. This pattern continues in Genesis 4 with the sin of their son Cain. In this account, Cain breaks the bounds placed on him by God, not this time as regards an inanimate tree, but as regards his own brother. His punishment is constant banishment: he must wander from place to place.

In Gen. 6.1-4 the pattern continues. This time, the 'sons of God' break the boundaries laid down by God and cross the boundary between heaven and earth to take mortals as their wives. Punishment is not declared, but the flood immediately follows and stands as a punishment against all humanity. Again, the punishment includes the theme of banishment: all animate creation is banished from the world made by God. The exception is Noah, his family, and representative animals of all types who remain as recipients of God's promises. In Gen. 9.20-29 a new element to the pattern emerges: Ham sins against his father by 'looking upon his nakedness' (an act of uncertain meaning). Therefore he is condemned, not by God, but by his father. The narrative of Genesis 1–11 concludes with a final story of boundary breaking and banishment sandwiched between two genealogies. Here the boundaries between heaven and earth are threatened not by heavenly beings, as in ch. 6, but by human beings. The tower of Babel is built as an attempt to invade the heavenly realms. The punishment declared is banishment from one another: God prevents communication between peoples and scatters them across the world.

The pattern of Genesis 1–11, therefore, can be seen as one of increasing violation of boundaries and the consequent increasing alienation of human beings. Certain boundaries are laid down to maintain the goodness of the creative order established by God. Attempts to cross these boundaries lead not to greater unity but to a greater separation. Nevertheless, the picture is not entirely dismal. God maintains a relationship with humanity throughout this cycle, and with each story of alienation comes a second chance, a token of mercy offered by God, which allows for the story to continue.

Creation and expulsion from Eden (Genesis 1–3)

The first three chapters of Genesis introduce a number of important themes, characters, and issues. Not surprisingly, these stories have been read and understood in a variety of ways. Interpretations interested in identifying the historical background of the text have generally concentrated on two major questions: the sources and traditions that lie behind the text as well as ancient Near Eastern parallels. Other approaches, meanwhile, have drawn insights from these texts on, among other things, anthropology, gender, and environmental issues.

The two accounts of creation

The first two chapters of Genesis describe the creation of the world. Out of chaos, a new world emerges by the word of God. However, a brief examination of the text indicates that Genesis 2 does not flow on easily from Genesis 1. Rather Genesis 1 (or, more precisely Gen. 1.1–2.4) and Genesis 2 (Gen. 2.4–25) offer two distinct accounts of creation. Genesis 1 describes creation as taking place in two sets of three actions. C. Westermann calls the first set 'three separations' and the second set 'three quickenings' (1988: 8, 9). The first set lays the foundations of the earth and the second calls life forth from it. Each of the separations more or less matches one of the quickenings, as Table 9.1 illustrates.

However, when we reach Genesis 2 none of this is mentioned. Genesis 2.5 specifically says that no plants have yet been created, despite the fact that in 1.11 God commands the earth to produce plants and trees of all kinds. However, this account cannot even be seen as a repetition of Genesis 1, because in Genesis 1 humanity is created after the plants and trees but in Genesis 2, before them.

Another difference is that the Genesis 1 account is concerned with portraying how creation took place, whereas the account in Genesis 2

Table 9.1 Separations and quickenings in Genesis 1

Day	Action	Day	Action
1	God separates **light** from **darkness**	4	God commands **lights** to hang in the sky
2	God separates the **sea** from the **sky**	5	God brings forth **sea creatures** and **birds**
3	God separates the **dry land** from the **sea**	6	God brings forth **animals** and creates **humankind**

acts as a prologue for Genesis 3, where the first act of disobedience and its consequences are described. Indeed, in this second account of creation, the act of creation seems subordinate in interest to the account of disobedience which immediately follows it. These two stories thus function in different ways.

These differences indicate that Genesis 1 and 2 may have originated from two separate sources or traditions. Genesis 1 is widely regarded as having been written from the Priestly tradition while Genesis 2 is deemed non-Priestly (or 'J' in traditional source criticism). Genesis 1 presents the account of creation almost as a list, or poem (day one, day two etc.), whereas Genesis 2 gives a much more flowing and story-like account of the events. In Genesis 1, God is a distant, transcendent being who commands and it is done. In Genesis 2, God seems more intimately involved with the act of creation, particularly as he is on the ground getting his hands dirty in creation, as well as attempting to find a companion for Adam. In the first account, God is referred to as *elohim*, a more generic name for the deity. In the second account, God's personal name (YHWH) is used throughout.

Ancient Near Eastern parallels with the Genesis accounts of creation

As noted above, a good deal has been learned in recent centuries from the discovery of texts from the ANE which shed light on biblical stories, including creation accounts and other stories of origins. Many of the important ancient Near Eastern texts are published in J.B. Pritchard, *Ancient Near Eastern Texts Relating to the Old Testament* (1969) (normally abbreviated as *ANET*). Abbreviated sections of the most important texts are available in a more accessible form in V.H. Matthews and D.C. Benjamin (2006).

Several motifs found in the accounts of Genesis 1–3 have striking parallels with various ancient texts, and these similarities exist on many different levels. Some similarities concern the motifs or details contained within a story. For example, there are minor resonances, such as the fact that Genesis 2 describes God forming Adam out of clay. This notion occurs in various ancient Near Eastern texts but the most remarkable is in the *Atrahasis Epic*. Here, the goddess Mami forms humans by pinching off pieces of clay (*ANET*, 99–100).

However, there are also more substantial similarities that reflect a similar view of the world or point towards a similar structure of the story. One such example is in the realm of cosmology. Although the Genesis 1 account has a limited description of the structure of the world, enough information exists to note parallels with, for example, the structure of the world given in the Babylonian epic *Enuma Elish*, a story which likely dates to the second millennium BCE. The primary similarity is the belief in the existence of a firmament. Genesis 1.6-7 describes God separating the waters by means of a 'dome' (NRSV). The Hebrew word is more vague and literally means something beaten or stretched out (e.g. a thin piece of metal). This means that God hollowed out a space in the middle of dense waters, in which he later created the earth. The waters flowed above the sky and under the earth but between them a space existed. A similar idea exists in the *Enuma Elish* which presents the creation of the world as a battle between the gods. Here Marduk, after conquering the goddess Tiamat, cuts her body in two and used half to form the sky and half to form the earth. This creative act hollowed out a space in the waters for life to exist by sealing out the waters of Apsu. This is not the only similarity between Genesis 1 and the *Enuma Elish*. Another striking parallel is the order of creation. Genesis 1 gives the order of creation as the creation of light; the separation between the waters; the creation of dry ground; the placing of the sun, moon, and stars in the sky; the creation of sea creatures; and finally the creation of animals and humans. The *Enuma Elish* presents a similar order of creation, culminating in the creation of human beings. However, unlike Genesis 1, it does not split each of these acts into periods of time.

These and other points of contact raise questions concerning the relationship (if any) of these traditions. Some suggest that Genesis 1 is indebted in some way to the *Enuma Elish* (or other ANE accounts), even if the function of the texts differs. Other scholars have concluded that the similarities reflect not direct borrowing but simply a similar view of the world. Whatever the reason for these similarities, one cannot fail to notice the differences that also exist. The most notable difference is the absolute power of God in the biblical texts. In the *Enuma Elish* creation takes place as a by-product of warfare between the gods; in Genesis the focus is on Israel's God (alone) as the creator. Further, in the Genesis account the peace and orderliness of creation contrast starkly with the chaos of the *Enuma Elish* account. While the authors of the Genesis accounts may have known of the other ancient accounts of creation, their view of God is fundamentally different. Nevertheless, such parallels are also an important reminder that the biblical texts did not emerge in a vacuum, but reflect ideas and themes known from elsewhere in the ancient world.

Literary and theological issues in Genesis 1–3

The interpretations of Genesis 1–3 discussed so far in this chapter have been concerned with understanding more about. Other interpretations explore literary, theological, and reader-centred questions, seeking, for example, to understand more about how these texts view God, humanity, and the environment.

These early chapters of Genesis have been of fundamental importance in theological discourse in both the Jewish and Christian traditions. Of particular import has been reflection on themes such as creation, anthropology, as well as disobedience and sin, and many of these relate to literary aspects of these chapters and how they are interpreted. We outline a few such examples here, in order to give a flavour of the different kinds of issues that emerge with reflection on these chapters.

The theme of creation stands at the centre of much Jewish and Christian theology. It occurs repeatedly in both the Old and New Testaments (see, for example, Job 38.4ff; Psalm 8; John 1 etc.) and features as an important part of doctrinal and ethical debate. Consequently, the account of creation given by the book of Genesis has been interpreted in different ways and used to demonstrate a variety of distinct positions. An interesting issue noted by interpreters relates to the nature of the 'beginning' at which creation takes place. A common idea in theological discourse is the notion of creation *ex nihilo*, the idea that God created the world out of nothing. While this seems a common-sense understanding to many, the text is actually somewhat ambiguous on this matter. In Gen. 1.1 the author paints a picture of a watery chaos without form, and continues by describing a wind which disturbs the waters as God begins to create. Water, then, is both present and seems to play a significant role in how these verses unfold. Thus, the Bible begins with God's creation and is clear about his role as sole creator, but whether this can be described as 'from nothing' is less clear.

Another area of enquiry which has been especially fruitful – extending well beyond biblical studies – has been engagement with the notion of humanity being created in the image of God (the well-known Latin phrase for this idea is *imago dei*). In Gen. 1.26-28 we read that humanity is created in the image (*tselem*) of God, though the reader is not given any further information on what this might mean. As one might imagine, this has led to considerable debate through the years, with the 'image' being equated with the soul, human rationality, human dominion on earth, or even the human physical form (see discussion on the history of interpretation in Clines 1968 and MacDonald 2013). More recently, biblical scholars have noted that in the world of the ANE, only the king was considered to bear the image of a god. This had the effect of validating the king's authority, while also connecting his authority and actions to the will of the gods. Scholars have increasingly suggested that the biblical statement in Gen. 1.27 needs to be read in light of this widely held belief. In this view, the Priestly tradition as seen in Genesis 1 is democratizing this royal ideology: all of humanity reflects God's image, and thus all of humanity functions as God's royal representatives on earth, carrying forward his purposes (Middleton 2005; Day 2013). Further, as Israel was forbidden from making images or icons of its God (Exod. 20:4-5), this reading suggests that humanity will serve this purpose.

These first chapters of Genesis have also brought to the fore a number of theological complexities related to the first act of disobedience and its consequences. One such issue revolves around God's statement that Adam and Eve will die if they eat of the forbidden fruit in the garden. This account has been taken up in a discussion between R.W.L. Moberly (1988, 2009) and J. Barr (1993, 2006). Barr questions the veracity of God's statements in these chapters, as humanity does not die as promised upon partaking of the fruit. Moberly, however, suggests that the Jewish and Christian traditions require a more nuanced reading that probes deeply the questions raised by this story, namely what the conditions of trust and disobedience in humanity's relationship with God might be, and whether death should be understood metaphorically (as in Deut. 30.15, 19) in light of the unfolding story.

This brings us to one final theological issue, and that is the notion of the fall and original sin. Christian tradition has long held that the initial act of disobedience by Adam and Eve led to 'the fall' of humanity, and ushered in a situation whereby humans are born into a state of sinfulness. This idea goes back to the church fathers, such as Irenaeus and Augustine, who themselves saw elements of this idea in Rom. 5.12-21 and 1 Cor. 15.22. However, not everyone views the story of Genesis 3 in this way. Barr (1993) doubts whether the story of Genesis 2-3 can bear the weight of traditional Christian understandings of 'the fall' into sin, and suggests instead that this is a story concerned with the loss of immortality. Others have suggested that alternative understandings of 'falling' may in fact be more appropriate. T.E. Fretheim outlines these various ideas:

> Traditionally, the metaphor refers to a fall 'down' or a fall 'short.' A variation stresses the 'becoming like God' theme, where human beings

assume God-like powers for themselves. This is a kind of fall 'up,' or a reaching up only to fall down, for humans are not able to handle what they have become. Yet, the primary metaphors in chapters 3–6 are those of estrangement, alienation, separation, and displacement, with ever-increasing distance from Eden, each other, and God. Perhaps these themes would allow for a variation on the 'fall' metaphor, namely, a falling 'out.' This metaphor would also be true to the basically relational character of what happens here.

Thus, Fretheim concludes,

> chapter 3 witnesses to an originating sin that begins a process, an intensification of alienation, extending over chapters 3–6, by which sin becomes 'original' in the sense of pervasive and inevitable with effects that are cosmic in scope. However generalizable the story in chapter 3, it alone cannot carry the weight and freight of the traditional view; the fall is finally not understood to be the product of a single act. But it is a beginning of no little consequence and chapters 3–6 together witness to a reality that subsequent generations can with good reason call a fall. (1994b: 152–3)

Feminist interpretations of Genesis 1–3

Genesis 1–3 has long stood at the centre of the debate about the nature of men and women and their relationship throughout history. As early as the New Testament, 1 Tim. 2.13-14 cites Genesis 2–3 as the reason for women's inability to have authority over men. This portrayal of woman as subordinate to man is often contrasted with Gen. 1.27, which states that both male and female were created in the image of God. H. Schüngel-Straumann presents a helpful survey of the history of interpretation of both passages, showing how even Genesis 1 has been used in what she calls 'anti-woman' arguments (1993: 64).

Unsurprisingly, many interpretations have reflected upon the significance of gender in the Genesis accounts. An important interpretation of this sort has been offered by P. Trible. Trible argues that the problem with Genesis 2–3 is not so much the text itself as the subsequent interpretations of the text. She calls the narrative 'A Love Story Gone Awry' (1978: 72–143), and her interpretation pivots on the Hebrew pun in Gen. 2.7. Here the man (Hebrew 'adam) is formed from the earth (Hebrew 'adamah). Trible maintains that this pun is deliberate and that 'man' here should be translated 'earth-creature' (77). Only after woman was created did the 'adam gain sexual identity. The story is a love story gone awry because in the fall their initial unity is separated: 'By betraying the woman to God, the man opposed himself to her; by ignoring him in her reply to God, the woman separates herself from the man' (120). The result of this, Trible maintains, is a 'hierarchy of division' (128). Trible here maintains that the problem for women lay not in Genesis but in subsequent misogynist interpretations of it (see also Bird 1981).

A reading with a different focus is offered by C. Meyers (1988). She is interested in the climate which produced the text and maintains that the Genesis 3 passage reflects the situation in Israel in the Iron Age I period. The context she paints for this passage is of settlement in the Palestinian hill country. Life at this time consisted of hard agricultural labour and required maximum commitment from both men and women. She maintains that the gender roles painted by Genesis 3 arise within this context and should be understood as such.

Environmental readings of Genesis 1–3

Recent years have seen the rise of readings which are concerned with the ecological and environmental dimensions of the Bible in general, including these early chapters of Genesis (Davis 2009; Habel 2011). As with the issue of gender, there are various ways in which the text can be interpreted on these matters. N.C. Habel (2009) has noted that while there are 'green' texts in the Bible which can be used constructively for engagement on these issues, there are also 'grey' texts which seem to devalue creation. Nevertheless, scholars have offered interpretations of these early chapters of Genesis which are increasingly sensitive to ecological concerns. Fretheim, for example, suggests that the God of the creation accounts in Genesis is one who shares creative activity with his creatures, and this relational model has 'significant implications for further reflection regarding creatures, their interrelationships, and their environmental responsibilities' (2012: 686).

N. Lohfink also concentrates on the relationship between humanity and the world, particularly the command in Gen. 1.28 to 'subdue the earth'. He criticizes certain readings of the text which support exploitation of the world's resources. Instead, he maintains, Gen. 1.28 should be read in the light of the Priestly tradition's understanding of 'artistic and technical achievement' (1994: 16) as set out in Exodus 25–31 and 35–40. The command to build and furnish the tabernacle, which these chapters contain, seems to continue the divine act of creation in Genesis 1. In the light of this and of humanity's creation 'in the image of God', Lohfink concludes that the command in Gen. 1.28 was 'so that the earth may be developed to resemble heaven, in order that the earth may become the dwelling place of God' (17). Far from supporting the exploitation of the earth, this verse encourages the transformation of earth into a heavenly dwelling place.

There is, then, a growing field of literature which explores these early chapters of Genesis in light of some of the most significant issues of our day, including gender and ecology, though such readings are not uniform in perspective or approach.

Cain and Abel (Gen 4)

The story which immediately follows Adam and Eve's expulsion from the Garden of Eden centres upon their offspring, Cain and Abel. This well-known story presents an account of the first murder. Cain's feeling of rejection, after God showed preference for his brother's sacrifice, leads him to kill Abel. The New Testament interprets this passage as presenting inherent 'righteousness' on Abel's part and inherent 'evil' on Cain's part (Mt. 23.35; 1 Jn 3.12). The epistle to the Hebrews even goes so far as to say that Abel's sacrifice was accepted because he made it 'by faith' (Heb. 11.4). Unfortunately, the text of Genesis 4 is not as clear as this. No reason is given for the acceptance of Abel's sacrifice and the rejection of Cain's.

G. Wenham (1987) enunciates five possible reasons for this: three concern God's attitude, two that of Cain and Abel. The first possibility is that God prefers shepherds (Abel) to gardeners (Cain), the second that God prefers animal to grain sacrifices, and the third that God's actions are inscrutable and the choice simply reflects the mystery of divine election. Of the final two possibilities, one refers to Heb. 11.4 as the solution and the other proposes that the difference was one of quality: Abel produced the finest from his flock; Cain just 'an offering of the fruit of the ground'. Whatever the reason for God's choice of one sacrifice over the other, this is not the central focus of the story (although in many interpretations it has become the central focus). Instead, the narrative focuses upon Cain's response to the rejection of his sacrifice, as well as God's continued engagement with Cain. It is his response that defines Cain's sin, not the nature of his sacrifice (see Kaminsky 2007).

G. West contrasts two liberationist readings of the story from South Africa. Both were interested in the conflict presented by the narrative, though one saw it as a support for the oppressed and the other as a support for the oppressor. A. Boesak reads the story as an account of struggle from a situation of struggle. His interest in the story is to identify an analogy with his present situation and his understanding of the narrative is that it maintains that there is no place for oppression in God's world. God unequivocally condemns Cain for his act of oppression in murdering Abel. In contrast, I. Mosala, while also writing from a 'situation of struggle', was more interested in the historical background of the narrative. Historical critics have long recognized, within the narrative of Cain and Abel, a reference to the tension that existed in the ancient world between nomads and settled farmers. Abel, a sheep farmer, represented the nomads and Cain, a tiller of the land, a settled farmer. Mosala maintained that the narrative supported the eviction of the settled farmers from their land: Cain, the settled farmer, sinned against Abel, his nomadic brother, and was forced to leave his land and wander over the face of the earth. This, Mosala argued, 'inaugurated a relentless process of land dispossession of the village peasants in Israel' (cited in West 1990: 307). These contrasting views of the narrative illustrate well the differences that can emerge in interpretations of the same text: Boesak views the story as a condemnation of oppression; Mosala as supporting it. For more on the ways in which the Cain and Abel story has been read and understood, see J. Byron (2012).

Genealogies

Genealogies appear regularly throughout Genesis 1–11. Their value is twofold. On the one hand, they allow the authors of the narrative to cover large periods of time without giving a detailed description of the events. On the other hand, they show how the ancient characters that feature in the story are related to the stories' original readers. This second feature of the genealogies allows the readers of the narrative to identify what happened as a story of their own 'beginnings'. This was continued by the New Testament writers, particularly Matthew and Luke (Mt. 1.1-16; Lk. 3.23-38), who used the technique of genealogies to tie Christianity to the story of Israel.

A detailed consideration of the genealogies contained in Genesis 1–11 indicates that there are two different ways of presenting genealogical-type material (this material includes both 'straight genealogies' and the table of nations found in ch. 10). The first type of genealogy (4.17-26; 10.8-19, 24–30) contains a certain amount of narrative and explains the origins of certain peoples (10.10), occupations (4.19-22), and sayings (10.9). The other type of genealogy in Genesis (5; 10.1-7, 20–23, 32; 11.10-32) seems to be more of a list of names and, in the case of Genesis 5, is interested in recounting the ages of the people recorded. Source critics generally attribute the first, more narrative style of genealogy to non-Priestly traditions, and the second, more list-like style, to 'P' (the latter often including the Hebrew word *toledot*, translated by the NRSV as 'descendants').

One interesting ancient interpretation of the biblical text focuses on the figure of Enoch, mentioned in Gen. 4.17-18 as the son of Cain and in Gen. 5.21-24 as the father of Methuselah. The phrase 'Enoch walked with God; then he was no more, because God took him' (Gen. 5.24) seems to have given rise to certain traditions about him. Ethiopic Enoch (often called 1 Enoch) and Slavonic Enoch (often called 2 Enoch) contain extended speculations about Enoch's ascent into heaven and his role in the heavenly realms. The importance of these speculations is highlighted by the fact that an Aramaic version of Ethiopic Enoch was discovered at Qumran and that the New Testament epistle of Jude (v. 15) gives a citation from the book as though citing from scripture. This is just one example of how seemingly inconsequential characters named in genealogies can have an impact in later tradition that far outweighs their role in the biblical material itself.

The sons of God and the daughters of humans

Between the genealogy of Genesis 5 and the flood narrative stands a brief yet strange account of the union between the sons of God and the daughters of humans, though no explanation is offered as to who these 'sons of God' might be (Gen. 6.3-4). The narrative is surprising on numerous levels. Although the 'sons of God' do appear elsewhere in the Hebrew Bible, most notably in Job 1.6ff, their appearance is sufficiently rare to be unusual. In addition, the narrative seems to have a double purpose. Verse 3 stresses that, despite union with the sons of God, humanity is mortal and will not live forever. Verse 4, meanwhile, uses the account to explain the presence of the Nephilim, giants with great power who appear again in Num. 13.33 and Deut. 2.10-11. Indeed, v. 4 provides a puzzle of its own. The origins of the Nephilim are traced to a time before the flood; the account does not explain how they survived the flood to be present 'also afterward' (v. 4).

The account seems to be reminiscent of myths from other cultures where gods and humans produce powerful offspring, and yet no accounts are sufficiently close to suggest any influence upon the biblical narrative. Perhaps the best explanation for the inclusion of the narrative is, like the creation accounts, to point to the differences between the Genesis tradition and other ancient Near Eastern texts. Elsewhere unions between gods and humans produce superhuman powers; here, v. 3 makes very clear that immortality did not result from the union. In the overall flow of the narrative from Genesis 1–11, a further boundary has been broken. In forming a union with the daughters of humans, the sons of God have broken the bounds between heaven and earth set down in Genesis 1.

Like the cryptic verses of Gen. 5.21-24, this narrative has become the subject of extensive speculation in Ethiopic Enoch. The first section of this lengthy work is known as 'the book of the Watchers' and concerns the fate of those 'angels' or 'watchers' who broke the boundary between heaven and earth as described in Gen. 6.1-4. The book of the Watchers contains several traditions about the actions of the fallen angels, including one which asserts that it was Azaz'el and his followers teaching the people divine secrets who were responsible for the fall of these beings. These Watchers have recently been given more popular expression in Darren Aronofsky's 2014 film *Noah*, where these characters are given a prominent role in the story of the flood. The Watchers are not present in the flood account of Genesis, but Aronofsky's interpretation seems to be one which reads the later tradition of Enoch back into the biblical story.

Flood accounts (Genesis 6–9)

As with other elements in the Pentateuch, the story of the flood has inspired much speculation relating to possible historical bases for the biblical account. Indeed, it is not uncommon to hear reports that Noah's ark has been discovered or unearthed on an archaeological expedition. However, like the chapters surrounding them, Genesis 6–9 are mythic in nature, and as will be outlined below, flood stories were well known in the ancient world. This is not to say that such stories did not originate with a purpose; the possibility of extensive, localized floods may have posed serious concerns for people of the ANE, and these accounts may reflect cultural memory of such events. Nevertheless, attempts to account for the historicity of the biblical account have offered little evidence, even while this story has proved very fruitful in literary, theological, and historical reflection. For examples of the wide-ranging use and interpretation of the biblical flood account, see Pleins (2003).

The two accounts of the flood

Just as scholars have identified two different accounts of creation in Genesis 1–2, so also they have pointed out the presence of two sources or traditions behind the flood narratives. Unlike the creation accounts, however, the two sources behind the flood account are not placed side by side in the text, with one beginning where the other ends. Instead, the accounts seem to be interwoven in the same narrative. While the flood narrative has a single overarching structure, different details stand next to each other in the flow of the story. For example, in Gen. 6.19-20, Noah is commanded to take two of each species of animal into the ark; in Gen. 7.2-3, he is commanded to take seven pairs of clean animals and one pair of unclean animals into the ark. Such discrepancies seem to indicate the presence of two separate accounts woven together to make a single one. In this case, the task of the source critic is made more complex by the fact that not all details are contained in both accounts. The task of 'unravelling' the narrative into its two constituent parts requires close attention to the style, theology, and terminology of the text. The complexity of the task means that, although there is a consensus about the sources of large portions of the narrative, there is no such consensus about smaller subsections of verses. The division of the account given in Table 9.2 is drawn from C. Westermann (1988: 45–50).

Table 9.2 The 'P' and 'non-P' elements of the flood narrative

'P'		'Non-P'	
Title and Introduction	6.9-10		
Divine punishment of human wickedness	6.11-13	Divine punishment of human wickedness	6.5-8
Noah commanded to build an ark	6.14-18a		
Noah commanded to take his family and two of every species into the ark	6.18b-22	Noah commanded to take his household, seven pairs of clean and one pair of each unclean animal into the ark	7.1-5
Age of Noah	7.6		
Date of flood	7.11		
		Rain falls for 40 days	7.12
Noah, his family, and animals went into the ark	7.13-16a	Noah, his family, and animals went into the ark	7.7-10
Flood comes on the earth	7.17a	Flood comes on the earth	7.16b and 17b
Description of flood	7.18-21	Description of flood	7.22-23
Flood lasts 150 days	7.24		
God stops flood	8.1-2a	Flood stops	8.2b-3
Waters recede and ark stops on Ararat	8.3b-5	Noah sends out birds to test the level of the waters	8.6-12
Date for drying up of the flood	8.13a and 8.14a	Noah sees that the earth is dry	8.13b
Noah is commanded to leave the ark	8.15-19		
		Noah sacrifices to God	8.20-22
God makes a covenant with Noah	9.1-17		
Length of Noah's life	9.28-29		

This type of breakdown of the text reveals various points. The first is that, although there is repetition between the verses attributed to 'P' and those attributed to 'non-P', we do not have two complete interwoven flood narratives. At various points, the 'non-P' narrative does not contain certain vital parts of the story, such as the building of the ark or Noah leaving the ark. In these instances, the reader must rely on the 'P' account for the narrative to make sense. Questions remain as to why particular parts of the story may have been dropped as the traditions were brought together, and scholars continue to probe these issues (see the discussion in Gertz 2012).

Ancient Near Eastern parallels with the flood narratives

The accounts of creation contained certain striking parallels with myths from other ancient Near Eastern civilizations. The flood narratives contain even more parallels with accounts from neighbouring countries. Accounts of flood are far from being unique to the book of Genesis, but those closest to the biblical accounts originate from the region of Mesopotamia. The accounts exist in various languages (the most important being Sumerian, Akkadian, and Assyrian), with various heroes (including Utnapishtim, Atrahasis, and Ziusudra) and in various degrees of completeness. The most complete version of the narrative is the *Gilgamesh Epic*, though it may well have drawn its flood narrative from its more ancient companion, the *Atrahasis Epic*, which places the flood in the context of a primeval history, after a description of creation.

The *Gilgamesh Epic* has been reconstructed from various different versions in different periods, the most complete coming from the Old Babylonian period (1750–1600 BCE) and the Neo-Assyrian period (750–612 BCE). (An accessible discussion of the text, its sources, and origins is given by Sasson 1992.) The account records the actions of the semi-divine king Gilgamesh, who, the story recounts, ruled in southern Mesopotamia in the third millennium BCE. The account contains a long description of the acts of Gilgamesh and his friend Enkidu. At the end of the narrative, though probably not original to it, Gilgamesh found a character named Utnapishtim, who recounted to Gilgamesh how he, Utnapishtim, achieved immortality.

This immortality was granted to Utnapishtim after he was saved from a universal flood, by which the gods intended to annihilate the earth. The general pattern of the narrative bears a remarkable resemblance to the Genesis account (English versions can be found in *ANET* 93–5). The god Enlil decided to flood the earth. Warned by the god Ea, Utnapishtim tore down his house and built a cube-shaped ship, into which he took treasure, his family, and both domestic and wild beasts. The storm raged for six days. On the seventh day the storm died down and the ark came to rest on Mount Nisir. The ship was grounded for six days. On the seventh day, Utnapishtim sent out a dove, which returned to him because she found no resting place. Then he sent out a swallow, which also came back. Finally, he sent a raven, which did not return. At this point, Utnapishtim released the creatures from the ark and sacrificed to the gods. They 'smelled the sweet savour' and 'the gods crowded like flies about the sacrifice' (lines 160–1). When the god Enlil saw that Utnapishtim had survived the flood, he was angry because he had intended to destroy all humanity. In order to preserve his plan, he made Utnapishtim and his wife divine and hence immortal.

The parallels between these accounts and the biblical accounts are obvious. Motifs such as the choosing of one person to survive the flood, the building of an ark, the preservation of his family and some animals, and the sending out of different birds at the end of the flood, all bear a certain resemblance to the biblical account. One of the most striking parallels is the reaction of the gods to the sacrifice after the flood. In both the *Gilgamesh Epic* and the *Atrahasis Epic* the gods smelled the sweet aroma of the sacrifice; in Gen. 8.21 we are told that 'the Lord smelled the pleasing odour' of the sacrifice. Such parallels between the accounts indicate that, at the very least, the biblical authors were aware of traditions about the flood also known by the Mesopotamian authors. Nevertheless, as was the case with the parallels between the creation accounts and the ancient Near Eastern myths, significant differences between the accounts indicate a very different view of God's relationship with the world. In Genesis, humanity plays a much more important part in the narrative. It is God's attempt to undo the sin of humankind that causes the flood and God's mercy that leads to the saving of Noah. While the biblical writers may have known of and even drawn from similar accounts about the flood, their purpose in writing appears to have been very different.

Literary, theological, and ecological approaches to the flood account

As with the creation accounts, a good deal of attention has been given to literary and theological dimensions of the flood story. For example, the flood, if viewed from the cosmology suggested by Genesis 1, is in fact a great act of 'un-creation'. In creation, God gradually separated out a space in the midst of the waters, in which humankind could live and multiply. In the flood, God filled in that space once more. The waters above and below the earth flowed back to where they had been before God separated them. If creation had been the imposition of order on chaos, the flood was the imposition of chaos on order. Nevertheless, the world does not remain in an uncreated state. D.J.A. Clines (1997) identified this as the Creation-Uncreation-Recreation theme: at the end of the flood the waters are separated once more, the command to multiply is reissued, and order over chaos returns. In this sense, the creation and flood accounts are linked thematically and literarily.

A number of theological questions also emerge from a reading of these chapters. One of the more obvious of these is the apparent disjunction between the biblical text and the way in which this story has been adapted for use with children; there are countless bibles, books, toys, and films aimed at children that highlight the unique story of Noah, the flood, and the animals on the ark (Dalton 2015). And yet, even a cursory reading of this story reveals that there is much more going on in these chapters than a simple children's tale. In fact, the use of this story with children is somewhat surprising given the rather dark picture which emerges: Gen. 6.6 states that God 'was sorry that he had made humankind on the earth' (NRSV) and resolved to undo his creative act with the destruction of the flood. Worth noting here is Aronofsky's 2014 film, which paints a picture of these chapters that is starkly different from those retellings aimed at children. Various critiques of this story have also been put forward that highlight the theological complexities of this narrative (Dawkins 2006).

Nevertheless, there has also been considerable theological reflection on these chapters, including explorations of the nature of God. Fretheim, for example, notes that 'Basic to the understanding of the God of this story is that God has entered into a genuine relationship with the world' (2010: 55–6). We see this in the fact that the motivating factor for God's action is not anger but regret and grief (Gen. 6.6-7). 'This regretful response of God assumes that humans have successfully resisted God's will for creation. As such, this text is a witness to divine vulnerability in the unfolding creation. This is a God who takes risks, who makes the divine self vulnerable to the twists and turns of creational life' (2010: 58–9). Further, God's promise to never destroy the earth in this way again comes in spite of the fact that humanity will go on being sinful and turning away from God's plan (8.21). 'This divine decision to go with a wicked world, come what may, means for God a continuing grieving of the heart ... the future of the creation that now becomes possible is rooted in this divine willingness to bear ongoing pain and sorrow' (61).

Other readings have focused on the way in which mercy and grace are important elements of the story. Moberly notes that in an ancient world where the notion of a cataclysmic flood is taken for granted, a tension emerges because, in the biblical worldview, there is no power other than Israel's God that could bring about such a flood. And yet, in the biblical account, 'the reasons for YHWH's actions are charged with moral concern' (2009: 109); God is concerned with the integrity of creation, and responds out of sorrow at how the story has unfolded. When read in this light, the saving of Noah and his family as well as the animals is a story of divine mercy: 'the text's overall emphasis remains YHWH's resolution to sustain life on earth in the future … Life for both Israel and for the world is a gift of grace' (118, 120).

Finally, recent studies have also begun to explore the ecological and environmental dimensions of this story. While there are environmental elements of this story that can be read in less positive ways (Habel's 'grey' texts), readers continue to find constructive ways of engaging with the creational aspects of this account. B.R. Rossing, for example, notes several points of connection between this story and our present ecological context. First, the story makes clear that human actions have consequences, and the corruption of humanity has implications for the physical world. Second, the story relates the saving of species from extinction, pointing towards a commitment to preserving and protecting life on earth. Third, in this story the curse on the ground is lifted (8.21), and God's commitment to the world and its well-being is reiterated in the covenant. Along with this, the story shows an awareness and appreciation of seasons and the agricultural year, urging us to be similarly aware of ecological concerns (8.22). Finally, the covenant of ch. 9 is with Noah and all of creation. In this sense, 'The Noah story underscores God's love for the integrity of the whole created world' (Rossing 2011: 115).

Priestly tradition and covenant

The conclusion of the flood story introduces another significant theme in the Pentateuch: the idea of a covenant, or special contract. God's making of a covenant with Noah at the end of the flood account is most often attributed to the Priestly tradition, and this theme of covenant has long been regarded as a defining element of the 'P' tradition. J. Wellhausen noted four major periods of history: the ages of Adam, Noah, Abraham, and Moses, each marked by a covenant. As F.M. Cross (1973) notes, it has regularly been recognized that God did not make a covenant with Adam but he did receive a blessing, which was also given to Noah, Abraham, and Moses, as Table 9.3 illustrates. In this light, the use of a similar formula in subsequent covenants marks a return to the original blessing given to humanity in creation. The covenants made with Noah, Abraham, and Moses all signalled the possibility of a return to the ideal state at creation.

Another noticeable element is that each covenant in each subsequent age became 'deeper and narrower', in that more was revealed to fewer people

Table 9.3 The blessings given to Adam, Noah, Abraham, and Moses

Name	Reference	Content of blessing
Adam	Gen. 1.28	God blessed them, and God said to them, 'Be fruitful and multiply, and fill the earth and subdue it; and have dominion over the fish of the sea and over the birds of the air and over every living thing that moves upon the earth.'
Noah	Gen. 9.7	'And you, be fruitful and multiply, abound on the earth and multiply in it.'
Abraham	Gen. 17.6	'I will make you exceedingly fruitful; and I will make nations of you, and kings shall come from you.'
Moses	Lev. 26.9	'I will look with favour upon you and make you fruitful and multiply you; and I will maintain my covenant with you.'

(Cross 1973: 296). As the covenants narrowed, from righteous humanity as a whole to Moses as the leader of the people of Israel, so also more of God's nature was revealed, culminating in the Torah for Israel. Thus, the covenant with Noah reaches back to the initial blessing given at creation, and points forward to Israel's covenant relationship with YHWH, serving as a thematic link for the Pentateuch as a whole. We return to the theme of covenant in Chapter 12 in our exploration of pentateuchal law.

The tower of Babel (Genesis 11)

The narrative of the primeval history ends with the account of the attempt to build a tower as far as the heavens, and the resulting dispersion of people and confusion of languages. In Gen. 6.1-4 the bounds of heaven were broken by the sons of God forming unions with the daughters of humans. Here, in ch. 11, the breach is made even greater by a human attempt to storm the heavenly realms by the building of a tower.

Various attempts have been made to understand the origins of this story. Somewhat surprisingly, there are no immediate ancient Near Eastern parallels to the narrative. On one level this story is etiological: it is an attempt to make sense of the experience of ethnic and linguistic diversity. Another possibility noted by many scholars is that this is a polemic against the Babylonians. The Hebrew text engages in a play on words, maintaining that the name 'Babel' was due to its connection to the Hebrew verb *bll*, which means 'confuse'. Both literary and archaeological evidence indicates that Babylon had many towers. The *Enuma Elish*, referred to above, celebrates the building of the

Esagil, a Babylonian temple, and it was a common belief in Babylon that the top of temples reached as far as heaven. In addition to this, archaeological evidence points to the existence of many ziggurats in Mesopotamia, which were pyramid-type towers (Rogerson 1991).

The Babel story is often understood as ironic. Even though the humans intend to build the tower as far as heaven, God is forced to come down from heaven to see it. The purpose of the story, therefore, seems to be to deride human attempts to reach heaven, particularly those of the apparently all-powerful Babylonians. As far as the overall structure of Genesis is concerned, this can be seen as the ultimate breaking of the boundaries set down by God in the creative order: human arrogance has reached so far that it now even attempts to invade heaven. However, others have offered more positive readings of this account. One such approach highlights the possibility that the diversity which emerges from the scattering of the people might be a positive development in the story of human culture and flourishing, one that allows for the further fulfilment of the blessing given in Genesis 1 to 'fill the earth' (see discussion in Briggs 2012).

Concluding remarks

While the Bible begins with a series of well-known stories, a close reading reveals that these narratives raise significant questions concerning history, gender, ecology, and theology. Indeed, these accounts have captured the imagination of readers in various ways for over two millennia, and their significance carries on to the present day.

The primeval history of Genesis 1–11 ends with a genealogy, which narrows down the focus of the story from the whole of humanity to Abraham, the father of the Israelites. With this, the focus of the Pentateuch switches from universal history to family history; from the whole world to that of one particular figure, Abraham, and his descendants. We explore these accounts of Israel's ancestors in the following chapter.

Further reading

The major commentaries noted in relation to Genesis in Chapter 2 are helpful places to begin for many of the issues here under discussion. Several further volumes are focused specifically on chs 1–11, including Miller (1978), Blenkinsopp (2011), Habel (2011), and Day (2013). Gertz (2012) offers a thorough and useful discussion on questions related to the origins and formation of the Primeval History. On Genesis and parallel texts from the ANE, consult Hays (2014). Theological concerns in these chapters are discussed in Moberly (2009). Hendel's volume (2013) on the reception of Genesis offers a number of fascinating examples of the way in which these texts have been used and understood down through the years.

The Ancestral Narratives (Genesis 12–50)

In Genesis 11 the story of the world's beginnings ends in the city of Babel, where language and culture become fragmented. Genesis 12–50 turns its attention away from the whole of humanity to one particular group of people: the family and descendants of Abraham. For the first time in the narrative so far, the beginnings of Israel become the focus of the narrative. The narrative of Genesis 12–50 follows the descendants of Abraham in their journey around the western reaches of the ANE and leaves them in Egypt, where the book of Exodus begins.

Roughly speaking, Genesis 12–50 falls into three sections, each focusing on particular members of the same family. Genesis 12.1–25.18 (often called the Abraham cycle) features the events surrounding the life of Abraham, his wife Sarah, his nephew Lot, and his sons Ishmael and Isaac. Genesis 25.19–35.29 (often called the Jacob cycle) turns its attention to Abraham's twin grandchildren, Jacob and Esau, and the tension surrounding their relationship. The final section, Genesis 37–50 (often called the Joseph narrative), deals with Joseph, one of Jacob's twelve children, and his experiences in a foreign land. These three sections, therefore, fashion their stories around three major characters, Abraham, Jacob, and Joseph, and around three major themes, the continuity of a line, fraternal conflict, and isolation in exile. Thus, as well as describing the lives of significant ancestors of old, these stories also explore central themes in the life of all societies: continuity, conflict, and place.

Readers have long referred to these chapters in Genesis as the 'patriarchal history', because they are concerned with the patriarchs Abraham, Isaac, Jacob, and Joseph. However, there are more than patriarchal figures in these stories. Indeed, women play particularly important roles throughout this collection of narratives. In light of this, it is perhaps more appropriate to refer to these as the 'ancestral narratives'; even if the cultural context is such that men receive the majority of the space in these chapters, these texts paint a picture of Israel's ancestors, both men and women, and the women in these stories should not be passed over lightly (Schneider 2008).

The origins and formation of the ancestral narratives

Traditional source critics regarded 'J', 'E', and 'P' as the major sources that lie behind Genesis 12–50, and some still hold to this breakdown, or modified versions of this. However, as outlined in Chapter 7, an increasing number of scholars are calling into question a number of the basic tenants of the Documentary Hypothesis, such as the notion of a coherent 'Yahwist' source that spans the Pentateuch. Rather, the trend has been to identify smaller units of tradition that were brought together over time, a development that has included the stories of the ancestors.

The notion that the traditions concerning Abraham, Isaac, and Jacob were not originally related, but that the stories about them were independent traditions about different ancestors which were joined later, is not a new idea; however, it is one which has gained significant traction in recent scholarship (Rendtorff 1990; Carr 1996; Schmid 2010). While 'P' is still identified in many of these readings, the once coherent 'J' source has been replaced by diverse 'non-P' materials that are considered unique to the individual ancestors. It has, for example, been noted that in these narratives, the three major patriarchs seem to be connected with different geographical locations: Abraham with Hebron, Isaac with Beer-sheba, and Jacob with Bethel. This may suggest that the traditions grew up in different areas with different tribes and only later came together to form a continuous strand (see the discussion in Gertz et al. 2012). Along with these developments relating to the sources and traditions behind the ancestors, the dating of these stories and traditions also continues to be debated. While traditional source critics date many of the these stories to the early monarchy, the recurring issues in these narratives relating to land, exile, and return have led to much speculation that the exile and its aftermath were the context that led to the bringing together of these traditions, even if parts of these traditions may well be much older.

The ancestors: Historical questions

Although Genesis 12–50 is quite different to Genesis 1–11, complex historical questions remain, including those related to the historicity of the ancestors. As mentioned above, Genesis 12 begins a story of a different quality to those in Genesis 1–11, as attention moves away from a universal story of earliest times to a particular family history. This concentration on the lives of a few individuals allows the account to provide a much more detailed insight into the way in which they lived their lives. This has inspired many scholars to attempt to locate Abraham and his descendants in a particular culture and

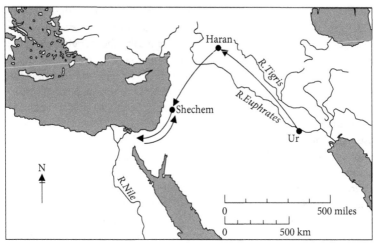

Map 10.1 Abraham's journey

time, notably Mesopotamia and Canaan in the second millennium BCE, the setting in which the text locates the ancestors.

A number of attempts have been made to demonstrate that various features within the Genesis stories could be traced back to the second millennium. Using archaeological evidence and evidence from the literature of other cultures from the second millennium BCE, such research aims to show that the patriarchal narratives contain features that are consistent with a second-millennium dating. Examples cited in such research include the fact that the personal names used in the stories, such as Terah, Abraham, and Jacob, fit with those used in the Mesopotamian region of the second millennium, and that migration was a common occurrence in the ANE during this period (Bright [1960] 2000). Others, meanwhile, have noted that these elements also fit in the first millennium BCE (Thompson 1974). The evidence may point to a second-millennium date, but may also point to a later period.

Scepticism about the historicity of the patriarchal narratives is not a new phenomenon. J. Wellhausen questioned the historicity of the narrative, suggesting that Abraham may be a 'free invention of unconscious art' (1885: 320). Indeed, certain elements within the Genesis account do seem to originate from a time later than the normal dating for Abraham in the early second millennium BCE. For example, Gen. 21.34 states that Abraham 'resided as an alien many days in the land of the Philistines', but the Philistines did not settle in Canaan until around 1200 BCE, later than the time of Abraham. Another anachronism is the reference to Abraham as the father of the Arabs (25.1-5), who are only recorded as a significant force from the 800s BCE. Both T.L. Thompson (1974) and J. Van

Seters (1975) remained unconvinced by the arguments in favour of the historicity of the patriarchal narratives. In detailed considerations of the evidence, they used the examples above, and many others, to argue that the narratives about the ancestors did not originate in the second millennium BCE but much later.

An alternative position is put forward by R. Hendel, who explores the issues from the vantage point of cultural memory. Hendel understands these narratives as composites of 'historical memory, traditional folklore, cultural self-definition, and narrative brilliance' (2005: 46). He is clear that there is no historical evidence regarding Abraham, Isaac, or Jacob as historical figures. What can be explored, however, are traditions that grew up around these figures, and such traditions can be situated historically. Looking at examples of geographical locations and other historical markers from Israel's history, Hendel posits that aspects of 'the patriarchal traditions have ancient roots. From these roots the stories grew and changed, adapted and embellished by storytellers of each age, until they came to be written down' (55). This, for Hendel, points again to the collective and cultural aspects of such remembering: 'Such stories of an epic past function as a symbolic shaper of community, joining people together around a common ethnic, cultural, and religious identity' (8).

The Abraham cycle (Genesis 12.1–25.18)

The Abraham cycle consists of one major theme supplemented by various additional accounts. The basic narrative focuses on the promise to Abraham to be a 'great nation'. The narrative returns to this promise repeatedly (13.14-18; 15.1-21; 17.1-27; 18.1-16a). Yet the plot of the narrative stresses the crisis that surrounds this promise: Abraham's descendants are to be blessed, but he has no descendants and his wife is old and barren. The unfolding of the solution to this crisis occupies most of the Abraham cycle. The crisis continues even when Isaac is born in ch. 21, since in the following chapter Abraham is commanded by God to kill him. Interwoven with this basic plot are various subplots: a war between Abraham and the kings of Canaan (14), the rescue of Abraham's nephew Lot from Sodom (18.16b–19.29), and the finding of a suitable wife for Isaac (24). The deaths of, first, Sarah (23.1-20) and then Abraham (25.1-18) are also reported in the account. (An accessible overview and commentary on the Abraham narratives can be found in Blenkinsopp 2015.)

Repetitions and inconsistencies in the Abraham cycle

At one level, the Abraham stories can be read as a coherent whole. However, upon closer inspection of the Abraham cycle, various inconsistencies and repetitions can be seen. For example, in Gen. 11.31-32, Terah took his family, left Ur-Kasidim, and came to Haran, where he died. In Gen. 12.1, God's command comes to Abraham to leave his land, his kindred, and the house of his father. Yet, according to the narrative in Genesis 11, he had already done all of this. Another example is the account of passing one's wife off as one's sister in a situation of danger. This account is attributed twice to Abraham and Sarah (12.10-20; 20.1-18) and once to Isaac and Rebekah (26.1-11), without any reference being made to it having happened before.

Traditional source critics attribute this type of inconsistency to the accounts having originated from different sources or traditions. Thus the tradition that Abraham came from Ur is attributed to 'P' and that he came from Haran to the 'non-P' tradition. The triple account of passing off a wife as a sister is often attributed to oral tradition, with 12.10-20 being regarded as the base tradition and 20.1-18 and 26.1-11 as embellishments of it.

Alternative interpretations, however, have viewed these accounts differently. D.M. Gunn and D.N. Fewell opt to read the story in its final form, rather than attempt to rediscover its origins. The picture they gain from the text of Abraham is somewhat different to the traditional portrayal of him. Abraham is renowned for his faith and ready acceptance of God's guidance. However, a close reading of the final form of the text reveals a different person. Rather than portraying a courageous, faithful figure, Gunn and Fewell propose that the text reveals 'a man of frequent surprise and great contradiction' (1993: 90). When God calls to Abraham, the call

> comes at an opportune time with an opportune content: Abram is to leave his native land, which he has already done, and his father's house, of which there is nothing left, to go to the land which is already the destination of his migration. We might ask ourselves, how much faith does it take to do what one has already decided to do? (1993: 91)

Gunn and Fewell suggest that the whole of the Genesis account portrays a man who acts uncertainly and at times foolishly, but who is constantly saved and protected by God. Their picture of Abraham is of a much less heroic, and much more human, figure.

The account of passing off a wife as a sister has also received alternative interpretations. R. Alter (1981), for example, suggests that these should be considered as 'type-scenes', stories told from a sort of narrative template, but with unique emphases depending on the concerns of the particular context of the story. A similar reading is offered by D.J.A. Clines (1990), who reads the stories not as one story embellished in three different ways but as three different stories. Through a close reading of the text, Clines demonstrates that although the vehicle of the story is similar, the purpose of each one is different. In each story, the danger described is a danger to the patriarch, not to his wife, but each narrative has a different function in its context. Genesis 12.10-20 focuses on Sarah. Immediately after the promise made to Abraham by God that he would be the father of many nations, the potential loss of Sarah becomes more crucial to the plot. The function is similar in Genesis 20 but here the danger seems cast more in the light of the potential loss of Isaac, who is born in the following chapter. The version in Genesis 26 has an entirely different function and the danger described is directed more to the Philistines, who would have suffered if they had mistreated Rebekah. This reading of the text illustrates the importance of studying each story in context, not simply as an isolated unit. Although when considered out of context these stories seem very similar, when considered in their context the function of each becomes much more important.

The promises to Abraham

The promises to the patriarchs are the focal points of the narrative in Genesis 12–50. Indeed, some have suggested that they are the key for understanding the whole of the Pentateuch (Clines 1997). The promise in 12.1-2 – which begins Genesis 12–50 – contains three themes which Clines maintains are drawn out in the rest of the Pentateuch.

> Now the LORD said to Abram, 'Go from your country and your kindred and your father's house to the land that I will show you. I will make of you a great nation, and I will bless you, and make your name great, so that you will be a blessing.' (Gen. 12.1-2)

These three themes are the promise of descendants ('I will make of you a great nation'), the promise of relationship with God ('I will bless you, and make your name great'), and the promise of land ('Go from your country … to the land that I will show you'). As well as being present throughout the Pentateuch, these promises are woven firmly into the fabric of the Abraham story itself (Baden 2013). The whole narrative portrays the slow unfolding of Abraham's relationship with God. The crises that surround the production of an heir are played out on the canvas of Abraham's new dwelling in the land of Canaan.

Although these promises appear throughout the Abraham cycle, they reach a particular climax in the double account of the making of a covenant between God and Abraham in chs 15 and 17. The covenant described in ch. 15 falls into two distinct sections: God's promise of descendants with Abraham's acceptance of this promise (vv. 1–6) and the ritual of the ratification of the covenant (vv. 7–21). One of the most striking elements of this covenant is the strange ritual of ratification described in vv. 9–18. Here Abraham is commanded to cut in two a calf, a goat, a ram, a dove, and a turtle dove. After dark, a smoking pot and a flaming torch are passed through the middle of the animals. The significance of this action is not entirely clear. Verse 18 states that God 'cut covenant' (NRSV translates the phrase 'made a covenant') with Abraham on that day. Thus, this action seems to provide the proof requested by Abraham (v. 8) that the promise would be fulfilled. This ceremony may explain the use of the term in Hebrew to 'cut a covenant', used in the Hebrew Bible to describe the making of a covenant.

The covenant in ch. 17, meanwhile, places an obligation, not on God, but on Abraham. In this account, the sign of the covenant is to take place regularly: the circumcision of every male person of the household. Again, the promise of the covenant is of descendants, relationship, and land. One of the most striking elements of this account is the change of name from Abram to Abraham. The name 'Abram', meaning in Hebrew 'the father of exaltation', is exchanged for 'Abraham', which is most often understood as 'the father of a multitude'.

Sarah, Hagar, and Ishmael

The account of the crisis surrounding the birth of a possible heir for Abraham is focused on Sarah's ability to bear children. This theme occupies a large portion of the Abraham cycle. Although the crucial need for heirs is Abraham's, the shame for barrenness is Sarah's. The narrative stresses the impossibility of the situation by indicating that, in addition to being infertile, Sarah is 90 years old. Tension is established in the story between God's promise and the apparent impossibility of its fulfilment. Although this collection of stories is known as the Abraham cycle, the character of Sarah is central to the account. In many places in the narrative she acts as silent foil to the male hero Abraham. Nevertheless, although present, she is often portrayed as irrelevant to the main narrative. Thus we do not know her opinion on the command to leave her home in Mesopotamia and journey to a new land, nor what she thought of God's command to Abraham in Genesis 22 to kill her only son (Trible 1991). However, in certain places, Sarah's voice is heard within the narrative. Perhaps the most important example of this is her interaction with Hagar, the Egyptian slave girl who at Sarah's behest bore a son for Abraham. Unsurprisingly, this sub-narrative has become the focus for many feminist interpretations of the text.

Sarah and Hagar's relationship is one of power and oppression. The powerful wife, Sarah, has need of the powerless slave, Hagar, and yet feels threatened by the shifting patterns of power when Hagar produces a son, the one thing Sarah cannot have. The relationship between Sarah and Hagar is set out primarily in two passages: Gen. 16.1-16 and 21.8-21. Source critics have traditionally identified these narratives as originating from different sources or traditions. However, although these stories do present a similar theme of the banishment of Hagar by Sarah, they can quite easily be read as complementary stories. In the first narrative, Hagar flees Sarah's cruel treatment while pregnant but is persuaded by an angel to return; in the second, she is evicted by Sarah and finds a new life with her son in Egypt. Both stories tell of God's increasing protection of Hagar as her situation worsens. This portrayal of power and oppression makes these stories of rival women even more interesting.

Sarah's role in this cycle of stories is complex. Although she is the wife of Abraham and the mother of the chosen son Isaac, her treatment of Hagar is oppressive and violent. The eviction of a slave into the desert would have been tantamount to murder, had not God protected Hagar and Ishmael. D.N. Fewell (1998) reflects further on this dynamic of power in her retelling of the story from Hagar's perspective. She focuses on the meaning of Ishmael's name, 'God hears', to draw out the theme of divine protection for Hagar. Trible also offers a reading of Hagar's story, noting that while it is a difficult story, it is one that 'shapes and challenges faith', not least because 'her story depicts oppression in three familiar forms: nationality, class, and sex'. She concludes that 'All we who are heirs of Sarah and Abraham, by flesh and spirit, must answer for the terror in Hagar's story' (1984: 23–4).

Hagar's story is intimately tied to that of Ishmael, Abraham's firstborn son who is passed over in favour of Isaac. Ishmael's story has much in common with other firstborn sons in Genesis and elsewhere who end up being the non-elect; that is, Ishmael will not be the son that is the bearer of promise in the line of Abraham. However, the portrayal of Ishmael again is a complex one (Heard 2001). While traditional interpretation has tended to read Ishmael in quite a negative light, a close reading of the texts concerning Hagar's son (Gen. 16.10-12, 17.20-22, and 21.11-13, 17–18) reveals that Ishmael is promised many descendants and a future that includes nationhood, as well as a promise of future blessing. While there are ambiguous and less positive elements to the various pronouncements concerning Ishmael, he is not cursed because he is passed over in favour of the younger Isaac. The prominent role that Ishmael would come to have in Islamic tradition, where he is also a prophet, has ensured that he has remained an important figure across the Abrahamic traditions (see, e.g., the discussion of Ishmael in rabbinic tradition in Bakhos 2006). Further discussion on both Hagar and Ishmael – including their relationship to Abraham, and their respective roles in Judaism, Christianity, and Islam – can be found in the volume of essays edited by M. Goodman, G.H. van Kooten, and T.A.G.M. van Ruiten (2010).

Abraham and Isaac

The birth of Isaac represents the climax of the whole Abraham cycle. The promises made to Abraham throughout this section are dependent upon Isaac's birth and subsequent survival. Isaac's long-awaited birth occurs in ch. 21, and yet this climax of the narrative is subtly undermined both in this chapter and the next. Chapter 21 also tells of the banishment of Hagar by Sarah and the near death of Ishmael, Hagar's son. The birth of Isaac almost causes the death of Abraham's other son, Ishmael. Even more surprising are the events of ch. 22, where the narrative describes God's command to Abraham to sacrifice Isaac. God's promise that Abraham will be the ancestor of many nations hangs in the balance once more.

In Chapter 8 we used Genesis 22 as an example of the various ways in which a biblical text can be interpreted. In addition to what was covered there, the significance of this story within the Jewish, Christian, and Muslim traditions is worth noting.

Rabbinic interpretations of the story of Gen. 22.1-19 are known as the *'aqedah* (binding) or *'aqedah Yishaq* (the binding of Isaac). P.S. Alexander (1990) has reviewed the major features of this rabbinic interpretation. Within rabbinic exegesis, the story of the binding of Isaac was a complex collection of ideas, covering numerous aspects of the narrative. When referring to the story, the rabbis based their discussion not only on the biblical version of the story but also on the traditions that had grown up around it within Judaism. Alexander has identified the three most important elements contained within these traditions. The first element found in Jewish tradition is that Isaac was a willing victim of the proposed sacrifice. The Targum *Pseudo-Jonathan* states that Isaac was not a young boy at the time of the sacrifice but thirty-seven years old. The decision to sacrifice him arose out of an argument between himself and Ishmael about who would give the greatest sacrifice to God – Isaac offered his whole body.

A second common element found in these traditions is that the sacrifice took place on the site of the temple in Jerusalem. Consequently, the sacrifice of Isaac acts as the ideal type for all subsequent sacrifices. Subsequent sacrifices are efficacious because they recall the *'aqedah*. The final most common element within these traditions is the belief that the *'aqedah* acted in some way for the benefit of Isaac's descendants. Alexander observes that this part of the tradition takes two forms. The first is that the obedience of

Abraham and of Isaac 'were works of supererogation which laid up merit for their descendants' (p. 45); the second that Isaac acted as a representative for his descendants. Thus, his action atoned for the sins of those that came after him. This final element of the traditions bears a remarkable resemblance to the Christian doctrine of the atonement. The parallels noted between these two have raised questions of a connection between them. While it is possible that the Jewish *'aqedah* tradition influenced the Christian tradition of the atoning sacrifice of Christ or vice versa, Alexander sees no reason to suppose a direct connection between the two. Instead, he argues that it is conceivable that the two traditions could have grown up independently of each other and that this is more likely than a direct borrowing of one from the other.

The fact that Genesis 22 depicts the (near) sacrifice of a beloved son has, not surprisingly, meant that this story has been the subject of much interpretive energy in the Christian tradition. A common approach has been to read this story typologically, with Isaac as a type of Christ and Jesus as the fulfilment. An example of this can be seen in the writing of the second-century theologian Clement of Alexandria. He comments as follows:

> Isaac is [a] type ... of the Lord. He was a son, just as is the Son (he is the son of Abraham; Christ, of God). He was a victim, as was the Lord, but his sacrifice was not consummated, while the Lord's was. All he did was to carry the wood of his sacrifice, just as the Lord bore the wood of the cross. Isaac rejoiced for a mystical reason, to prefigure the joy with which the Lord has filled us. (Clement of Alexandria, *Christ the Educator* 1.5.23, cited in Sheridan 2002: 105)

This type of reading was widespread in the early church, and remains popular today. R.W.L. Moberly, however, has suggested that a more significant parallel is to be found in Abraham and Jesus, both of whom respond with faithful obedience when tested. He notes,

> When all is said and done, Genesis 22 remains a demanding and unsettling text, not least because it will not neatly fit into our preferred tidy categorizations. It is surely in this respect that, for the Christian reader, an imaginative and existential linkage between Genesis 22 and the passion of Jesus ... becomes appropriate. The linkage is not a matter of details – carrying the wood/cross, the location of Jerusalem – but rather in the fact that when Jesus is at Gethsemane and Golgotha and the Easter Garden, then, as with Abraham at Moriah, all 'explanations' ... become inadequate to do justice to the subject matter of the text ...

Christians believe that, rightly understood and appropriated, these texts point to an entry into anguished darkness that can also be a way into light and life. (2009: 198–9)

Finally, this story is retold in the Qur'an (37.99-109), and this retelling has had a complex history in the Islamic tradition. In the version found in the Qur'an it is not said which son was sacrificed, Isaac or Ishmael, and both sons appear elsewhere in the Qur'an. Older Islamic tradition seems to have held that Isaac is the son mentioned in the Qur'an, but it was the great Islamic commentator of the fourteenth century, Ibn Kathir, who popularized the interpretation that it is indeed Ishmael that is offered by Abraham, a notion that has gained widespread acceptance in the modern period (Mirza 2013).

Despite the importance of the birth and survival of Isaac for the patriarchal narrative, his character remains remarkably undeveloped. With a few exceptions (e.g. Genesis 24), the focus of the narrative passes straight from Abraham to Isaac's two sons, Jacob and Esau. Isaac is portrayed as a shadowy figure, significant primarily for his continuance of Abraham's line. J.C. Exum and J.W. Whedbee (1990) reflect upon the elusiveness of his character and the significance of his name. The name Isaac means, in Hebrew, 'he laughs'. Yet Isaac is only portrayed as a joyful figure at his birth. Sarah's cynical laughter of 18.12, when she heard God's promise of a child, turned to laughter of joy at his birth: 'Sarah said, "God has brought laughter for me; everyone who hears will laugh with me"' (21.6). For the most part, in the rest of the narrative Isaac is portrayed as a 'victim through and through, characteristically acquiescent to personages stronger and more clever than he' (Exum and Whedbee 1990: 130). Even in the passages in which Isaac features, his role is a passive one. For example, in several scenes it is his wife Rebekah who is the strong character, not Isaac, as one would expect. Isaac is the passive bearer of the promise of God, whereas Rebekah is the active character who ensures that the promise is passed on to her favourite son, Jacob. For more on the portrayal of Rebekah in these stories, see A.J. Bledstein (1993), T.J. Schneider (2008), and M.R. Jacobs (2007).

The Jacob cycle (Genesis 25.19–35.29)

In contrast to Isaac, the character of Jacob is well defined in the biblical narrative. Even his name fits his character better than that of Isaac. The biblical narrative gives two etymologies for the name Jacob. Genesis 25.26 ties the name to the Hebrew word '*aqeb*, which means 'heel', as Jacob is said to grab Esau's heel as they leave the womb. Genesis 27.36, meanwhile, associates it with *'aqab*, meaning 'cheat'. Both these etymologies of the name give the impression of an active character who is determined to achieve his aims by any means possible. In Gen. 32.29 and 35.10 he is renamed Israel, the former explaining the name as highlighting the fact that Jacob struggles with both God and humanity. Such is the character of Jacob in the biblical narrative.

The whole cycle of stories circles around Jacob's bearing of the promise of God, achieved by tricking his elder brother Esau out of his blessing. The tensions which surround God's promise still form the focus of the narrative. This time the crisis is not concerned with continuity but with the land. Jacob tricks the birthright from his brother and is driven from the land. As a result, the question which hangs over the whole of the Jacob narrative is whether God's promise can be fulfilled outside the land. It is only with Jacob's return in Genesis 32 that the crisis is resolved once more.

R. Alter draws out some of the complexities of the conflict between Jacob and Esau. The text of Gen. 25.23 identifies Jacob and Esau as 'the eponymous founders of two neighbouring and rival peoples' (1981: 42). The descriptions of Esau as red and hairy-skinned (25.25) with a large appetite (25.29-34) can be understood as associating him with primal, almost beast-like qualities. Such a portrayal would seem to be in line with the harsh portrayal elsewhere in the Hebrew Bible of Esau's descendants – the Edomites – by Jacob's descendants, the Israelites. As with Ishmael, however, the portrayal of Esau in these chapters is complex. While there are elements that can be construed negatively, Esau's gracious and brotherly welcome of Jacob in Genesis 33 ensures that Jacob's (and Israel's) story continues, and Jacob even likens seeing Esau's face to seeing the face of God (33.10; see Anderson 2011).

In fact, there is even more to the story than this. Whatever one thinks about Esau's character in these stories, Jacob is revealed as an ambiguous character, mercenary and scheming. A significant question raised by these chapters is how to understand Jacob's character and actions in light of the fact that he is the chosen son who bears the promise of Abraham. Some through the years have defended Jacob and his actions, assuming that if he is the patriarch he must in some way be worthy of the role (see, for example, J. Calvin [1554] 1850). A more popular approach in recent years has been to understand Jacob as a trickster hero, a character type known in the ancient world. Here Jacob's mental acumen and ability to outwit his father, brother, and uncle is understood to prove his superiority and these are to be celebrated (Niditch 1987). Finally, there are some who suggest that Jacob's role as the chosen son is another example of the mystery of election; Jacob is no more deserving than Esau, and is the bearer of promise in spite of his various shortcomings. Indeed, some of these imperfections are elements with which Israel as a nation would be able to identify. As F.E. Greenspahn comments,

Just as the portrayal of her ancestors reflects Israel's sense of worth, her fate cannot be divorced from their experience, and particularly those of her namesake Jacob. Oppressed, ravaged, defeated, and exiled, her history was not what one would expect for God's chosen people. The Bible's heroes are thus appropriate to its understanding of the nation's own worth. Convinced God had chosen her, Israel was no less cognizant of her being an unlikely and maybe even undeserving choice … Her sense of superiority is leavened with a substantial, and frequently overlooked, element of humility and self-derogation, laying the groundwork to counter any arrogant inclinations Israel, or her eventual daughter traditions, might otherwise have felt. (1994: 131–4)

In this same vein, Alter points out that there is a certain 'symmetrical poetic justice' (1981: 45) in the fact that Jacob himself is tricked as he tricked his father and brother. Jacob took advantage of his father's bad eyesight to cheat Esau out of his birthright (Genesis 27), but Laban used the bridal veil to trick Jacob into marrying Leah instead of Rachel (Genesis 29). Jacob may be a trickster, but what is less clear is if this is something of which the biblical tradition approves.

The characters of Rachel and Leah are not as well defined as that of Rebekah (Schneider 2008). Where Rebekah is shown to be an active, thinking subject, Rachel and Leah, on the whole, play a much more passive role in the story. However, J.E. Lapsley (1998) has attempted to understand more about Rachel in the context of the Genesis narrative. She focuses her attention on Rachel's response to her father in Gen. 31.35: 'Let not my lord be angry that I cannot rise before you, for the way of women is upon me.' This response allowed Rachel to deceive her father and steal the household gods for which he was searching. Lapsley regards this as a hint of a female voice within a male narrative. She maintains that, while the words are a lie, they convey truth in that they represent the inequity of Rachel's position in patriarchal society and constitute a resistance and protest to this position.

Another woman featured in the Jacob cycle is Dinah, Jacob's daughter (Genesis 34). This narrative does not appear to fit easily into the flow of the Jacob cycle and is more concerned with the action of Dinah's brothers than that of her father. The narrative tells of the rape of Dinah by Shechem, the son of a city chief, and the vengeance wreaked upon the city by Dinah's brothers. Traditional interpretations of this passage understand it in similar terms to the author of the text: as an act of 'burning shame done to the brothers' (von Rad [1956] 1972: 334). S. Scholz (1998), however, directs her attention to the feature in the text, generally accepted by scholars, that Shechem attempted to woo Dinah after raping her. This is often regarded as mitigation for the act of rape which precedes it. By means of a detailed consideration of the verbs used in the text, Scholz maintains the importance of recognizing that this account is not a love story but is a story that recounts sexual violence.

For more on the origins and development of the Jacob Cycle, see E. Blum (2012), while various literary and thematic issues are helpfully unpacked by M. Fishbane (1975).

The Joseph narrative (Genesis 37–50)

The final section of Genesis turns its attention to the life of one of Jacob's twelve sons, Joseph (Clifford 2012). Joseph was the eleventh son of Jacob and the first son of Jacob's favourite wife, Rachel. Although a part of the patriarchal narrative, the Joseph narrative stands out as unusual. The Abraham and Jacob cycles consist of small units loosely bound together to form a chronological history. The Joseph narrative seems to be a much more complete narrative, with a clear plot and progression from one section to another (Westermann 1996). For this reason, it is common to refer to Genesis 37–50 as the Joseph narrative, not the Joseph cycle (as in the Abraham and Jacob cycles). The chapters seem to form a novella with a clear beginning and end, and development of character throughout. The overall narrative tells of the success of Joseph in the face of familial conflict. Joseph, the favourite son of his father, alienates his brothers, who send him into slavery (Genesis 37). Various factors lead to success in the Egyptian court and a position of great authority (41.46-57). A severe famine drives his family to beg for aid in Egypt. Joseph provides the help that they need and becomes united with his family once more (chs 42–50). Interwoven with this basic narrative are two other narratives: the account of Judah and Tamar, another story which explores gender and power imbalance in the ancient world, and the cycle of stories about Joseph's time in Egypt, outlining his rise to success in the Egyptian court.

The apparent unity of the text is one of the striking features of this account. This has led some critics to propose that the Joseph narrative was a complete, originally independent, text, inserted as a whole into the Genesis narrative. For example, C. Westermann (1988: 257-8) regards the account as a 'single, self-contained document' dating to the period of the early monarchy. Others, however, see a story that developed over time and date it as late as the fourth century BCE in the post-exilic period, noting strong themes related to Diaspora (Schmid 2002). Whatever the case, the story shows familiarity with Egyptian life and customs. Life in the Egyptian court, including the existence of court officials and counsellors, is accurately portrayed in the narrative. In fact, the account of Joseph and Potiphar's wife in ch. 39 finds an interesting parallel in Egyptian literature. The Egyptian account of the Two Brothers (*ANET*, 23–5) tells of a younger brother who worked for his elder brother. One day, the wife of the elder brother attempted to persuade the younger brother to sleep with her. When he refused, the elder brother's wife accused him falsely to her husband. This account bears obvious parallels to the Joseph story, though it does not necessarily indicate that the author of the Joseph narrative drew from it.

It has been observed that the whole Joseph narrative revolves around knowledge (Alter 1981). The hero, Joseph, has divinely inspired knowledge, given through dreams and interpretation of dreams, which allows him to foresee what will happen to his brothers (they will bow down and worship him, Gen. 37.5-11), to his fellow prisoners (the cup-bearer will be freed and the baker executed, Gen. 40.1-19), and to Egypt (it will have seven years of plenty followed by seven years of famine, Gen. 41.25-36). Alongside this are the counter-figures who do not have knowledge: Pharaoh (who does not know the meaning of his dream, Gen. 41.1-8) and Joseph's brothers (who do not know Joseph when they meet him again, 42.8). Alter maintains that this theme is one which makes the Joseph narrative such a compelling story. This and other elements have led some to speculate that the Joseph narrative has a connection to wisdom traditions (von Rad 1966), though others have called this idea into question (Fox 2012).

Genesis 12–50 in extra-biblical Jewish texts

The importance of Genesis 12–50 for later Jewish writers is ably demonstrated by the existence of numerous books based on the biblical account. The book of *Jubilees* is a retelling of the narrative of Genesis 1 to Exodus 20, which features a lengthy retelling of the patriarchal narratives (see Hayward 2012). Fragments of the book were found in the excavations at Qumran and have helped to fix a date for the book, which most regard to be around 161–140 BCE. The whole book is set in the context of Moses' receiving of the law on Mount Sinai and seems to account for Moses' authorship of at least the first part of the Torah. The narrative of Genesis 1 to Exodus 20 is revealed to Moses by 'the angel of the presence', and he wrote down the account as the angel spoke. Chapters 2–10 of *Jubilees* contain a retelling of the primeval history and chs 46–50 comprise stories about Moses. The rest of the book is occupied with a retelling and elaboration of the narratives about the patriarchs with various parts abbreviated or omitted and additional parts added. Thus, for example, Sarah's harsh treatment of Hagar in Gen. 16.4-14 is omitted but various additional stories are included. Particularly noticeable are chs 11–19, which tell a series of tales about Abraham's youth, and chs 37–38, which describe a war between Jacob and Esau. The presence of fragments of the book at Qumran demonstrates how important this reworking of the Genesis tradition was in ancient Judaism. This is made even more interesting by the presence of a second retelling of Genesis among the Dead Sea Scrolls: the *Genesis Apocryphon*. Although only fragmentary, it is possible to identify that it uses a similar technique to that of the book of *Jubilees*, of retelling and embellishing the Genesis narrative.

Another embellishment of the biblical narrative, though of a different type, can be found in the story of *Joseph and Aseneth*. This is thought to be a Jewish text written in Egypt between the first century BCE and the second century CE. It is an expansion of a single verse from Gen. 41.45, which records that Joseph married Aseneth, the daughter of Potipherah, priest of On. This brief statement seems to have caused considerable consternation among Jews of the time, for whom marriage outside Judaism was forbidden. This marriage was particularly problematic, as Aseneth was the daughter of an Egyptian priest. The story is a romance. Aseneth fell in love with Joseph but he would not consider her because she was a heathen. Heartbroken, Aseneth fasted for a week and at the end of the week was visited by an angel who announced that God had accepted Aseneth and had written her in the 'book of the living'. Thus it was proper for Joseph to marry his Egyptian bride.

Other collections are also based on Genesis 12–50. *The Testaments of the Three Patriarchs* consists, as its name suggests, of three 'Testaments' of Abraham, Isaac, and Jacob respectively. Written one after another, probably between the first and third centuries CE, they are based upon the deaths of the patriarchs and contain accounts of visits to them by an angel before they die. *The Testaments of the Twelve Patriarchs* are likewise based on the deaths of Jacob's twelve sons and purport to contain their last words to their families before death. It is interesting that both collections of Testaments were adopted by Christianity and became important texts within the Eastern Church.

The ancestors in early Christianity and Islam

Abraham was also a figure of importance within early Christian texts. For the apostle Paul, the figure of Abraham played a vital part in his argument about the relationship between Christianity and the law. In his interpretation of the narrative, he uses various different techniques to support his argument of the inclusion of the Gentiles in the promises of God. In Romans 4 he concentrates on the order of the text of Genesis. He argues that, as Abraham's faith was reckoned to him as righteousness (Rom. 4.3, based on Gen. 15.6) before circumcision was instituted (Gen. 17.24), Abraham can be regarded as the ancestor of the uncircumcised as well of the circumcised.

The argument of Galatians 3 is based upon Paul's use of various specific verses from the narrative. The crucial verses for Paul are Gen. 15.6 and 18.18 (also Gen. 12.3) and Gen. 12.7 (also Gen. 22.17-18). Genesis 15.6 allows him to consider the significance of Abraham's faith. Genesis 18.18 and 12.7 are important for the promises they contain. Paul interprets the promise that 'all the nations of the earth shall be blessed' (Gen. 18.18) as referring to the Gentiles and the words 'to your offspring' (12.7) as referring in the singular to Christ, not to the Jews. Thus these verses helped him to support his argument that the promises to Abraham were fulfilled in Christ and Christianity. Paul's use of the Hagar and Sarah story (Gal. 4.21–5.1) is also interesting. His interpretation of the birth of Ishmael and Isaac is entirely allegorical. Ishmael, he maintains, stands for slavery; Isaac, for freedom. Christians are to consider themselves as Abraham's heirs according to Isaac, not according to Ishmael. There can be no doubt that the Abraham story was well known to Paul. It was so important for him that he returned to it repeatedly in different ways in order to support his case.

It is worth noting that Abraham is also an important figure in Islam (Bakhos 2014). As G.R. Hawting (2010) points out, this connection can be found in the Qur'an, as well as in later Islamic literature and tradition, the latter offering fuller detail and exposition than that which is found in the sacred text of Islam. An important connection between Abraham and Islam is Abraham's son Ishmael, who will later be considered the ancestor of the Arabs. However, the importance of Abraham can also be seen in the fact that he is noted as a prophet in the Qur'an, and Islam understands itself as the (true) continuation or restoration of the religion revealed to Abraham. Consequently, Sura 2.127 in the Qur'an notes that Abraham and Ishmael built the Ka'ba, the building at the centre of the sacred mosque in Mecca and Islam's most holy site, while Muslim tradition also holds that Abraham brought monotheism to Arabia. There is thus both a historical and religious connection that is claimed with Abraham.

Concluding remarks

As outlined above, in the course of Genesis 12–50, numerous interpretive issues emerge for the attuned reader, including historical, literary, theological, and reader-centred concerns. One such issue is the tension which surrounds God's original promise to Abraham of descendants and the gift of land.

Despite the extended account of God's intervention to save Joseph, given in Genesis 37–50, the account ends with Jacob and his whole family living in Egypt, away from the land of Canaan. The scene is set, therefore, for the next stage in the story of the beginnings of Israel, a stage in which Abraham's descendants become a people, and journey once again towards the land of promise.

Further reading

The major commentaries noted in Chapter 2 are a good place to begin study on the ancestors, and volumes focusing specifically on Genesis 12–50 include Westermann (1986, 1995), Moberly (1992a), and Wenham (1995). Issues related to the origins and formation of these chapters are discussed in Carr (1996). Further questions related to the historicity of the ancestors are dealt with in Blenkinsopp (1992). The stories of the women in these chapters are investigated in Brenner (1993) and Schneider (2008). Theological dimensions of these chapters are explored in Fretheim (1994a) and Moberly (2009).

Moses and the Exodus Tradition
(Exodus 1–15)

The book of Exodus begins where Genesis ends: in Egypt. In this sense, it acts as a sequel to the events described in the Joseph narrative. Exodus 1.8 in particular ('now a new king arose over Egypt, who did not know Joseph') seems to indicate that we are to understand what follows as the next episode in the story. Almost as soon as it begins, however, it becomes clear that the nature of the account has changed. The story no longer describes a family history, with a single significant 'patriarch' as leader. Joseph's descendants are now 'numerous' and 'powerful' (Exod. 1.9). The altered nature of the people also leads to a different kind of leader. Moses is chosen by God to lead the people, not by virtue of rank or birthright, but by virtue of divine calling. Although Exodus clearly follows on from the Genesis narrative, the situation is very different. As Genesis 12–50 moved the story of beginnings on from a universal history to the history of a chosen family, so Exodus also moves the story on from a family history towards the history of a people.

The book of Exodus falls easily into four sections (for an introduction to and overview of the book of Exodus, consult Chapter 3). Exodus 1.1–12.36 describes the situation of the people in Egypt and the rise of Moses; Exod. 12.37–15.21 recounts the exodus from Egypt; Exod. 15.22–18.27 describes the wandering in the wilderness; and Exod. 19.1–40.30 narrates the giving of the law to Moses on Sinai. The first two sections are the focus of this current chapter, which highlights a number of critical issues related to Moses and the account of the liberation of the Israelites in the exodus event. The latter two sections of Exodus present the themes of wilderness wanderings and law, themes which are also found in the remaining books of the Pentateuch (Leviticus, Numbers, and Deuteronomy). For this reason, Exod. 15.22–40.30 will be explored in more detail in Chapters 12 and 13. In what follows we explore literary and thematic elements, historical issues and concerns, as well as religious and theological implications of these first chapters of Exodus.

Literary and thematic elements of Exodus 1–15

Origins and relationship to Pentateuch traditions

In the traditional Documentary Hypothesis, the narrative of the exodus traditions found in Exodus 1–15 was considered to come from a combination of Yahwistic, Elohistic, and Priestly sources. However, as outlined in Chapter 7, developments in pentateuchal studies over the past several decades have had a significant impact on research into the origins of the exodus tradition, as well as its relationship to the broader pentateuchal materials. Most notably, questions surrounding the feasibility of the 'E' source, as well as the possibility of a coherent 'J' source that spans Genesis-Numbers, have led to a reappraisal of these issues. Further, recent research has suggested that the Moses story was originally an independent account of the origins of Israel, distinct from the ancestral narratives of Genesis. In this reading, the connection of the stories of the ancestors and Moses comes at quite a late stage, and may be a Priestly development (Schmid 2010; Berner 2014). Nevertheless, it does seem clear that there are different traditions in this account, and the 'P' materials are, as elsewhere, quite recognizable. Thus, while it is far from settled, there is some consensus that the narrative of Exodus 1–15 is a combination of 'P' and 'non-P' traditions.

The Moses birth narrative (1.1–2.25)

The book of Exodus begins with an overview of the 'family of Abraham', which has now become a great people in a foreign land, but very quickly focuses on one particular member of this people: Moses. The narrative differs from that of Genesis because this is no longer a family history, but it remains similar in that the story is told through the eyes of one person. It consists of a number of vignettes apparently unconnected and many years apart. It begins with the birth of Moses, then moves on to Moses' flight from Egypt in disgrace, his marriage to Zipporah, and subsequent calling by God to return to Egypt. In the space of two chapters, the history of Moses before his call to confront Pharaoh is told in short, economical yet effective units.

The narrative begins with the account of the birth of Moses in adverse circumstances, as the young baby is hidden away by his parents – first in their home, later in the river Nile – to escape the Pharaoh's decree that all sons born to the Hebrews are to be killed. These early stories also recount how his life is saved by the actions of various women. The Hebrew midwives Shiprah and Puah, Moses' mother and sister, and Pharaoh's daughter are all instrumental in saving him from death (Römer 2015). The account is enhanced by various twists in the plot: the one who saves Israel is saved from death at birth; Moses' life is threatened by a decree of Pharaoh and saved by Pharaoh's daughter; and Moses' mother gives up her son to save him and gets him back as his wet nurse.

The tale of Moses' birth is a familiar one in folktales from many different cultures, in particular the legend of Sargon of Akkad, whose mother concealed him at birth in a basket made of rushes and sealed with bitumen. Sargon was later rescued by Akki and raised as his son. Meanwhile, the name given to Moses by Pharaoh's daughter when she saved him has caused considerable debate among scholars. The biblical text ties the name (*mosheh*) to the Hebrew word *mashah*, which means 'to draw'. An alternative is that this name originates from the Egyptian *mesu*, meaning 'son', which can be found in other Egyptian names such as Ahmose and Thutmose (Dozeman 2009).

The second episode in Moses' life also sees him in danger of death, this time for killing an Egyptian overlord who Moses sees mistreating an Israelite slave. Here again a certain symmetry enhances the tale: Moses is forced to flee from the land from which he will later deliver the people of God. This episode is quickly followed by the third major episode. This part of the story takes place in the land of Midian, where Moses defended the daughters of Reuel, a Midianite priest, against shepherds who prevented them drawing water from a well. R. Alter regards this as a 'betrothal type-scene', echoing the stories of both Isaac and Rebekah and Jacob and Rachel. There are certainly close similarities between the accounts, most notably the motif of drawing water from a well. Alter notes, however, that the Moses account seems to be 'so spare a treatment of the convention as to be almost nondescript' (1981: 57). Whereas in the other stories the narrative develops the characters of Rebekah and Rachel and their respective fathers, this episode gives only the scantiest details about Zipporah and Reuel. This mirrors the treatment of Zipporah in the rest of the narrative – she is little more than a shadow in the background of the account. What is interesting about this account is that, just as Moses' flight from Egypt anticipated the exodus to come, so also this narrative contains elements which anticipate future action by Moses. For example, the verb used of Moses' action by the well, *hoshi'a*, comes from the same root as the word *moshi'a* or 'saviour' – Moses' future role in relation to the Israelites. There is also a connection between Moses' action to aid the daughters of Reuel to draw water from the well and Moses himself being drawn from the water of the river (Propp 1999).

These vignettes at the start of the book of Exodus function not only to introduce the major characters but also to point to what has gone before and what is to come. The betrothal type-scene in Exod. 2.14-22 ties the narrative back into the accounts of the patriarchs in Genesis. At the same time, motifs such as salvation or drawing water show both the active and passive role of the hero Moses: Moses is both saved and saves; he is drawn from the water and draws water. Although the hero of the narrative, Moses does not stand alone. He is helped, just as he helps others.

The calling of Moses (3.1–7.7)

The next stage of the narrative turns to the events running up to the exodus itself and features the calling and sending of Moses to Egypt. This section appears to contain two parallel accounts of the call of Moses (Exod. 3.1–4.23 and Exod. 6.1–7.7), generally ascribed to 'non-P' and 'P' traditions, respectively. These two accounts stand on either side of an account of failure on the part of Moses and Aaron in persuading Pharaoh to release the Israelites. The first account of Moses' calling contains a theophany or revelation of God. Although the biblical account states that an 'angel of the LORD' appeared to Moses in a 'flame of fire out of a bush', the subsequent account makes it clear that it was God himself that Moses encountered. Theophanies occur frequently in the pages of the Hebrew Bible and this one contains many motifs which occur regularly elsewhere (see, for example, Exodus 19; Isaiah 6; Ezekiel 1). The theophany takes place on Mount Horeb (elsewhere called Mount Sinai), where numerous other theophanies take place, most notably the great theophany which was accompanied by the giving of the law (Exodus 19). Other motifs which stand out are the presence of fire and Moses' fear in the presence of God. In other theophanies, God's presence is accompanied by similar natural phenomena, such as thunder and lightning or hail, and in most the motif of fear in the presence of God can be found.

One of the most significant episodes of this section is the revelation of the divine name to Moses. In Hebrew the divine name is rendered by four consonants, YHWH, and is consequently known as the tetragrammaton (or four letters). It is well known that the sacredness of the divine name in Jewish tradition meant that it was never pronounced. Consequently the word has no vowels and a pronunciation of the word as 'Yahweh' is a guess on the part of Christian scholars. Within Jewish tradition, whenever the tetragrammaton was encountered, the word *adonay* or Lord was pronounced instead (hence the rendering in the NRSV of 'The LORD' whenever YHWH appears in the text). In order to remind readers of this fact, the vowels of *adonay* appear under the consonants YHWH. This is the origin of the form of the name 'Jehovah', which is a combination of the Latin form of the letters of the tetragrammaton with the vowels of *adonay*. The meaning of the divine name is disputed. Exodus 3.14 associates the name with the verb 'to be', though whether this is an accurate rendering of the form of the word is unclear (see discussion in Dozeman 2009). For more on the divine name and its use in the ancestral narratives along with the Moses story, see R.W.L. Moberly (1992b).

The figure of Aaron appears for the first time in this section alongside Moses. Aaron is an elusive character in the narrative, appearing in 126 verses in the Pentateuch but portrayed varyingly by the authors of the account. He is depicted both as a chosen priest from whom a line of priests emerges and also as a flawed character who is part of the Israelites' creation of the golden calf. The contrasting ways in which Aaron is depicted by the text has led scholars to explore possible explanations for these differences (Wellhausen 1885; Watts 2011). In this particular section, Aaron is an elusive character who appears for the first time in Exod. 4.14 as a proposed mouthpiece for the nervous Moses. No explanation is given of Moses' continued connection with a brother from whom he was separated both while growing up and while in the Midian desert.

The plagues (7.8–12.32)

Moses' second visit to Pharaoh features the ten plagues which God brought on Egypt to persuade Pharaoh to release the Israelites. This section concerning the plagues also contains the well-known notion of God hardening Pharaoh's heart, an idea which has inspired much theological debate through the years. The plagues fall into three groups of three with the tenth, the death of the firstborn son of the Egyptians, as the climax of the narrative, as Table 11.1 illustrates. It is this final plague which persuaded Pharaoh to let the Israelites go. T.E. Fretheim (1991) has noted the connection of the plagues to ecological disasters, thus highlighting the way in which these function as part of a theology of creation. It is also possible that these plagues are part

Table 11.1 The plagues which afflicted the Egyptians

First set of plagues	Second set of plagues	Third set of plagues
First plague:	*Fourth plague:*	*Seventh plague:*
Pollution of the Nile	Invasion of flies	Hailstorm
Second plague:	*Fifth plague:*	*Eighth plague:*
Invasion of frogs	Disease of livestock	Invasion of locusts
Third plague:	*Sixth plague:*	*Ninth plague:*
Invasion of gnats	Boils	Darkness falling
Tenth plague: Death of the firstborn sons		

of a polemic against Egyptian deities, such as Ra, the sun god (Rendsburg 1988). In either case, it is the supremacy of Israel's God that is highlighted. (For more on the plagues, consult Lemmelijn 2009.)

Across the Red Sea (12.33–15.31)

The exodus continues with the account of the flight from Egypt (Exod. 12.33-39; Exod. 13.17–14.31). The crossing of the Red Sea is one of the most iconic images in the Hebrew Bible, and is one that has been captured in numerous ways in art and film. Readers have long wondered about the logistics of such a crossing, and there have been various reconstructions through the years to explain the phenomenon from a natural or scientific perspective. It is noteworthy that the biblical text itself says that a strong wind played a part in the event (Exod. 14.21), though it also makes clear that it all takes place on divine initiative.

An important theme in the exodus tradition is the defeat of Pharaoh and his army at the crossing of the sea. Just as the plagues showed God's power over nature, so to does the escape through the sea. Indeed, the prominence of the sea in the scene is notable, as the sea played a crucial role in numerous mythologies and worldviews of the ANE. As T.B. Dozeman notes, 'The story of Yahweh's control over the sea is influenced by liturgical motifs from ancient Near Eastern religion where the sea represents the forces of nature at war with the god of creation' (2009: 298). Examples include Baal's victory over the god of the sea in Canaanite lore, and the Babylonian creation myth Enuma Elish, where the creation begins with Marduk splitting Tiamat, god of the sea. The crossing features elements which point to 'P' and 'non-P' parts to the narrative, and Dozeman suggests that these may be influenced by both the Canaanite ('P') and Babylonian ('non-P') traditions. However, there is more to the exodus account than simple appropriation of other traditions, as Israel's God is battling Pharaoh, rather than the sea. This may be reflective of the idea that Israel's God is the only God (Genesis 1), and thus there are no other gods with who he can do battle (Edelman 2012). In this case, God's control over the sea becomes part of the means by which Pharaoh and his armies are defeated. Nevertheless, the sea and God's power over it would become an important aspect for how the exodus was understood by other biblical writers (Isa. 5.9-11; Psalm 114).

The flight from Egypt concludes with Moses' and Miriam's song of triumph after the crossing of the Red Sea and the destruction of the Egyptian force. This song of triumph (Exod. 15.1-21) occurs in two forms in the text: a long form in the first person (Exod. 15.1-18) and short form in the third person (Exod. 15.21). The short form, sung by Miriam and 'all the women', contains the first stanza of the long form sung by Moses. It has long been suspected by scholars that Miriam's song may be the older of the two, later taken up and elaborated in Moses' song, which bears a remarkable similarity to hymns of thanksgiving in the Psalter (see for example, Psalms 69 and 101). This theory has proved attractive to feminist scholars who are interested in locating the lost female voice in the biblical text. If this episode can be demonstrated to be both ancient and giving priority to the voice of women, then a strong case can be made that this is another example of how the voice of women has been subsumed by later male biblical writers (see Trible 1994; Bach 1999). In fact, a text found at Qumran (4Q365) indicates a longer form of Miriam's song, which may point to the antiquity of this idea (Brooke 2005).

History and the exodus tradition

Although the exodus is considered one of the foundational events of the Hebrew Bible and would remain important for later Judaism and Christianity, there are complex questions relating to the origins, historicity, and dating of the event. We offer here an introduction to some significant elements in discussions on these matters (for helpful overviews, see Grabbe 2014, as well as the essays in Levy, Schneider, and Propp 2015).

The exodus event: Dating, participants, and route

There is a good deal of disagreement as to the historicity of Moses and the larger exodus tradition. For those who understand the exodus account as narrating a historical (or historically plausible) event, certain questions, and complexities still emerge in relation to the date for this event, the identity of the participants, and the route that might have been taken.

Two major periods have been proposed for the date of the exodus in historical reconstructions: the fifteenth century BCE and the thirteenth century BCE (Geraty 2015). A fifteenth-century date for the exodus is suggested by 1 Kgs 6.1: 'In the four hundred and eightieth year after the Israelites came out of the land of Egypt, in the fourth year of Solomon's reign over Israel, in the month of Ziv, which is the second month, he began to build the house of the LORD.' The fourth year of Solomon's reign is commonly dated to around 966 BCE. This would place the exodus 480 years earlier, in 1446 BCE. For many years, this date was commonly accepted. There are, however, numerous problems with a fifteenth-century date for the exodus and settlement. One of these is that, if the generations between the exodus and the fourth year of Solomon's reign are combined, the number of years reached is over 553 years, not 480. This raises questions about how the ancient biblical writers calculated dates and generations.

Problems such as this led some to abandon a fifteenth-century date in favour of a date in the thirteenth century. Evidence which suggests the thirteenth century includes the reference in Exod. 1.11 to the building of the store cities Pithom and Rameses by the Israelites in Egypt. Rameses II was king in Egypt from 1304–1237 BCE and the city Pi-Ramesse was built during his reign and named after him. The city of Rameses mentioned in Exod. 1.11 may well be this city, Pi-Ramesse. This date may be supported by the Merneptah Stele. Merneptah, the son of Rameses II, ruled in Egypt between 1212 and 1202 BCE. Archaeologists have found a stele, a large standing block of stone, engraved with a record of his many victories. One of these victories was a subjugation of Israel, which suggests that by the time of Merneptah the Israelites had already settled in Israel, though how best to understand this reference to Israel is debated.

Two questions arise in a consideration of the people mentioned in the exodus narrative. The first concerns the number of people who left Egypt. Exodus 12.37 states that the number of people who left in the exodus was 600,000 men, plus women and children. If most of the men were married, then the total number of leavers would be around 2 or 3 million. As indicated in Chapter 3, this causes some problems with the biblical account. It would be impossible for so many people to cross a stretch of water in the space of a night or to be able to survive in the desert for forty years. There are two possible solutions to this problem. Either the Hebrew '*eleph* should be taken to mean family (rather than a thousand), as it is in Judg. 6.15 and 1 Sam. 10.19 or the number 600,000, like other statistics in the Hebrew Bible, is not accurate, with proposals ranging from a few thousand to a few tribes that left Egypt. J. Wellhausen (1885), while accepting the basic veracity of the exodus tradition, proposed that those entering and subsequently leaving Egypt were a small group of tribal shepherding peoples. H.H. Rowley (1950) maintained that those who left were members of the Joseph tribes (Ephraim and Manasseh), while J. Bright ([1960] 2000) suggested they were a mixed group who later spread their exodus tradition to all the Israelites.

Other attempts to identify the characters involved in the exodus try to associate those mentioned with groups known from extra-biblical sources. Two of these groups of people are the Hyksos and the Habiru (the latter also known as the Hapiru, 'Apiru, or Khapiru). The Hyksos were the rulers of Egypt in the 'second intermediate period' (roughly 1786–1529 BCE).

Records indicate that they invaded Egypt and were probably of Semitic origin. The Jewish historian Josephus, who claimed to have taken his information from an Egyptian historian, Manetho, associated Joseph's arrival in Egypt with that of the Hyksos. If the tradition in Gen. 15.13 that the people were in Egypt for four hundred years is correct *and* if a thirteenth-century date is accepted for the exodus, then Joseph's arrival in Egypt would correspond with that of the Hyksos. While this theory is attractive, other biblical verses suggest that the sojourn in Egypt was much shorter, only four generations (Gen. 15.16; Exod. 6.16-20), making a connection with the Hyksos less likely.

The Habiru are a group of people referred to in numerous sources from the second millennium BCE, most notably in one of the Amarna letters from a Jerusalemite chieftain to Egypt in 1375 BCE. This band of people was an invading force that troubled many different regions around this period. The similarity between the name Habiru and 'Hebrew' inevitably led scholars to propose a connection between the two groups. Indeed, if there was a connection between them, this would further support a fifteenth-century date for the exodus. A detailed consideration of the texts referring to *Habiru*, however, indicates that the term was not an ethnic one but a social one. It referred to groups of people who lived on the outskirts of society, and their presence seems to have been a general phenomenon of the Late Bronze Age period. Consequently, while the Israelites might have been identified as Habiru, it would be hard to prove that the Habiru referred to in the Amarna letters were in fact the Israelites. While the connections proposed between the Hyksos, the Habiru, and the biblical narrative are alluring, there is insufficient evidence to substantiate these views with any certainty.

Another historical question raised by the text is the location of the sea crossed by Moses and the people as they left Egypt (Moshier and Hoffmeier 2015). The English phrase 'Red Sea' (cf. Exod. 15.22) translates the phrases used in the Vulgate and Septuagint, both of which mean 'Red Sea' and are used elsewhere to refer to the north-west section of the Indian Ocean which separates Africa from Arabia. The northernmost sections of the sea split into two gulfs: the Gulf of Suez, which runs between the Sinai desert and Egypt, and the Gulf of Aqabah, which runs between the Sinai desert and the desert of Arabia. The 'Red Sea' can refer to either one of these gulfs or the main section of the sea. The slight complexity is that the Hebrew *yam suph* can mean 'sea of reeds'. This has led to considerable debate about its location. The question facing scholars is whether the phrase 'sea of reeds' refers to a description of what the sea was like or whether it was the name of the sea. There is little consensus on the issue. Some point to the presence

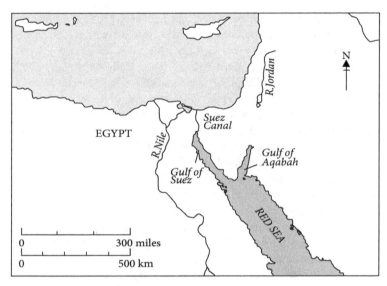

Map 11.1 Possible locations of the 'Red Sea'

of a marshy area along the route of the modern Suez canal as a possible
location for the 'sea of reeds'. Others note that 1 Kgs 9.26 refers to the Gulf
of Aqabah as the 'sea of reeds', suggesting that the traditional 'Red Sea'
might be an appropriate description here (see Map 11.1).

Alternative theories for the exodus traditions

One of the difficulties of dating the exodus is that it is not something that can
be done in isolation. The date of the exodus is integrally linked with a number
of other issues, including the date of the settlement of the people in Canaan, the
account of which is recorded in the books of Joshua and Judges. The biblical
account places the exodus approximately forty years before the people settled
in the land of Canaan. Consequently, the date proposed for the settlement
clearly affects the date proposed for the exodus. However, issues such as the
large numbers of those said to have been part of the Israelite group leaving
Egypt, as noted above, have led some to question how useful these traditions
are for historical reconstruction. Further, archaeological work has shown little
evidence of violent conquest in Canaan in the eras normally associated with
the exodus and conquest. Thus, employing archaeological and sociological
research, various theories regarding the origins of the people Israel have
emerged over the past half century, many of which suggest that the Israelites

emerged whole or in part from within Canaan itself – that is, that a mass exodus from Egypt did not occur but that the Israelites were indigenous to Canaan (Gottwald 1979).

How, then, to explain the emergence of the exodus tradition? One approach is to consider more closely the relationship of the narrative world and the world of the narrators, as those who put these stories together were likely doing so from a significant historical distance to the stories they are narrating (Schmid 2015). As noted in previous chapters, the emergence of these traditions is increasingly considered to be from later in Israel's history. Thus, theories have emerged that might make sense of exodus motifs in these later eras, either in relation to the tense relations with the Assyrians, where the Egyptians become a symbolic representation of Assyria, or in correlating the exodus and the return from exile in the Persian period, often considered a second exodus (Isa. 51.9-11).

Others, meanwhile, have put forward theories that connect the exodus tradition more closely to memories of Egypt, even if this differs from how the account is portrayed in the book of Exodus. Some have suggested that the tradition of the exodus is based on the harsh treatment of the Canaanites by the Egyptians in the early second millennium, a period in which Egypt's rule would have extended north into Canaan. In this view, memories of the harsh Egyptian rule *in Canaan* were later transferred geographically *to Egypt*, where a new exodus story was created (Na'aman 2011). It is also likely that some slaves would have been moved south from Canaan to Egypt during this period of Egyptian dominance. Thus, a related theory is that the exodus tradition could be founded on a small group of slaves, perhaps originally from Canaan and taken down to Egypt, who decamped from Egypt and banded together with native Canaanites upon their return (Knauf 2010). Together this 'mixed multitude' developed a new, communal identity, part of which entailed remembering the ruthless Pharaoh and the escape from his rule. In these readings, the exodus is understood as cultural memory, where, in the words of R. Hendel, 'historical memory, folklore, ethnic self-fashioning, and literary artistry converge' (2015: 65). Hendel expands on the implications of this cultural, collective memory:

> Even if some or many of these formative events did not really happen in the way that they are told, they were – and still are – felt and understood to be a shared memory of a collective past. Such stories of an epic past function as a symbolic shaper of community, joining people together around a common ethnic, cultural, and religious identity … Jewish identity, from its beginnings to the present day, is formed in no small part by the recitation of these stories. (2005: 8)

Religious and theological issues

The exodus in biblical tradition

The account of the exodus would become a central theme in other biblical narratives, notably those that involved leaving or returning to a land. The account of entry into the Promised Land across the river Jordan (Joshua 4) seems to be consciously based on the crossing of the Red Sea. Likewise the return from exile, envisioned by the prophets Isaiah and Ezekiel, also seems to be related to the exodus narrative (see particularly Isa. 43.14-21; Ezek. 20.32-44). One of the major ways in which the tradition is used in theological reflection is to define and celebrate the salvific nature of God's relationship with the Israelites. It is in the exodus event that God's nature, as one who saves God's people from slavery and oppression, is defined. There are many interesting examples of the use of the exodus tradition within the Hebrew Bible to highlight such redemption, particularly in the Psalter and the writings of the prophets (e.g. Hos. 11.1; Ps. 78.12ff; see Römer 2011b). Even in the New Testament, God's redemptive act in the incarnation is, on occasion, interpreted in terms of the exodus. Thus the flight of Joseph, Mary, and Jesus to Egypt and their subsequent return is interpreted as a second exodus by the author of the Gospel of Matthew (Mt. 2.15).

The figure of Moses

As is the case with the stories of the ancestors, there is little proof outside of the biblical material with which one might verify the historicity of Moses. Some, such as M. Noth ([1954] 1960), have been sceptical about any ability to speak of the historicity of the figure Moses, whom Noth regarded as the editorial glue which joined together the otherwise-independent strands of the patriarchal and exodus traditions. Other scholars such as G.W. Coats (1988) have questioned such a stance, arguing that the importance of Moses within the tradition indicates that he was something more than an editorial device. Whatever the historical basis of the tradition, the figure of Moses stands out from the pages of the biblical narrative. Moses is the first leader of the nascent people of Israel, called to be God's agent in one of the most significant acts of divine redemption recorded in the biblical narrative. He is a figure of such importance that it is difficult to imagine the biblical narrative without him.

Indeed, in the traditions of Judaism, Christianity, and Islam, Moses has remained a vitally important figure, not least because of his association with divine revelation. In fact, such is the influence of Moses that research concerning this biblical figure is now taken up in a variety of contexts well beyond traditional biblical studies. Two well-known examples along these lines include a book by S. Freud (1939), who offered a psychoanalytic reading of the Moses story, as well as that from J. Assmann (1997), who traces the cultural and social memory of the traditions concerning Moses and Egypt. Moses has also been an important figure in cultural dimensions ranging from visual arts, to literature, to cinema (Britt 2004; Shepherd 2008). Moses, then, is a character whose legacy in many ways far exceeds his role in the biblical story. For more on the reception of Moses in biblical tradition and historical perspective, see the essays in J. Beal (2014).

Festivals and the exodus

An interesting and complex element of the exodus tradition is the establishment of certain cultic regulations which are woven into the narrative: two festivals and the practice of the dedication of the firstborn to YHWH. The festivals of the Passover and unleavened bread are associated with the account of the exodus, where they explain how the Israelites are to avoid the final plague, the death of the firstborn, and prepare for their hurried exit from Egypt. Exodus 12.1-13, 21–27, and 43–50 set out the regulations which must be observed at the feast of the Passover; in this case we have the unusual situation where the description of the first celebration of the event is accompanied by instructions for future commemoration. The Israelites must choose a blemish-free lamb on the tenth day of the Jewish month of Nisan and keep it until the fourteenth day, when it should be slaughtered. That evening, its blood should be sprinkled on the doorposts of the house and it should be roasted and eaten. Interwoven with this account in Exod. 12.14-20 and 13.3-10 are the regulations for the feast of unleavened bread, which the biblical account states is a seven-day continuation of the feast of the Passover (i.e. it runs from the fifteenth to the twenty-first day of Nisan). The eating of unleavened bread, which in part symbolizes the haste with which the Israelites had to flee Egypt, marks the festival. Exodus 13.11-16 contains the regulations for dedicating the firstborn to YHWH.

These three practices, the festivals of the Passover and unleavened bread and the dedication of the firstborn, are interwoven with the account of exodus. However, many have suggested that these festivals were originally independent and only later associated with each other within the framework of the biblical narrative, gaining additional significance as a result of their association with the exodus account. W. Johnstone (1990, 2003), among others, suggests that the festivals of the Passover and unleavened bread actually originated in different cultures (see also Edelman 2012). He associates the Passover with nomadic practices and the feast of unleavened bread with settled, agricultural festivals, noting the similarities between the Passover and the practice of the Sinai Bedouin tribes called the *fidyah*. This practice was designed to ward off cholera and consisted of smearing the entrance of a dwelling with the blood of a slaughtered animal and consuming its flesh in a community meal. In contrast to the Passover, Johnstone suggests that the feast of unleavened bread originated in a farming community and originally marked the beginning of the barley harvest, drawing his evidence from Exod. 23.14-19 and 34.18-26, which contain additional regulations for the festival. T. Schneider (2015), meanwhile, notes connections between Passover and elements of Egyptian culture, suggesting that there may well be Egyptian motifs that underlie the final plague and the related Passover.

Whatever the historical reality behind these traditions, there can be little doubt that the cultic regulations contained in Exodus 12–13 took on enormous significance due to their association with God's act of redemption in the exodus. Both in Judaism and Christianity these two feasts, together with the associated practice of the dedication of every firstborn male, gained central importance. The feast of the Passover and unleavened bread became one of the three obligatory pilgrimage festivals, alongside the feast of weeks and the feast of Tabernacles (see, for example, Exod. 23.14-19), celebrated in the temple every year. Consequently it stood at the heart of Israelite worship year by year. Even after the fall of the Temple in 70 CE, the festival maintained its importance. *Pesahim*, a tractate of the Mishnah and Talmud, contains regulations for the celebration of the Passover after the fall of the Temple. Their reinterpretation of the festival makes it a family celebration, associated with redemption, both past and future.

The Passover would also become important within Christianity, through its association with the crucifixion and resurrection of Jesus Christ. For Christians, the notion of the dedication of the firstborn male, associated with the Passover in Exodus, gives the tradition additional significance. Thus the twin notions of Jesus as the paschal lamb and the firstborn son of God are intertwined. The gospel accounts do not agree about the precise correlation between the events of the crucifixion and the feast of the Passover. The Synoptic Gospels maintain that the Last Supper was the Passover meal celebrated by Jesus and his disciples (Mk 14.6, 12–17; Mt. 26.17, 19–20; Lk. 22.7-9, 13–14), making the crucifixion take place at the beginning of the feast of unleavened bread. By contrast, John's Gospel has Jesus crucified at the same time as the paschal lambs, on the last day of the feast of the Passover (Jn 19.14). Either way, the association of the Passover with the concept of redemption makes it an appropriate backdrop for the celebration of the Christian notion of salvation.

Pharaoh's hardened heart

As noted above, an element of these chapters that has long interested interpreters is the repeated reference to the hardening (or stiffening) of Pharaoh's heart, an idea which occurs twenty times in these chapters (see, for example, Exod. 7.3, 7.13, 8.19, 10.20). Some of these refer to God hardening Pharaoh's heart (4.21, 7.3), while others state that his heart was hardened (7.13, 7.22). Readers, particularly in the Christian tradition, have struggled with how to understand this notion, notably God's role in hardening Pharaoh's heart. This is heightened by the fact that Paul cites Exod. 9.16 in Rom. 9.17, using the hardening of Pharaoh's heart as an example of God's freedom in electing Israel as the chosen people. This has led to much theological and philosophical speculation through the centuries. Does the fact that God hardens Pharaoh's heart mean that God takes away Pharaoh's free will? This question has received the attention that it has in part because it touches on core issues related both to the character of God (as all-powerful) as well as the nature of humanity (as active and free agents).

From antiquity, readers have noted this issue, and many, particularly the church fathers, 'ended up with a compromise position which combined God's power with man's free will' (Childs 1974: 166). The Reformers, notably J. Calvin, would seize on Paul's use of this motif and focus on predestination, or the idea that some things are preordained and thus destined to happen. Recent decades have introduced new interpretive approaches. For example, one approach is to read these texts psychologically, where hardening is seen to be idiomatic, describing 'the inner human reaction of resistance which once begun could no longer be reversed by the individual will' (Childs 1974: 170). Thus, it has been suggested that the movement in the text from Pharaoh hardening his heart (8.15) to that of God hardening Pharaoh's heart (9.12) is indicative of such a development. N. Sarna notes that this movement 'is the biblical way of asserting that the king's intransigence has by then become habitual and irreversible; his character has become his destiny' (1991: 21).

B.S. Childs, meanwhile, focuses on literary elements and suggests that the hardening motif is closely connected to the plagues as signs in these chapters:

> the [hardening] motif sought to explain a tradition which contained a series of divine signs but which continued to fail in their purpose. Hardening was the vocabulary used by the biblical writers to describe the resistance which prevented the signs from achieving their assigned task. The motif has been consistently over-interpreted by supposing that it arose from a profoundly theological reflection and seeing it as a problem of free will and predestination. (1974: 174)

According to Childs, there is no theological dilemma in the biblical account; rather, this terminology is a literary motif that highlights why the plagues continued to be unsuccessful.

Exodus and liberation theology

We have already noted the importance of redemption for an understanding of the exodus event. The specific nature of the salvation described in the exodus account is of liberation from oppression and slavery. It is unsurprising, therefore, that the exodus account has been one of the crucial texts for liberation theologians. For those who currently experience oppression in any form, the portrayal of a God who hears the cry of the oppressed and acts to liberate them is vital. Liberationist readings of the Bible see its central message as one of liberation for the poor and the nature of God as one who is particularly on the side of the poor. Liberationist readings of the Bible became popular in Latin America in the 1960s and arose out of the reflections of those who experienced poverty and oppression. Unlike other methods of biblical interpretation, it began not in the academy, but among people who joined together to read the Bible and share their experiences. Helpful surveys of the origins of liberation theology and its impact on the academic world can be found in C. Rowland (2007).

The significance of the exodus for liberation theology is expressed in G. Gutierrez's seminal work, *A Theology of Liberation*, as 'the suppression of disorder and the creation of a new order' (1974: 88). Gutiérrez notes Moses' struggle not only to achieve liberation for the people of Israel but also to persuade them of the extent of their oppression and their need to struggle against it. Thus the account functions not only as an image of what God has done for the people but also as a model of how people should behave in a situation of oppression. This involves becoming aware of the roots of their oppression, struggling against it, and looking forward to a future in which they can 'establish a society free from misery and alienation'. The impact of this approach to the exodus story is that the interpretation of the text becomes a dialogue, with similar experiences shedding light on the text and the text, in its turn, shedding light on those experiences. An even more thorough liberationist approach to the book of Exodus can be found in G.V. Pixley's commentary on the book (1987), which is based around the concept of liberation.

While this idea of the exodus as representative of wider concerns of liberation seems intuitive to many, it has come in for some criticism, particularly from the Jewish scholar J.D. Levenson (1993b). Levenson focuses on the fact that the Israelites are to be set free so that they can serve (only) God. In this sense, the exodus is a change of ownership – from Pharaoh to YHWH – rather than general liberation. Further, it is both Israel crying out and the fact that these are the descendants of Abraham, Isaac, and Jacob (Exod. 2.23-25) that leads to God's action on their behalf. Thus, while the suffering of the people is a factor, so too is the particularity of Israel as the chosen people, and this needs to be kept in mind with any universalizing moves. (For a response to Levenson on these matters, see Brueggemann 1995.)

Nevertheless, the exodus has played an important role in a number of diverse contexts through the years related to liberation. We find exodus imagery in Negro spirituals in the face of slavery, in twentieth-century social movements in South America, and in Martin Luther King Jr's rhetoric in the civil rights movement. From its use in the larger story of the Bible to its appropriation throughout history, few biblical stories have had as far-reaching an impact as the exodus tradition.

Concluding remarks

Taken on its own, the exodus is one of the defining moments within the story of the people of Israel. In addition to its importance within the literature of the Hebrew Bible, the exodus would become central to the cultic life of Israel as three of the major festivals are all connected, in some way, with the events of the exodus. This cultic significance has ensured that the exodus functions as a central event for future generations. In fact, the Babylonian Talmud states, 'In every generation a person is duty-bound to regard himself as if he personally has gone forth from Egypt' (*Tractate Pesahim*).

However, the account of the exodus is also part of a larger context that needs to be kept in mind. These chapters introduce the reader to Moses, a character who is prominent throughout the rest of the Pentateuch, particularly at the giving of the law, while they also serve as a preface for Israel's journey through the wilderness and towards the Promised Land. We turn our attention to these related aspects of the pentateuchal story in the next two chapters as we explore the law (Chapter 12) and the wilderness wanderings (Chapter 13).

Further reading

Commentaries which explore some of the issues outlined above in relation to the exodus traditions include Childs (1974), Fretheim (1988), Propp (1999), Meyers (2005), Dozeman (2009), and Johnstone (2014). Critical issues are explored in the collections of essays edited by Dozeman (2010); Dozeman, Evans, and Lohr (2014); and Levy, Schneider, and Propp (2015). The relationship of the exodus tradition and the ancestors in Genesis is discussed in Schmid (2010). The role of Moses in the biblical tradition and his reception in later history are explored in the edited collection of Beal (2014).

'The Law' in Exodus–Deuteronomy

As the Israelites escape from Egypt, they begin their long journey towards Canaan. It is in this context that we encounter the dual themes of law and wilderness wanderings, which are interwoven in the remaining texts of the Pentateuch. The present chapter will consider the collections of laws and legal material in more detail; Chapter 13 will explore the narrative framework of the wilderness wanderings.

For many readers of the Bible, 'law' seems mysterious or (perhaps worse, in the modern world) irrelevant and boring. Indeed, for some, particularly Christians, the law has a very negative connotation, in part because of the way in which it has been understood in later Christian theology. However, in the Jewish tradition, the law plays a central and positive role. The law, or Torah, is seen as life-enhancing rather than something that is limiting; here it is worth recalling that the word *torah* means much more than law, but encompasses ideas such as teaching and instruction. Further, there are a number of elements of the law traditions in the Pentateuch that are vitally important for understanding the theology and orientation of the Hebrew Bible as a whole, not to mention significant portions of the New Testament. Thus, the law traditions of the Pentateuch are issues we ignore at our own peril if we wish to understand the biblical material.

In this chapter we explore a number of elements related to these traditions, including theories on the origins and formation of the law, broad issues related to the law and legal materials, and finally a closer look at law in the individual books of Exodus, Leviticus, Numbers, and Deuteronomy. It will become clear that, while it is possible to speak of 'law' in the Pentateuch, this heading includes diverse materials that differ in content, style, and perspective.

Origins and formation of law traditions

Although it is common to speak in general of 'law' in the Pentateuch, there are in fact quite distinct collections of laws to be found when we examine Exodus 19 to the end of Deuteronomy. Exodus 20 contains the best-known collection:

'the Ten Commandments', also known as the Decalogue, which is repeated in Deut. 5.6-21. Also to be found in the book of Exodus are the 'Covenant Code' (Exod. 20.22–23.19) and a collection of cultic commandments about the setting up of the tabernacle (Exod. 25.1–31.17). The 'Covenant Code' or 'Book of the Covenant' takes its name from Exod. 24.7, which recounts how Moses read out the collection of laws to the people of Israel after his descent from Sinai. The book of Leviticus, meanwhile, contains what is known as the 'Holiness Code' (Leviticus 17–26), a collection which, as the name suggests, is concerned with issues of holiness. In addition to these there are collections of laws to be found in the first part of Leviticus, the book of Deuteronomy, as well as the miscellaneous laws in Numbers.

The relationship of these smaller collections to one another, and the place of law in the formation of the broader Pentateuch, has been an area of increasing interest in recent decades. As noted in the discussion of Chapter 7, developments in theories relating to the origins of the Pentateuch have led to a reconsideration of several factors. Rather than the bringing together of extensive documents that span the pentateuchal material, a growing number of scholars suggest that the Pentateuch came together as smaller units or traditions were edited together. We have seen how this is the case with the ancestral and exodus traditions in Chapters 10 and 11; similar processes seem to be at work in the law and legal materials in the Pentateuch.

The Covenant Code of Exodus is generally understood to be the oldest of the biblical law codes, and most likely pre-dates both the Priestly and Deuteronomic traditions. This collection of laws is similar in a number of ways and may have even drawn from Hammurabi's law, a Babylonian collection from eighteenth century BCE (Wright 2009). While the date for the Covenant Code is thought to be much later than Hammurabi's code, dated anywhere from the tenth to the eighth/seventh centuries BCE, the connections between Hammurabi's law and the Covenant Code offer one prominent example that suggest a close relationship between Israel's law and other law codes from the ANE.

Along with this connection to ANE law, there is also (re)interpretation of laws within the biblical corpus itself. For example, it is likely that, following the Covenant Code, the next legal tradition to develop is that found in Deuteronomy, notably chs 12–26 (or parts thereof). There is a striking resemblance in this collection to material found in the Covenant Code, though there is also a development of particular ideas. An example of this can be seen in the laws concerning the manumission of slaves which are expanded to include female slaves in Deut. 15.12-18 (cf. Exod. 21.1-6). Whether the Deuteronomic material was meant to replace the Covenant Code or merely interpret and update it for a new era is a matter of some debate (Levinson 1997). Nevertheless, the textual points of contact between the traditions suggest a dynamic relationship that includes interpretation of and response to earlier materials.

A significant portion of the remaining law materials in the Pentateuch are associated with the Priestly tradition. This Priestly material, as discussed in Chapter 7, contains both narrative and law, and is usually dated to the exilic or post-exilic periods, though some do hold that this material emerged at an earlier stage, perhaps during the age of the monarchy (Milgrom 1998). However, 'Priestly' should not be understood as referring to one author or a single historical setting for these materials. Rather, as J.N. Lohr notes, it is 'a statement about the orientation and genre of this block of literature. The P material in this block is distinctive for its emphasis on instruction (or list) and matters relating to holiness, worship, and purity' (2012: 88).

When focusing on the law elements of the Priestly tradition, it is generally thought to include much of the final half of Exodus (including material relating to the tabernacle), as well as a good deal of Leviticus. Of special note here is the Holiness Code of Leviticus 17–26, which we noted above. This collection of laws was long held to be an independent collection that was older than Deuteronomy. However, a growing contingent of scholars places the Holiness Code in the post-exilic period (perhaps the fifth century BCE), in part because it seems to be mediating between the Covenant Code and Deuteronomic laws (Nihan 2007). In a similar manner, the laws of Numbers can also be seen to negotiate between legal positions found in other parts of the Pentateuch, and so are increasingly considered later material. Taken together, it is clear that the laws and legal traditions were an important part of how and why the Pentateuch took shape as an authoritative collection, demonstrating a dynamic process of development not dissimilar to the narrative stories of origins (Kazen forthcoming).

An issue related to the origins and formation of these traditions revolves around the question of how much law as found in the Pentateuch might have actually been practised in ancient Israel. Some argue that the law traditions developed early in Israel's history and thus a good deal of the biblical law was instituted and implemented in Israel. Others, however, suggest that it is not the date but the genre of the material that is important. Comparative work with other ancient Near Eastern material suggests that ancient law most often operated by customary rather than written law. Thus, the writing of law codes such as Hammurabi's code and the biblical law materials seems to have served other purposes, such as royal propaganda or education of scribes (Westbrook 1988). Whatever the case, we do know that many of these laws were adapted for later use, particularly in the Jewish tradition, long after their original setting and function were obsolete. Thus, even if we know little of their original use, their later appropriation has ensured that they have had a long afterlife, and continued significance down to the present day (Watts 2013).

General issues relating to pentateuchal law and legal materials

Before looking at elements of law as seen in Exodus, Leviticus, Numbers, and Deuteronomy, there are some general issues worth noting that relate to law and the legal materials.

Law as interpretive framework for reading the Pentateuch

The broad range of material that might be considered 'law' in the Pentateuch is extensive. Indeed, the second half of Exodus, all of Leviticus, and significant portions of Numbers and Deuteronomy are dedicated to issues that fall broadly under this notion of law. And yet, for a variety of reasons, law has not generally received the same attention in academic research as have the narrative elements of the Pentateuch.

J.W. Watts, however, has proposed that the legal material was intended to be read alongside the narrative material of the Pentateuch and that, if the first five books of the Hebrew Bible are read in this way, our understanding of them is improved. Watts notes that the most common references to reading in the Hebrew Bible are to the reading of the law. This occurs both publicly (see, for example, Exod. 24.7; Deut. 31.11; Josh. 8.34-35; 2 Kgs 22.10; 2 Chron. 34.18; Neh. 8.1) and privately (see, for example, Deut. 17.19 and Josh. 1.8). Furthermore, these references to the public reading of the law refer to the reading of the 'whole law,' or at least large portions of it' (1999: 22). He concludes that this emphasis on the reading of the law suggests that it was written down with the purpose of reading in mind. From this starting point, Watts explores an interpretation of the Pentateuch which takes into consideration the possibility of a public reading of the Pentateuch and the laws it contains.

Watts demonstrates the existence of other texts from the ANE and Mediterranean world which use a combination of stories, lists, and sanctions in order to persuade their readers. The Pentateuch, he maintains, uses a similar rhetorical strategy to persuade its readers. This view of the Pentateuch transforms the law from being an uninteresting addition to the narrative of the text into a central component of the Pentateuch's rhetorical technique. The interrelation of law and narrative was the element that helped the readers to locate their identity within Israel. One value of the approach outlined by Watts is that it allows the title 'Torah' to be used for the first five books of the Hebrew Bible in a way that takes seriously the combination of both law and narrative.

Categorizing Israel's law

Material which can fall under the heading 'law' in the Pentateuch is actually quite varied. It ranges from moral commands, to legal advice, to ritual and cultic instruction. The Pentateuch presents these issues using a number of terms, including *torah* ('law', 'instruction'), *mitzvah* ('commandment'), and *mishpat* ('ordinance'). As we have noted elsewhere, the word *torah* has far-reaching implications; while it can be translated as 'law', its broader connotations include 'teaching' and 'instruction', and for this reason it is used as the name for the collection of the five books in the Jewish tradition.

Given the broad-ranging nature of this material, a number of attempts have been made to categorize the laws found in the Pentateuch. Though similar divisions can be found earlier in the Christian tradition, one influential example was offered by Thomas Aquinas in his *Summa Theologica* (1265–74) where he put forward a three-part division of the law into moral, judicial, and ceremonial (or ritual) elements. Aquinas' approach has been very influential in Catholic theology, but also in the Lutheran and Reformed traditions; J. Calvin, for example, makes explicit reference to this division in his *Institutes of the Christian Religion* (1536). More recently, a similar division has been offered by C.D. Stanley (2010); using slightly different terminology, he notes that these laws, commandments, and instructions encompass a number of dimensions of human life, which he labels social, ritual, and ethical dimensions.

Whatever labels we use, it is clear that the biblical material includes laws that cover issues such as theft, murder, civil disputes, and adultery (the judicial or social dimension); others which focus on issues of purity, cleanliness, and cultic observation (the ceremonial or ritual dimension); and those which prescribe moral behaviour towards parents, neighbours, and foreigners (the moral or ethical dimension). What is surprising for many readers is that laws from across these various dimensions are often found in close proximity to each other in the biblical text. This boundary crossing between social, religious, and ethical dimensions might sound foreign to contemporary ears, but it is important to remember that these texts took shape in a culture where there was no separation between religious and secular space. Everything was in some sense related to God, and so Israel's Torah relates to the varied aspects of human life. In this sense the law serves as a blueprint for what

Israelite society is to look like, though, as noted above, the extent to which this vision might have been implemented is unclear.

Another approach to categorizing the law relates to how the laws are formulated. Using the technique of form criticism, A. Alt ([1934] 1966) argued that there are two basic forms of law in the Pentateuch: casuistic and apodeictic. Casuistic laws are expressed with a conditional clause, 'If ...', and those concerned are spoken of in the third person. An example of this type of law, given by Alt, comes from Exod. 21.18-19:

> If individuals quarrel and one strikes the other with a stone or fist so that the injured party, though not dead, is confined to bed, but recovers and walks around outside with the help of a staff, then the assailant shall be free of liability, except to pay for the loss of time, and to arrange for full recovery.

Apodeictic law, he maintained, exists in a list of short, simple clauses, normally worded in a similar way and expressing a prohibition of some sort. A good example of this kind of law can be found in Lev. 18.7-17:

> You shall not uncover the nakedness of your father, which is the nakedness of your mother; she is your mother, you shall not uncover her nakedness.
>
> You shall not uncover the nakedness of your father's wife; it is the nakedness of your father.
>
> You shall not uncover the nakedness of your sister, your father's daughter or your mother's daughter, whether born at home or born abroad.
>
> You shall not uncover the nakedness of your son's daughter or of your daughter's daughter, for their nakedness is your own nakedness.

Another of the features that Alt noted was that casuistic law stipulated for general misdemeanours not necessarily specific to Israel, whereas, on the whole, apodeictic law seemed to contain laws more pertinent to Israel. In addition, Alt found various laws in the Code of Hammurabi that bore the same form as the casuistic laws in the Pentateuch. He therefore concluded that the apodeictic laws of the Pentateuch originated in Israel, probably during the covenant-renewal festival, but the casuistic laws originated outside Israel and were adopted by the Israelites over time. While Alt's views have been influential in the field of biblical law, they have been challenged by some as overly simplistic (Patrick 1985). Nevertheless, the recognition that there are different types of laws which might serve different purposes has had a lasting impact on the study of biblical law.

Law and ethics

The presence of the law codes within the Bible inevitably raises the question of how they should be treated in a modern context (Barton 2003). Particularly relevant here is the question of whether (and for whom) they might be considered binding in the modern world. The problems of this issue are exacerbated by the fact that the biblical law codes are not complete. They do not contain laws which are pertinent to every question of daily living, even though it is clear from texts elsewhere in the Hebrew Bible that such laws existed. Thus, for example, there is no law contained in the Pentateuch which governs the sale of property, but Jer. 32.11 mentions a 'deed of property' which was sealed and which he obtained when he bought the field of Anathoth. This indicates that property law existed in ancient Israel, even if the law codes do not legislate for it.

Jewish and Christian traditions allow for this difficulty in different ways. Jewish tradition supplements the laws contained in the Hebrew Bible with those contained in the Mishnah, a collection of rabbinic laws and sayings compiled around 200 CE. The Mishnah purports to contain oral law given to Moses on Mount Sinai and handed down throughout subsequent generations. Thus many areas which are not legislated for in the Hebrew Bible are, nevertheless, covered in other Jewish texts. Christian tradition takes the opposite approach and regards many of the laws of the Old Testament as no longer binding upon modern Christians.

An exception to this view of the Hebrew Bible in general and the law codes in particular is the Decalogue. The Ten Commandments have, traditionally, been given a place within Christian ethics denied to the other law codes of the Pentateuch. As early as St Augustine, the Decalogue was used to instruct Christians in morality. They were particularly important for the Reformers and formed the bedrock of much teaching that arose from a Reformed tradition. When used in this way, they were often isolated from their historical and literary context and regarded as a permanent moral code. The place of biblical law in the public sphere is an issue that persists to this day, as seen, for example, in debates about the appropriateness of displaying the Ten Commandments in public spaces in the United States, or in discussions concerning sexual ethics which are often informed by biblical tradition. (We return to these issues in Chapter 14, where we explore the reception of the Pentateuch.)

Law in Exodus

In the book of Exodus, the giving of the law on Sinai and the exit from Egypt are both vitally important parts of the story. The first half of the book contains a description of leaving Egypt (Exodus 1–18); the second half (Exodus 19–40) contains an account of the giving of the law to Moses at Sinai. While it has been argued that the exodus and Sinai originated as separate traditions (Wellhausen 1885; von Rad [1938] 1966), in the world of the text, the one is firmly accompanied by the other. God's action of liberation in leading the people out of Egypt is one side of the covenant made with the people. The people's side of the covenant is to obey the requirements laid upon them in the law given at Sinai. Exodus and Sinai form two sides of the same covenantal coin: the former establishes God's responsibility; the latter sets out the people's responsibility.

Theophany and Mount Sinai

The laws found in the second half of Exodus and the book of Leviticus are presented against the background of a theophany at Mount Sinai (Exod. 19.1-25; 20.18-21; 24.1-18; 34.1-10). Like the theophany to Moses described in Exodus 3, the revelation of God prior to the disclosure of the law took place on Mount Sinai (or Horeb, as it is called elsewhere, as in Deuteronomy) and involved certain characteristic natural phenomena such as thunder, lightning, and clouds. Also present is the motif of fear at the presence of God, which is expressed here in terms of the potential danger that existed for the people who came near the mountain (see, for example, Exod. 19.12: 'You shall set limits for the people all around, saying, "Be careful not to go up the mountain or to touch the edge of it"'). Numerous religions located the dwelling place of their gods on the top of mountains. Indeed, F.M. Cross (1973) argued that Ugaritic tradition about Baal's residence on the top of a mountain was influential on Israel's belief in YHWH. Whether or not this is true, considerable evidence exists which points to a strong and early connection between YHWH and Mount Sinai. Particularly interesting are references in the Psalms to YHWH as the 'God of Sinai' (e.g. Ps. 68.9), a title which seems to indicate an early belief that Sinai was the dwelling place of God.

Although the essential account of the theophany and giving of the law on Mount Sinai is clear, the details are confusing. For example, the narrative presents a confusing picture of Moses' ascent and descent of the sacred mountain. In Exod. 19.3 Moses ascends the mountain to speak to God, he then descends to speak to the people in 19.7, goes up again in 19.8, and comes down again in 19.14. Exodus 19.20 has Moses ascend the mountain once more and descend again in v. 24. After the communication of the Decalogue to the people in Exod. 20.1-17, Moses ascends the mountain once more in 20.21. This confusion has indicated to source critics the presence of numerous sources behind the final version of the text. There is little agreement, however, about how these different sources were woven together to provide the final narrative contained in the book of Exodus. The crucial chapters, Exodus 19 and 24, are particularly problematic. On the whole, most scholars are agreed that it is possible to identify the presence of 'P' and 'non-P' materials, with possible editorial influence from the Deuteronomic tradition (Dozeman 2009).

Whatever difficulties remain in historical reconstructions of these accounts, the role of Sinai in the Pentateuch cannot be overstated. From Exodus 19 to Numbers 10 (including all of Leviticus), the pentateuchal story is situated at Sinai. Indeed, for this reason, Sinai has in many ways become synonymous with Moses, the law, and revelation itself (Levenson 1985; issues related to the location of Mount Sinai are discussed in Chapter 13).

Law and covenant

It is in the context of this theophany to Moses on Mount Sinai that the covenant relationship between God and the people is defined. Although there are many interlocking and overlapping strands in the Pentateuch, the essential structure is clear. The theophany established a two-way relationship between the one God and the people of Israel. The revelation of God established one side of the relationship; the law codes dotted throughout the remainder of the Pentateuch established the other. The formation of this relationship placed obligations on the people which must be fulfilled. Although varied in nature, these law codes create vertical and horizontal structures for Israelite society: the vertical structures stipulate the correct worship of God, while the horizontal ones established obligations between human beings. In various instances, the precise nature of the obligations that exist between humans is dependent upon their relationship with God. So, for example, the laws requiring the fair treatment of slaves, recorded in Deut. 15.12-18, are supported by the Israelites' own experience of slavery in Egypt. Just as YHWH redeemed the Israelites from Egypt, so also the Israelites are obliged to treat their own slaves with fairness and compassion.

Discoveries from the past century have highlighted points of contact between the biblical covenants and political treaties from the ANE. Treaties were common in the ancient world and existed in various forms. Examples of such treaties include those which came from the Hittites between 1460 and 1215 BCE. The Hittite Empire was roughly located in the region of Anatolia and northern Syria. The rulers of this empire established relationships with the peoples they conquered (their vassals) by means of a treaty, which laid out the obligations of the people to their overlords (the suzerain). G.E. Mendenhall and G.A. Herion (1992), among others, have advocated that the

Sinai covenant was modelled on the earlier Hittite treaties. In particular they note seven characteristics, listed in Table 12.1, which both the Hittite treaties and the Sinai covenant share.

Although this theory has been influential in arguing for an early date for the concept of covenant in the history of Israel, there are a number of problems with it, many of which have been pointed out by D.J. McCarthy (1978). Perhaps the most important of these is that, while all the major features of a Hittite treaty can be found in the biblical account, they are not all found in one place. For example, the Ten Commandments found in Exod. 20.2-17 contain many of the features of the early Hittite treaties but not all of them (as Table 12.1 illustrates). Various features of the Hittite treaties occur elsewhere in the Pentateuch but not always alongside the account of the drawing up of the Sinai covenant. If the Sinai covenant had been modelled on a Hittite treaty from an early date, one would expect to find all its parts in one place in the biblical account.

Table 12.1 Parallels between Hittite treaties and the Sinai covenant

Element of treaty	Form in Hittite treaty	Biblical parallels identified by Mendenhall
(1) Identification of covenant giver	Begins 'The Words of ...' and gives name, titles and genealogy of king,	'I am the LORD your God, who brought you out of the land of Egypt ...' Exod. 20.2
(2) Historical prologue	The Hittite king recounts the deeds which have benefited the vassal	As (1) above
(3) Treaty stipulations	Describes the vassals' obligations	The Ten Commandments (Exod. 20.3-17)
(4) Provision to deposit treaty in temple	Sets out that the treaty should be deposited in the vassals' temple and read out regularly	Tablets deposited in the ark of the covenant (e.g. Exod. 25.21)
(5) List of witnessed to treaty	Lengthy lists of deities who acted witnesses to the treaty	E.g. 'Give ear, O heavens, and I will speak ...' Deut. 32.1
(6) Curses and blessings formulae	List of the consequences of obedience and disobedience	See, for example, Deuteronomy 28
(7) The ratification ceremony	The formal ritual which brought the treaty into being	Sacrifice, e.g. Exod. 24.5-8

The particulars of how Israel's notions of covenant relate to ancient Near Eastern treaties remain contested; however, in outlining Israel's covenant relationship with their God, the pentateuchal texts and traditions do seem to be drawing on well-known and common ideas from the ancient world.

The Decalogue

In Exodus 20 we encounter a list of commands that has become known as the Ten Commandments or the Decalogue. While the Ten Commandments are the most well-known element of Israel's law, many casual readers are not aware that this list exists in two slightly different forms in the Hebrew Bible, in Exod. 20.2-17 and Deut. 5.6-21. The major differences between the two lists are the motivation behind Sabbath observance and the prohibition against covetousness. In Exod. 20.11 the reason given for Sabbath rest is following the divine example after creation; in Deut. 5.15 the reason given is the exodus. Exodus 20.17 records a prohibition against covetousness in which the wife of one's neighbour is counted among his possessions; Deut. 5.21 contains the same list but separates the wife of a neighbour from the rest of his 'belongings'. These differences indicate that the Ten Commandments may have existed in more than one form before they reached their current form in the biblical text. This observation is made even more pertinent by the form of the commands contained in the Decalogue. On the whole, each of the Ten Commandments contains some form of basic prohibition with, in some cases, additional material. For example, the third commandment ('You shall not make wrongful use of the name of the LORD your God, for the LORD will not acquit anyone who misuses his name', Exod. 20.7) contains a basic prohibition against irreverent use of the name of God, with an additional clause giving a reason for the command.

Those who seek the original form of the commandments suggest that they were originally basic prohibitions that have been subsequently expanded. J. Blenkinsopp (1992: 208) suggests that they may have looked something like the list below:

1. You shall have no other gods before me.
2. You shall not make for yourself a graven image.
3. You shall not utter YHWH's name for wrong purposes.
4. Observe the Sabbath day to keep it holy.
5. Honour your father and your mother.
6. Do not commit murder.
7. Do not commit adultery.
8. Do not steal.
9. Do not bear false witness against your neighbour.
10. Do not covet your neighbour's house.

In spite of the fact that the biblical text itself terms this collection of laws Ten Commandments or Words (e.g. Exod. 38.28; Deut. 4.13; 10.4), Jewish and Christian traditions are not agreed on how they should be enumerated or divided. Jewish tradition and the Reformed Churches enumerate the commandments as in the list above, whereas the Roman Catholic Church and the Lutheran Church count commandments two and three in the list above, about false worship, as one commandment and split the tenth commandment, about covetousness, into two.

On the whole, commentators tend to regard the Ten Commandments either as timeless moral instruction or as a historical insight into the workings of early Israelite society. An exception to this can be found in an article by D.J.A. Clines (1995), who enquires into the motivations which lie behind the writing and reading of the commandments. Clines resists the natural meaning of the text and asks instead whose interest the commandments served. It is quite clear, from even the most superficial reading of the text, that they are written in the interests of those with property, hence the prohibitions against stealing and covetousness. This approach is supported by traditional historical-critical treatments of the text which suggest that they seem to be written from the point of view of a settled society in which many people lived in houses and owned property. Here Clines reads against the grain to highlight possible ideologies motivating the text and its creation.

Whatever their origins, these commandments have had pride of place in both the Jewish and Christian traditions, and by extension, broader Western society and culture, with many still championing the enduring significance of these commands. Indeed, it is this privileged place that has led to some disagreement in recent years about the place of religious law in ostensibly secular societies, such as whether replica stone tablets of the Ten Commandments should be hung in courtrooms and other public spaces, an issue which has been particularly contentious in the United States. For more on the historical context of the Decalogue as well as its use in later tradition, see the volume from P.D. Miller (2009).

The Covenant Code

A second collection of laws found in the book of Exodus is commonly known as the Covenant Code (Exod. 20.22-23.19). It receives its name from the reference in Exod. 24.7, which records Moses taking the book of the covenant and reading it to the people. The code contains a variety of material, beginning and ending with cultic regulations. The cultic regulations at the beginning of the code oppose idol worship and at the end of the code regulate for worship at the three major agricultural festivals of the year, which took place during the barley harvest (the festival of unleavened bread associated with Passover), the wheat harvest (associated with Pentecost), and the fruit and grape harvest (associated with the feast of Tabernacles). Between these cultic regulations are a whole host of general laws that govern the peaceful continuation of society, covering slavery, murder, stealing, and other such crimes.

As noted above, the Covenant Code is often considered the most ancient of the law codes in the Pentateuch, and bears some resemblance to the Code of Hammurabi. An example of this is found in the famous law of 'an eye for an eye and a tooth for a tooth' (Exod. 21.24), which can be compared with Hammurabi 196: 'If a citizen has destroyed the eye of one of citizen status they shall destroy his eye' (Johnstone 1990: 54). This, W. Johnstone suggests, points to the fact that the Covenant Code contains laws which were in line with ancient Near Eastern legal tradition but which were subsequently assimilated by the authors of the Hebrew Bible as stipulations within Israel's covenant.

The tabernacle

Regulations governing the correct worship of God can be found both in Exod. 25.1–31.17 and throughout the book of Leviticus. Scholars generally accept that these passages of cultic regulation stem from the Priestly tradition. Exodus 25.1–31.17 is primarily concerned with establishing the construction of the tabernacle and the ordination and actions of the priests. Exodus 35–40 repeats much of the substance of chs 25–31 as it describes in minute detail how the laws contained in the earlier chapters were to be carried out. The tabernacle, as outlined in Exodus, is a tent sanctuary and place of worship, constructed by the Israelites for their time in the wilderness. This structure is presented by 'P' as vital within the cultic life of early Israel as it was the central focus of worship, the place where the Ark of the Covenant was deposited and, most importantly of all, the symbol of God's active presence among the people (Klein 1996). Within the structure of the narrative, the tabernacle is instituted at the giving of the law to Moses. It functions, therefore, not only as the place in which the law was deposited but also as the place where God could be revealed. Consequently, the tabernacle symbolized God's dwelling among the Israelites.

As the Priestly materials are generally thought to have developed in the exilic or post-exilic eras, scholars have long argued that the tabernacle did not exist but was a creation of Priestly tradition in the exilic period (Wellhausen 1885). There are logistical issues that make the reality of the tabernacle being carried through the wilderness as depicted in Exodus unlikely, not least the cumulative weight of the gold, silver, and bronze said to be part of the structure. Others, such as F.M. Cross (1981), have suggested that the tabernacle may have existed, though Cross maintains that it dated to the time of David, not the time of Moses. Others still have posited that it may have been a smaller element housed within Solomon's Temple. In these readings, the tabernacle represents an example of cultural memory, drawing on historical elements that are mapped on to an earlier period in Israel's story. As seen in our discussion of the exodus (Chapter 11), one's approach to these questions depends in large part on how one understands the historical basis of the exodus and wilderness traditions and when they might have emerged.

Whatever its historical basis, the tabernacle is given considerable space in Exodus, and so should not be overlooked in thinking about these texts and traditions. Recent research on the tabernacle has looked at a number of issues relating to the structure and its portrayal. Such research has explored (1) the spatial rhetoric of these texts, including the social and symbolic dimensions highlighted in the portrayal of the tabernacle as sacred space (George 2009), as well as (2) how the tabernacle can be seen to encourage the later community in their religious life, including the justification of the Aaronide priesthood. Indeed, it is important to note that the priesthood first appears on the scene at this point in the Pentateuch (Exodus 28). Thus, 'This narrative implicitly summons readers to follow the example of Moses, Aaron and the exodus generation in setting up the cultic community. By returning to this old Mosaic pattern, they would experience the living presence of God and go forth into God's future' (Klein 1996: 275). Whether such traditions took shape in the monarchic period as the religious community and Temple took shape or in the exilic/post-exilic eras as a way to cope with the loss of the Temple remains a point of debate (see discussion in Utzschneider 2015).

In the Christian tradition, the tabernacle has proved especially popular in figural and typological interpretation, notably in light of its use in Hebrews 8–9, where the tent and related elements (priests, vessels) are seen as pointing to spiritual issues such as the priesthood of Jesus and the New Covenant.

Law in Leviticus

The book of Leviticus, as noted above, continues the giving of the law at Sinai, which begins in Exodus. This book contains regulations for the maintenance of purity within the people of Israel, focusing particularly on regulations for worship. The book falls roughly into two sections. Leviticus 1–16, sometimes called the 'Priestly Code', contains regulations governing the actions of priests: chs 1–10 lay out the requirements for priestly service in the sanctuary, including the correct offering of sacrifices (chs 1–7), and chs 11–16 present the laws of purification to be carried out by the priests. Leviticus 17–27 turns to the purity of Israel as a whole and lays out the requirements for holy living by all Israelites. These chapters regulate in detail the day-to-day life of Israel, laying down stipulations about how Israelites should behave towards one another. Scholars generally attribute the book of Leviticus as a whole to 'P' but identify within it a 'holiness code' ('H', chs 17–26, with ch. 27, acting as an appendix) which may originate from a different period (Stackert 2007). The dating of 'P' and 'H' is discussed in Chapter 7.

Holiness, purity, and ritual

As noted in Chapter 4, there are a number of interrelated elements that are important to consider when reflecting on Leviticus, and we focus here on three: holiness, purity, and ritual. These concerns are broad in focus, dealing with issues such as food, clothing, sexual practices, bodily fluids, and significant times and places.

Central to this worldview is the idea that Israel's God, YHWH, is holy and set apart from all else. Because God is holy, that which is set apart for him is to be holy as well, including God's covenant partner, Israel. Israel, because it belongs to God, needs to strive for holiness in order to sustain its relationship with this God, including the ability to approach God in his holy place, the tabernacle.

In several dimensions of life the biblical material indicates that there are levels or gradations of holiness. Think, for example, of the tabernacle (and elsewhere the Temple): while most buildings in ancient Israel would simply be profane, the tabernacle is to be a holy place. Not only that, but there are levels of holiness within this sacred place: an outer court, an inner court, and the 'holy of holies', the sacred place to be entered only once a year by the high priest (the holiest of the priests). The same can be said with regard to people and times of the year, which also seem to exhibit gradations of holiness. Thus, holiness seems to function on a spectrum, with God as the ultimately holy one. As J.S. Kaminsky and J.N. Lohr note, these orders of holiness can seem like oppressive hierarchies to modern readers. However, the repeated calls throughout the book for Israel as a whole to be holy (11.44-45; 19.1-3) could suggest 'a bold attempt to make Israel a nation of priests' (2011: 117). Further, it is also the case that the actions of one impact the greater whole; in this sense, the entire community is interrelated and responsible for right living before God (Kaminsky 2008).

Related to notions of holiness are those of purity and impurity. In the world of Leviticus, if something is holy it is pure or clean. And conversely, if something is impure it is unholy, unfit for the requirements of approaching God's holiness. However, as with notions of holiness, the idea of purity is complex. First, some elements discussed in Leviticus are considered forbidden and unclean, even when there is no obvious moral connection. There are, for example, things such as pigs (Lev. 11.1-8) that are considered unclean with no exceptions – they are to be avoided. Here that which is unclean is fixed as forbidden and impure. There are also practices and natural occurrences in Leviticus that make one unclean; again, these do not seem to be related to immorality or sinfulness, but, unlike forbidden food, many of these are time bound. Thus, menstruation and ejaculation make a woman or man unclean; however, these are common occurrences that render the person ritually unclean for a period of time, and are not considered sinful. Such a person can be purified, and it is rituals that are the avenue for such purification to help restore order (Klawans 2000). Finally, some things in Leviticus are forbidden and are clearly considered morally wrong or sinful (e.g. murder in Lev. 24.14). These types of prohibitions are not usually spoken of in terms of purity, and tend to be found in the second half of the book. Thus, prohibitions and notions of purity and cleanliness are complex in Leviticus: some prohibitions relate to issues that are always forbidden and lead to impurity, while others refer to time-bound issues of impurity that can be ritually cleansed; and while some prohibitions relate very clearly to morality, others seem to be issues of importance for ritual purity, but their relationship to morality or sin is not evident.

This brings us to a final prevalent theme in Leviticus, and that is ritual. Rituals vary from religion to religion, but very often are formalized versions of ordinary activities (Smith 1992). Leviticus is a book that is full of ritual, and much of this relates to the notions of purity and holiness outlined above. Rituals, particularly as found in the legal portions of the Pentateuch, provide a way for people to move from impurity to purity, from profanity to holiness. Of particular importance in Leviticus are sacrifices and offerings. There were several different forms of sacrifices, including burnt offerings, where an animal was completely consumed, and the sacrifice of well-being, where the animal was eaten by those offering the sacrifice. Grains and cereals could also be offered as sacrifices, and again some of this was burned in its entirety while other parts could be eaten. These rituals provided the path by which one could move from an unclean state to that of purity, and most often it was the priestly class who could appropriately undertake such rituals.

How should these interrelated issues of holiness, purity, and ritual be understood? As is often the case, the worldview underpinning these ideas is not explained for us in the biblical text. Several models and theories have been put forward, and we introduce a few of these here.

Through the years many have assumed that such purity rules were simply superstitious without any logical or coherent basis. Others have suggested that there are social or environmental reasons for such purity systems. Thus, from medieval times it was suggested that the forbidden animals, such as pigs (11.7), carried disease, and this was the reason they were to be avoided. Others have suggested that the reason that camels (11.4) should not be eaten is because they were needed for work more than they were for food. Accordingly, these laws were meant to maintain the health as well as the social and environmental stability of ancient Israel. Another possible reason for the purity laws was that they were to help distinguish Israel from the other nations, a theme which recurs throughout the Pentateuch and indeed other books of the Hebrew Bible, and which is also mentioned in Leviticus (18.3).

Over the past century, driven in large part by anthropological research, an increasing number of scholars have begun suggesting that these purity laws and ritual instructions reveal an ordered, unified system, a structure of thought that is internally coherent, even if not immediately evident or logical to the reader. Various attempts have been made to 'decode' just what this system of thought might be in Leviticus.

One of the most influential of such studies was produced by the anthropologist M. Douglas, in her study of the concepts of pollution and taboo. This study explores the notion of 'uncleanness' from the perspective of comparative anthropology. Her study explores pollution in many different 'primitive religions', including Israelite religion. In the chapter on Leviticus, she maintains that 'uncleanness is matter out of place' ([1966] 2002: 50). Thus, in Leviticus the unclean animals are those that do not fit fully into their type. She argues that Leviticus takes up the threefold classification of animals given in the Genesis 1 account of creation: those on the earth, those in the waters, and those in the firmament. Each of these types of creature has a prevailing characteristic: 'in the firmament two-legged fowls fly with wings. In the water scaly fish swim with fins. On the earth four legged animals hop, jump or walk. Any class of creatures which is not equipped for the right kind of locomotion in its element is contrary to holiness' (2002: 69).

So, for example, animals in the water that do not have fins or scales are unclean (Lev. 11.10-12) and so also are four-footed creatures that fly (Lev. 11.20-26). The purpose of these regulations, according to Douglas, is to emphasize the completeness of God. Holiness requires the Israelites to imitate the oneness and completeness of God. The avoidance of any 'incomplete' animal is a physical symbol of this desire for holiness.

In a later article (1993a), Douglas returned to the question of forbidden animals in Leviticus, noting, this time, how unusual the levitical laws are in comparison with purity regulations in other cultures, where purity regulations function politically to support the *status quo*; in Israel their concern was not so much politics as justice. Keeping the purity regulations served to remind the Israelites of their obligation to maintain justice for all. Later again, Douglas would return to Leviticus (1999), this time suggesting that the laws of taboo were to protect those animals which could not protect themselves, thus allowing them to flourish. Hence, Douglas' own thought developed on these issues, at several points as a response to the work of others in the field. Nevertheless, her theoretical framework focusing on a unified system of thought in Leviticus has remained influential.

J. Milgrom (1993) also advocated for understanding the purity and ritual elements of Leviticus as a structured and ordered system. He differed from Douglas, however, in focusing on death as the central concern of Leviticus, as opposed to the created order. Thus, rituals are needed for menstruation, ejaculation, or skin diseases because these relate to the continuum of life and death. Milgrom also differentiated between ritual and moral impurity, noting that much of purity-related material in Leviticus is not necessarily concerned with morality. Some of these ideas have been taken up in various ways by G. Wenham (1979), D.P. Wright (1992), and J. Klawans (2000, 2006), among others.

J.W. Watts (2007, 2013) has also focused on ritual dimensions of Leviticus, and in doing so has suggested an alternative perspective to that offered by Douglas and Milgrom. Watts begins by noting the fact that we have access to only the textual description of a ritual rather than direct access to the ritual itself. Thus, rather than attempting to figure out the logic of rituals and a unified system of thought that undergirds them – about which the text tells us very little, which in turn can leave the interpreter to provide their own system – he argues a more profitable approach is to investigate the rhetoric of the text, probing who is trying to convince whom of what. Whose purposes does the text serve, and to what end? With this in mind, Watts employs rhetorical criticism to argue that the rituals portrayed in Leviticus served to legitimize the Temple and its ritual traditions, along with those who carried out these duties, the Aaronide priests. This had a corollary, in that the texts portraying these rituals took on greater significance, a phenomenon found elsewhere in the ancient world:

> texts were used in a variety of cultures to establish correct ritual performance and to legitimize the ritual practices of priests, kings, and temples. Thus the idea of enacting written instructions, that is, 'doing it by the book', involved first of all doing rituals. There is also some evidence that texts began to be manipulated and read as part of the rituals themselves. Therefore as texts validated the accuracy and efficacy of rituals, rituals elevated the authority of certain texts to iconic status. (2007: 208)

Watts suggests that this is the case with Leviticus and the Pentateuch more broadly: 'in addition to legitimizing the Aaronide priests, the Torah's ritual rhetoric serves to establish itself as the supreme authority for ritual practice' (2013: 97). Thus, whatever their historical origins, the rituals portrayed in Leviticus legitimized the authority of those performing the rituals – the priesthood in the line of Aaron – which in turn served to help establish the authority of the Torah, an important part of the process that led to its status as 'Scripture'.

Sacrifices and offerings

As noted above, sacrifice is an important element in the ritual world of Leviticus, particularly in chs. 1–7. In these chapters, five different sacrifices are outlined:

1. The burnt offering (Leviticus 1): here an animal is sacrificed and is wholly consumed in the fire, and this is said to be a 'pleasing odour' to the LORD (Lev. 1.17). This sacrifice is said to make atonement for those who offer it (1.4), though how this works and what is being atoned for are left unsaid.
2. Grain offerings (Leviticus 2): offerings of grain or cereal are presented as a gift to the LORD from that which is produced on the land; some of this is burned, while the rest is eaten by the priests.
3. Offerings of well-being (Leviticus 3): in this case an animal is sacrificed, but only part of the animal is burned; the rest is shared between the priests as well as those who bring the offering. Further instructions are given in Leviticus 7, where it is made clear these well-being offerings can be given in thanksgiving or as a votive offering, taken as part of a vow.
4. Sin or purification offering (Leviticus 4–5): the first three sacrifices are voluntary, but the fourth is required when there is sin that has occurred due to accidence or ignorance. Here different rituals take place depending on who is involved, from the high priest, to all of Israel, to individuals.
5. Guilt or reparation offering (Leviticus 5–6): this is another required offering, and relates to acts that include the misuse of sacred things or those where a neighbour has been wronged. In these cases a ram is offered, but there is no distinguishing between peoples or groups for this offering. Proper restitution for the wronged person is also outlined.

As with holiness and purity, the underlying logic of sacrifice is not spelled out in Leviticus. Some have put forward that sacrifice in the ancient world was food or a 'pleasing aroma' for the gods, the latter being an idea we do find in Leviticus. Others suggest sacrifices showed honour and respect for the gods, or represented an exchange of favours, giving something of worth to the gods (such as an animal) in return for favour or blessing. However, comparative research from other cultures and traditions has highlighted the fact that practitioners often do not themselves understand the logic of their sacrificial practices, or they have conflicting views on the matter. What is often more important in such cases is the purpose for which the ritual is performed and that it be performed accurately, rather than finding reasons for doing it in this particular way (Watts 2007).

While much of this worldview is difficult and foreign for modern readers, it is important to remember how widespread such activities were in the ancient world, and, indeed, how prevalent the concepts still are today. For example, while sacrifice on an altar is not as important a ritual in the contemporary world as it once was, many cultures have retained the *notion* of sacrifice, replacing the action with symbolic representation. Thus, fasting (sacrificing food) is common in many religious traditions, as is worship (sacrifice of praise) and financial giving (sacrifice of possessions). Indeed, Christianity speaks of Jesus' death as the ultimate example of sacrifice (Jn 1.29; Rom. 3.25). We even find these notions in broader society, where we are told that people have sacrificed for their country by serving in the military or taking on the burdens of economic hardship. Thus, although physical sacrifice on an altar is an increasingly foreign concept, symbolic usage of this idea remains ever-present in our world, a reminder that we are perhaps closer to the world of Leviticus than we often assume.

Jubilee

Many of the details of the Levitical regulations seem alien to modern society and pertaining only to ancient Israelite society. However, the principles that lie behind the laws are sometimes picked up in surprising ways. A good example of this is the concept of 'jubilee' set out in Leviticus 25. The year of jubilee is an important socio-economic concept within the book of Leviticus, although it is unclear whether it was ever practised in Israel. It was to take place at the end of 'seven times seven years' (Lev. 25.8). At the end of each seven-year period, a 'sabbatical year' took place in which the agricultural land lay fallow (Lev. 25.17). At the end of seven of these sabbatical years, a jubilee year began, though there is a disagreement among scholars about whether the jubilee year began on the seventh sabbatical year (forty-nine years) or after it (fifty years).

The concept of jubilee demands that any land that has been sold due to financial difficulty must be returned in the year of jubilee. This ensures that wealth remains shared equally among families and tribes. This concept was used extensively by the 'Jubilee 2000' campaign for the relief of international debt at the turn of the millennium. Supporters of the 'Jubilee 2000' campaign took up the principle of the return of property to the poor by the rich in a particular year and called upon the governments of first-world countries to cancel the debts of developing countries. This movement was a significant one and achieved a considerable level of success. In this sense, principles set out in what many consider the most obscure part of the Pentateuch have been picked up by those advocating for issues of justice.

Law in Numbers

The book of Numbers, like its neighbour Deuteronomy, is a mixture of law and narrative (for an overview, see Chapter 5). However, unlike Deuteronomy, in the book of Numbers law and narrative are interwoven throughout the book. Laws appear in chs 5–6; 9; 15; 18–19; 26.1–27.11; and 33.50–36.13, alongside census lists and more descriptive narratives. The laws presented in Numbers share many concerns with those in Exodus and Leviticus, such as purity and ritual, and for this reason they have long been associated with the Priestly tradition. However, as noted earlier, an increasing number of scholars see Numbers as offering a bridge between the Priestly and Deuteronomic traditions in the Pentateuch, and because of this a growing number of scholars suggest that the book is a later development in the pentateuchal material (see the essays in Frevel, Pola, and Schart 2013).

Although the chapters containing law codes in the book of Numbers may appear from their numbering to be haphazard, it is possible to identify three major portions of law in the book, given at Sinai (1–10), Kadesh (15; 18–19), and the plains or steppes of Moab (28–30; 33.50–36.13). Thus, the narrative shapes the giving of the law in the book of Numbers.

The laws contained within Numbers cover a wide range of different topics, governing how the ancient Israelites live together. Of particular interest are four case studies of legal problems. These legal conundrums are represented as problems that arose in the Israelite community and upon which Moses was called to adjudicate. Moses, in his turn, put the case before God, who made a judgement on the matter. Like the other laws in Numbers, these case studies cover a variety of different concerns: the keeping of the Passover by people rendered unclean (9.1-14), the collection of firewood on the Sabbath (15.32-36), the inheritance of property by women (27.1-11), and the inheritance of tribal property (36.1-12). Unlike the other laws in the Pentateuch, these commands are given in response to particular problems, although the question of whether such laws arose in relation to historical situations or were literary creations remains a point of debate (Wenham 1997; MacDonald 2012b). While situated as part of the wilderness wanderings, the various laws concerning issues such as land rights, inheritance, and priestly functions suggest that many of these reflect a time when Israel was settled.

The *Sotah*: **Numbers 5.11-31**

The laws in Numbers are complex, and various methods noted in previous chapters have been employed in trying to understand them. For example, in Num. 5.11-31 (an episode sometimes called the *Sotah*), regulations are given for a ritual to be performed if a husband suspects his wife of infidelity. This passage is problematic on a number of levels. For example, there are literary issues, such as repetition of words, which have led to discussion about multiple sources or traditions in this account (Shectman 2010). Others have explored the ancient Near Eastern background of this ritual and the broader elements of this episode that might be related to magic (Gudme 2013). Another notable issue relates to gender, in that the text seems to assume the guilt of the woman while privileging the rights and suspicions of the husband, while no similar ritual is offered for a wife who might suspect her husband of betrayal (Bach 1993). Finally, it has been suggested that the episode actually encourages the reader to be suspicious of the husband's suspicion, as the book of Numbers as a whole is interested in the issue of trust; in this case, the episode functions in a literary manner to reinforce a larger theme of the book and in doing so subverts the expected societal gender norms (Briggs 2009). Thus, the legal material found in Numbers presents the reader with a number of issues, and, as is the case with other parts of the Pentateuch, various perspectives have been used in order to better understand this material.

Law in Deuteronomy

As in the book of Numbers, law and narrative in Deuteronomy appear side by side. Unlike the book of Numbers, however, the law forms a central core (12.1-26.15), preceded (1-11) and succeeded (26.16-34.12) by narrative. The setting of the giving of the law is a speech by Moses to the people of Israel. This gives the book a characteristic hortatory style. Although it flows fairly well from beginning to end, it is not a unified whole. It contains two prologues in the form of an address by Moses (1.1-4.40; 4.44-11.32), a set of curses (27.15-26), a set of blessings and curses (27.11-13; 28.3-6; and 28.16-19), and certain appendices, including the Song of Moses (31.30–32.47) and the blessing of Moses (33.1-29). Most contemporary scholars are agreed that it has reached its current form through a process of expansion, rather than redaction of separate sources.

Deuteronomy and treaty

As with Exodus, there is also debate concerning the relationship of Deuteronomy and ancient treaties. The book exhibits many characteristics of treaties such as a description of the relationship between the parties involved, stipulations for the parties, blessings and curses, and public reading of the accord. Again, as in relation to Exodus, various historical parallels have been offered; second-millennium BCE Hittite treaties have been suggested as a possible source for Deuteronomy (Berman 2011), while seventh-century BCE Assyrian treaties have also been proposed (Levinson and Stackert 2012). The case has been made that Deuteronomy is a subversive response to Assyrian treaties, proclaiming YHWH's lordship rather than a foreign power, though the specificity of this argument has recently come in for some criticism (Crouch 2014).

Deuteronomy and the Covenant Code

Many of the laws contained in Deuteronomy are adaptations of earlier laws found in the Covenant Code in Exod. 20.22–23.19. G. von Rad ([1964] 1966) noted the many similarities between Deuteronomy and the Covenant Code and argued that where differences existed it was clear that Deuteronomy was the later text. More recent studies have suggested that Deuteronomy was not just reinterpreting earlier material, but that a more systematic replacement was in mind (Levinson 1997). Perhaps the most striking illustration of Deuteronomy's use of earlier laws is a movement away from laws that govern those who live an agricultural lifestyle to those who live in cities. A good example of this is the law of release which, in Exod. 23.10-11, refers simply to allowing land to lie fallow, but is expanded in Deut. 15.1-11 to refer to release from debt. This movement represents a shift towards a more economically sophisticated society.

Centralization and oneness

Alongside the expansion of the Covenant Code lies an expansion of certain cultic regulations. One of the most distinctive cultic themes in Deuteronomy is the centralization of worship in a single sanctuary. The placing of this command in Deut. 12.1-31, at the very start of the section outlining the laws of Israel, emphasizes its importance within the book. Israel should not worship YHWH anywhere but in the central sanctuary. The traditional practice of worship at various shrines throughout the country is condemned. Indeed, it is the importance of the central sanctuary within the reforms of King Josiah, described in 2 Kgs 23.1-20, that indicates that the book of the law found by Hilkiah the priest in the temple (2 Kgs 22.8) should in some sense be seen as related to Deuteronomy.

Worship is one of three strands within the commands of Deuteronomy which give the book its characteristic flavour. The other two are the oneness of God and covenant. These three strands are dependent upon each other. Deuteronomy 6.4 begins with the words 'Hear, O Israel: The LORD is our God, the LORD alone' (NRSV), alternatively translated as 'the LORD is one'. This verse is known within Jewish tradition as the *Shema*, from the Hebrew word for 'hear', with which it begins. This one God has formed a special relationship with one people – the people of Israel – through the covenant and calls them to worship him in one place – the central sanctuary.

One of the significant elements within the covenant relationship, established through theophany and law, was monotheism or at the very least henotheism. The difference between the two is that monotheism requires a belief that only one God exists, while henotheism allows for the existence of many gods but requires that only one is worshipped. Absolute monotheism is expressed in only a few places in the Hebrew Bible, an example being Deutero-Isaiah (see, for example, Isa. 45.5: 'I am the LORD, and there is no other; besides me there is no god'). Elsewhere, the existence of other gods seems implicit (see, for example, Ps. 95.3: 'For the LORD is a great God, and a great King above all gods'), though the command to worship only YHWH remains. The requirements of the covenant relationship, unequivocally expressed at the start of the Decalogue (Exod. 20.4-6; Deut. 5.8-10), are that YHWH alone is to be worshipped by the Israelites (Moberly 2013).

Together, these different emphases – one place of worship, one God, one people – point towards the themes of 'oneness' and centralization that permeate the book (Kaminsky and Lohr 2011).

Concluding remarks

Law is a significant element within the Pentateuch and, as we have seen, is a central component in Exodus, Leviticus, Numbers, and Deuteronomy (in fact, traces of law can even be seen in Genesis; see Gen. 9.4; 17.9-14). Although different writers present law in different ways, a single theme connects all the law codes and legal dimensions of the Pentateuch: the God who has established a special relationship with the people of Israel requires certain actions from them. In this light, law (or, perhaps better, *torah*), has a special place within the story of Israel's emergence, as it lays down the foundations for the continuing relationship of God with his people. This dynamic relationship between God and Israel is highlighted – and, indeed, will be tested – during Israel's sojourn through the wilderness. We turn our attention to the wilderness wanderings in Chapter 13.

Further reading

A summary of the place of law and legal traditions in the formation of the Pentateuch can be found in Kazen (forthcoming), with more specific discussions founds in Levinson (1997), Nihan (2007), and Stackert (2007). On the rhetoric of law and the role of law in the Torah, see Watts (1999, 2007). The relationship of Israel's law to other ANE law codes is discussed in Wright (2009), while the essays in Hagedorn and Kratz (2013) look at the interplay of law and religion in the ancient world, including the Hebrew Bible. Further discussion on issues related to purity can be found in Schwartz et al. (2008). Theological dimensions of law are explored in Lohr (2015).

The Wilderness Wanderings

The narrative sections in the books of Exodus, Numbers, and Deuteronomy describe the journey of the people of Israel from captivity in Egypt to the borders of the land of Canaan. This journey is commonly known as the wilderness wanderings, due to verses such as Num. 32.13, which give the reason for the lengthy journey through the desert as a punishment from God ('And the LORD's anger was kindled against Israel, and he made them wander in the wilderness for forty years, until all the generation that had done evil in the sight of the LORD had disappeared'). In this reading, the wandering is a time of punishment: those who left Egypt in the exodus sinned against God by their rebellion and lack of trust and, consequently, were punished by not reaching the Promised Land.

While this is the dominant understanding of the wilderness wanderings, it is not the only one. Deuteronomy, in particular, construes the time in the wilderness as one of testing, where God tests Israel to see if they are able to truly follow God and his commands (Deut. 8.2). In this view, the wilderness is a time of testing and refinement before Israel enters the Promised Land. (It is this latter notion of the wilderness as a time of refinement that has become dominant in Jewish, Christian, and other religious traditions, as seen, for example, in the 'desert fathers' who were some of the early practitioners of Christian monasticism.) Whether the journey was punishment or a time of testing, its significance in the story of the Pentateuch remains paramount. In the journey across the desert the people prepare themselves as a community for the new beginning that they are to experience.

In this chapter we explore the various traditions related to the wilderness. We begin by addressing some issues that relate to the wilderness traditions as a whole, before exploring the distinct depictions of the time in the wilderness in Exodus, Numbers, and Deuteronomy.

Origins, formation, and historical setting of the wilderness traditions

The question of the origins and formation of the wilderness traditions is closely linked with questions concerning the historicity of the accounts (see Chapter 11 for a discussion of similar issues in relation to the exodus).

Some have suggested that the wilderness stories and itineraries offer an account which reflects accurately the geography of the second millennium BCE, and so, along with the exodus, can be situated in the era of Moses and the deliverance from Egypt (Wenham 1981; Hoffmeier 2005). There are aspects of these narratives that do indeed reflect ancient geographical and cultural elements; however, proving that traditions originate from this period is difficult. First, writers can and do often appropriate ancient aspects in their writing to give a sense of authenticity and antiquity, and thus it is difficult to judge a text's date by the plausibility of its account. Second, the wilderness wanderings exhibit many of the tensions and contradictions found elsewhere in the Pentateuch, including references that seem to come from a much later period, as well as multiple accounts of events or stages in the journey of the Israelites.

These issues have led to other suggestions for the setting and origins of these traditions. A common understanding in the twentieth century was that the wilderness wanderings consist of different sources, some quite ancient, which were brought together with other traditions in the monarchical period as part of the larger story of Israel's salvation history. The work of G. von Rad ([1938] 1966) moves in this direction. In von Rad's view, the wilderness theme is part of the Yahwist's great story of salvation and connects the exodus tradition to the conquest of the Promised Land. While such approaches suggest that these texts were compiled in the monarchical period, and so at quite a distance from any purported time in the wilderness, such approaches do allow for some collective memory of a historical past: 'If ... a group whose later significance greatly exceeded its size had been in Egypt and adopted the worship of Yahweh of Sinai, it is highly likely that the Pentateuch preserves some relics of their existence in the desert' (Davies 1992b: 913). This theory, too, has encountered objections. For example, a difficulty with a dating from the monarchic period is that, in literature that is commonly dated to this period, reference to the wilderness theme as part of Israel's history of salvation is not present (Albertz 2014). In Hosea, for instance, the idea of the wilderness occurs often, but not in ways that are suggestive of the wilderness wanderings. Meanwhile, such usage becomes much more prominent in exilic and post-exilic material (Jer. 2.6; Isa. 40.3).

For these and other reasons, an increasing number of scholars situate the wilderness wanderings in the late monarchic, exilic, or early post-exilic eras (Van Seters 1994; Dozeman 2009; Roskop 2011). Here, as in other aspects of pentateuchal research that we have outlined elsewhere in this volume, the exile and its aftermath play a prominent role: the wilderness imagery reflects a 'wandering' people – either as exiles or in the emerging Diaspora – dealing with and trying to make sense of their new situation away from the land of promise.

Developments in relation to the origins and setting of the wilderness traditions are closely related to questions concerning the formation of these traditions and the relationship between them. Traditional source criticism saw evidence of material from 'J' and 'P' in the accounts in Exodus and Numbers, while the Deuteronomic material was recognized as a different tradition, and often assumed to be later than the material in Exodus and Numbers. As noted in Chapter 7, however, serious questions have been raised about the plausibility of a 'J' source that spans the Pentateuch, while the role of Numbers in relation to the rest of the Pentateuch has also been revisited. These developments have had significant implications for how we might envisage the formation of the wilderness materials. For example, in Numbers 33 we find a list that outlines in brief fashion Israel's journey through the wilderness. It has long been thought that the wilderness wanderings originated with this list, which was then supplemented and expanded with stories and further travel announcements (Davies 1992b). However, A. Roskop (2011) has suggested that Numbers 33 is in fact a summary of the wilderness accounts, rather than their originating source, a theory that fits well with broader trends which are rethinking the place of Numbers in the formation of the Pentateuch (Frevel, Pola, and Schart 2013). Thus, the wilderness traditions have become increasingly important for investigations into the formation of the Pentateuch/Torah in its present shape (Dozeman 2011).

The geography of the wilderness wanderings

In line with the various ideas concerning the origins and historical context of the wilderness wanderings, a good deal of work has been done in relation to the geography presented in the wilderness wanderings, all of which are set in the Sinai peninsula and the Transjordan, the area south and east of the Jordan river.

For those interested in reconstructing the history of the wilderness wanderings as well as those trying to make sense of the account as presented in the Bible (i.e. the narrative as presented, even if it comes from a later date), a major issue concerns the location of Mount Sinai and how this affects the route taken through the wilderness. These two are unavoidably linked, because the position taken on the location of Sinai affects one's choice of route for the wilderness wanderings. Just as there is difficulty in identifying, with any certainty, the location of the Red (reed) Sea (see Chapter 11), so also there exists a problem in locating Mount Sinai. An initial complexity is that the mountain appears to bear two different names in the biblical tradition: Sinai and Horeb. M. Noth, among others, used source criticism to account for this difference and argues that Sinai is used in early texts, whereas Horeb is used in texts from the later Deuteronomic tradition (Noth [1954] 1960).

The difficulty surrounding the mountain's location is not so easily solved. The major problem arises from the vagueness of the biblical text. The way in which the mountain is described could, and indeed has, led to its location being identified anywhere from the southern Sinai Peninsula to modern-day Saudi Arabia. The first, and traditional, proposal is that Mount Sinai is to be equated with the mountain Jabal Musa, in the southern Sinai Peninsula ((1) on Map 13.1). This location seems to be supported by Deut. 1.2 ('By the way of Mount Seir it takes eleven days to reach Kadesh-barnea from Horeb'). Against this location, however, is the lateness of this association, which seems to have arisen in the third century CE. A second possibility is that the mountain is to be found in the northern Sinai Peninsula, in the region of Kadesh-barnea ((2) on the map). This location is suggested by the length of time that the Israelites spent in Kadesh ('after you had stayed at Kadesh as many days as you did', Deut. 1.46) but seems unlikely, given the description

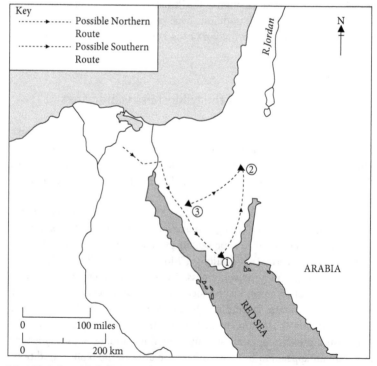

Map 13.1 Possible locations of Mount Sinai

in Deut. 1.2 quoted above. Another theory supporting the northern Sinai Peninsula identifies the mountain with Jabal Sinn Bishar, just south of Suez ((3) on the map) and fulfils the criteria of being three days journey from Egypt and eleven days from Kadesh. A fourth suggestion, supported by Noth, places Sinai not in the Sinai Peninsula but further east in Northwest Arabia. The reason for this is the reference to smoke and fire on the mountain, which Noth believes suggests that it was a live volcano. As no active volcanoes exist in the Sinai Peninsula, this pushes the location of the mountain further east to Arabia, where volcanoes are known to have been active around this time.

The route taken in the wilderness wanderings is also hard to ascertain. The text indicates that the Israelites travelled from Rameses to Moab via Kadesh-barnea, but the precise route of their journey is difficult to plot, and many of the place names offered in the itineraries are difficult to locate with any certainty. One factor which affects the route is obviously the location of Mount Sinai. If the mountain is believed to be in the south, then a more southerly route through the wilderness may have been envisioned; if in the north, a more northerly route becomes possible. A detailed discussion of both the location of Sinai/Horeb and the wilderness wanderings is offered by G.I. Davies (1979; 1992a, b).

A further complexity in the geography of the wilderness traditions is that Numbers and Deuteronomy seem to be at odds at several points. An example of this is the encounter with the Edomites as Israel moves towards Canaan. In Num. 20.14-21, the encounter with the Edomites is hostile, and Israel goes *around* Edom. In Deut. 2.1-8, however, there is a more cordial account, and Israel passes *through* Edom. While attempts have been made to harmonize these accounts, it is relatively clear that there are different traditions at work in the accounts in Numbers and Deuteronomy (Anderson 2012; MacDonald 2012a).

Interpretive approaches to the wilderness traditions

A further issue worth noting relates to different ways in which readers have attempted to understand the function of wilderness wanderings. What role does the time in the wilderness play in the larger story of Israel, and why is it presented in this way?

An element of the wanderings which has long been noted relates to how the people are depicted in the various accounts, and some have tried to make sense of the wanderings in light of this component. There are two sets of what are sometimes referred to as the 'murmuring stories' in the wilderness material: those in Exodus 14–18 and those in Numbers 11–21. Here various challenges and complaints are raised over issues such as food, water, health, and leadership as Israel makes their way through the wilderness. The murmurings in Exodus can be understood as more positive in nature, and function as times of (mutual) testing between God and Israel in this initial phase of their relationship following the exodus. In Numbers, however, the murmuring is much more negative, and often relates to Israel's disobedience and lack of trust. Some have suggested that this difference indicates early and later sources, where originally positive stories of testing were transformed into negative stories of grumbling and disobedience on the part of Israel (Coats 1968). Others have suggested that this is a literary device, highlighting a shift in Israel's relationship with God, from mutual testing to that of disobedience and mistrust (Dozeman 2009).

Another aspect of the wilderness wanderings relates to the *movement* of the people, and interpreters have used this as a framework for understanding the wilderness traditions. M.S. Smith (1997), among others, has suggested that the wilderness journeys can be understood as part of a pilgrimage, with the Promised Land as the final destination. Others, such as Roskop (2011), have posited that a military-like movement of a travelling army is envisioned, an idea which is already noted in Numbers 33: 'These are the stages by which the Israelites went out of the land of Egypt in military formation under the leadership of Moses and Aaron' (Num. 33.1). Roskop points out that this is a common trope in other writings of the ANE, and may be used in the biblical account to highlight the role of God as Israel's king, leading his army on their journey.

Finally, interpreters have drawn on the anthropological study of ritual and rites of passage to suggest that the time in the wilderness is 'liminal space' in the story of Israel (Dozeman 2009; Sacks 2011). In rites of passage, individuals or groups move from a place of settled norms, to an unstable 'liminal' state of transition, to reincorporation into a new settled sphere (van Gennep 1960; Turner 1969). Applying this to the biblical wilderness traditions, the wilderness is understood as an interim, unsettled (liminal) phase of transition between the settled states of Egypt and the Promised Land. Here Israel learns to live outside of slavery, while developing social structures and their life with YHWH before entering the land of promise.

Exodus

The description of the Israelites' sojourn in the wilderness is concentrated in Exod. 15.22–18.27. The account contains three major sections. The first, Exod. 15.22–17.7, describes the Israelites' shortage of water and food in the wilderness and the miraculous provision of sustenance in the form of manna, quails, and water. The other two accounts report a battle with the Amalekites along with the visit of Moses' father-in-law Jethro to the Israelite camp, where he instructs Moses on some elements of how he is approaching his role as leader. The account of the visit of Jethro seems to be out of place in the order of the narrative: Exod. 18.5 reports that Jethro visited the camp at the mountain of God, whereas the arrival of the Israelites at this mountain is not described until Exod. 19.2. This suggests that the account has been moved out of its natural order. Although out of place chronologically, thematically these three incidents fit together well: the three strands of divine intervention to provide food, defend against attack from enemies, and address the need for internal organization seem appropriate at this point in the narrative, placed as it is between the exodus and the giving of the law on Sinai.

The story of manna

One of the more well known of these accounts from Exodus is the story of manna. In Exodus 16, the Israelites are a month and a half into their journey away from Egypt and towards Sinai and find themselves lacking food in the desert. They begin to complain about this situation, and so God miraculously provides food for the people: in the morning, a food appears on the ground which is called *manna*, a wordplay on the fact that the people did not recognize it and so asked, 'what is it?' (Hebrew *man hu*; see Propp 1999 for further possible wordplays). The people are only to collect enough food to see them through each day, as any extra food which is gathered goes bad.

This story has elicited a variety of responses through the years, including attempts to explain manna from a natural perspective, and figural interpretations, such as those which understand manna as symbolic of wisdom (Philo), or Jesus as the new 'bread of heaven' (John 6). R.W.L. Moberly (2013), drawing on the Jewish and Christian impulse to read the story metaphorically, suggests that the narrative can be understood metaphorically while staying true to the spirit of the story. In his reading, the account points to the spiritual discipline of daily living, where faith is needed on a daily basis for God's provision. In this sense, the 'testing' (16.4) which the people face is a way to develop and cultivate trust during their journey in the wilderness. As noted above, the challenges which the people face in Exodus can be construed more positively than those in Numbers, as these are times of mutual testing between God and the people of Israel. Testing is an important theme that is found throughout the Pentateuch and elsewhere in the Bible that is suggestive of the dynamic relationship between God and his people, and the story of manna seems to fit this pattern (Moberly 2000).

Numbers

The book of Numbers contains a much longer description of the time spent in the wilderness by the Israelites. Indeed, the Hebrew title of the book, *Bemidbar* ('In the wilderness'), sums up how important the journey through the wilderness is to it.

As we have discussed elsewhere, Numbers is a complicated book (see Chapter 5, for an introduction to Numbers). It begins in the wilderness where Leviticus ends, ends in Moab where Deuteronomy begins, and weaves together material of different types including narrative about the wilderness wanderings, law codes, and census lists. The book has a more fluid form than some of its counterparts elsewhere in the Pentateuch. For this reason, one of the major questions surrounding the book relates to its composition and structure. Some treatments of Numbers propose a triadic construction for the book, based on the three blocks of material associated with law-giving at Sinai, Kadesh, and Moab, though there is little agreement among scholars about where these sections begin and end (Wenham 1997). An alternative suggestion on the book's structure has been made by M. Douglas (1993b). She proposes that Numbers has a cyclical structure which, she maintains, is a commentary on the book of Genesis. In her structure the book contains six themes matched by six 'anti-themes'. The six themes describe God's ordering of Israel, the six anti-themes Israel's rebellion against God. More recently, scholars such as R. Achenbach (2003) have suggested that the lack of structure in Numbers is related to the late date of its composition, and the fact that it seems to be offering a mediating position between the Priestly and Deuteronomic traditions. In this reading, the wilderness traditions in Numbers are some of the last portions of the pentateuchal material to take shape.

Death, birth, and generations

As noted at the outset of the chapter, the story of the twelve spies recorded in Numbers 13–14 is a pivotal section in the book, as it offers the rationale as to why the Israelites will not be going directly to the land of promise, but will wander in the wilderness for forty years. These chapters tell the story of spies who are sent into the land of Canaan to get a view of the land before the Israelites make their entry. The spies return, noting the size of the people and the fortifications of their cities. The people are frightened by the report of the spies and, rebelling against Moses, decide they do not want to attempt to enter the land of Canaan. According to Num. 32.13, because of this lack of trust, the whole generation who left Egypt will die off in the wilderness during this wandering. Only the two spies who suggested the people should move forward – Joshua and Caleb – are the exceptions to this rule.

This story – another example of the murmuring motif – introduces several important themes in the book of Numbers, namely, death, (re)birth, and generations. As D.T. Olson (1985) has noted, these issues punctuate the book: the censuses in chs 1 and 26, along with the death of the old generation and the birth of the new generation, serve to highlight the rebirth of Israel as it prepares to enter the land of promise, while also juxtaposing these generations as faithless and faithful. As J.S. Kaminsky and J.N. Lohr point out, the text seems to indicate that 'within each generation … comes tendencies to rebel and not trust, yet also to listen and obey. … The message of Numbers is to avoid the pitfalls of the past and walk in the ways of those who learn to trust and obey' (2011: 140).

The Book of Balaam

One of the most memorable episodes in the book of Numbers is the story of Balak and Balaam. Numbers 22–24 contains the account of Balaam, a seer from Pethor in Babylonia who was paid by Balak, the king of Moab, to curse Israel but was prevented from doing so by an angel of YHWH who appeared first to Balaam's donkey and then to the seer himself. In the end, Balaam offers a blessing for Israel, rather than a curse.

The best-known element of the story is the account of the talking ass (Num. 22.22-35). G. Savran (1994) noted the significance of this account in the light of the only other reference to talking animals in the Hebrew Bible, which is the serpent in the Garden of Eden (Gen. 3.1-5). Savran noted that an angel with a sword features in both texts (Gen. 3.24 and Num. 22.31) as do the themes of blessing and curse. When read alongside the Genesis account, further insights can be gained into the story of Balaam and the ass, most notably the progression of theme from universal cursing in Genesis (Gen. 3.14-19) to the blessing of Israel by Balaam (Num. 23.7-10) – a movement which mirrors the movement of the Pentateuch as a whole.

Another reason why Balaam is such an interesting figure is that he is one of the few examples of a biblical character who also appears in non-biblical materials. Balaam is mentioned in the Tell Deir Alla inscription, discovered in 1967 on the east bank of the Jordan river, and thought to be from the eighth century BCE (Hackett 1984). Here a figure named Balaam also seems to have a role as a prophet or diviner, offering an important connection between biblical material and traditions from the ANE.

Deuteronomy

Although most of Deuteronomy consists of law, the book has a narrative framework, in chs 1–3 and 34, which describe Israel's journey in the wilderness and Moses' death in the steppes of Moab. M. Noth ([1943] 1981) maintained that the feel of a historical survey given by the narrative indicated that it was intended to be an introduction not only for Deuteronomy but also for the whole collection of writings known as the Deuteronomistic history, which runs from Deuteronomy to the end of 2 Kings.

Even more important than the narrative, however, is the fact that the whole of the book is cast as a farewell speech by Moses to the people of Israel prior to their entry into the Promised Land. This technique of putting speeches in general, and farewell speeches in particular, into the mouths of major figures is characteristic of ancient historians. It can be found not only elsewhere in the Hebrew Bible (see, for example, Joshua 23) but also in other historical writings in the ancient world. Thucydides, a Greek historian writing in the fifth century BCE, specifically indicated that he placed speeches in the mouths of characters in his histories (*The History of the Peloponnesian War* 1.22.1). This technique allows the writers of history to comment on what is taking place. The striking element of Deuteronomy is that the book as a whole is cast as the final speech of Moses before his death. Within the Pentateuch, therefore, it acts partly as a summary and restatement of much of what has gone before.

Deuteronomy and other wilderness traditions

This brings us back to the wilderness material in Deuteronomy. There are many similarities between the wilderness account in Deuteronomy and those found in Exodus and Numbers, even if there are, as noted earlier, some differences, such as the descriptions of the encounter with the Edomites/ sons of Esau. While the 'D' wilderness material was long thought to be later than, and indeed was assumed to use, the wilderness accounts in Exodus and Numbers, this theory has been challenged in recent years. Instead, it has been put forward by some that the material in Numbers 20, which is similar to Deuteronomy 1–3, may in fact borrow from Deuteronomy, or that both traditions draw from an earlier, common source, and provide their own variants (Fleming 2012). N. MacDonald (2012a) has suggested that there may have been several editions of both accounts, which would indicate a complex interdependence that developed over time, rather than a one-dimension relationship of source material.

Another notable difference between Numbers and Deuteronomy and their portrayal of the wilderness is how the traditions account for Moses not being allowed to enter the Promised Land. In Numbers 20, God instructs Moses to speak to a rock in the wilderness at Meribah, from which he will provide water for the Israelites. Instead of speaking to the rock, however, Moses strikes the rock in frustration. Numbers 20.12 relates that God told Moses (and Aaron) that they would not enter the Promised Land because of this act of disobedience. In Deut. 1.37-38, however, Moses seems to indicate that he is not allowed to enter Canaan because of the disbelief of the people after the episode with the spies. In this account, Moses will be part of the generation that dies off in the wilderness. Jewish tradition has through the years offered a number of reasons for this discrepancy. One notable harmonization comes from Rabbi Saadia Gaon (d. 942 CE), who pointed out that because the people sinned after the report from the spies, Israel was forced to wander for a further thirty-eight years, during which time Moses would strike the rock at Meribah. Thus, the spy episode leads indirectly to the striking of the rock.

Concluding remarks

The account of the journey of the people of Israel through the wilderness spans the narrative of three out of the five books of the Pentateuch and, like other parts of this collection, has been the subject of considerable historical, literary, and theological reflection. The account of the journey is, at times, like its content: rambling and drawn out, interspersed with other stories which do not at first appear to fit. Nevertheless, this period in the story of the Pentateuch is significant as it signals a time of transition. As the Pentateuch draws to a close, a new generation of Israelites faces an unknown future, without Moses to lead them. They are also, however, encamped on the borders of the land of Canaan, and so the Pentateuch ends on the brink of possibility. In this sense, the wilderness is both an ending and a beginning, concluding the story of the Pentateuch while pointing to the future.

Further reading

Davies (1992b) offers a helpful introduction to both the wilderness traditions as well as the various critical issues involved in these traditions. Roskop (2011) offers wide-ranging discussion on the wilderness traditions as a whole and their place in the study of pentateuchal origins. MacDonald (2012a) explores some of the differences between accounts given in Numbers and Deuteronomy, while the essays in Frevel, Pola, and Schart (2013) look at the role of Numbers in the formation of the Pentateuch. Lohr (2009) and Moberly (2013) explore some of the literary and theological dimensions of the wilderness traditions, in particular the manna and Balaam episodes.

The Reception of the Pentateuch: The Use, Impact, and Influence of the Five Books

The death of Moses at the end of Deuteronomy brings us to the conclusion of the Pentateuch. It is worth remembering, however, that the study of the Pentateuch includes more than the exploration of these five books. An important part of the study of the Pentateuch is reflection on the *reception* of this collection; that is, how these texts and traditions have been used and the impact which they have had down through the centuries. It should be noted that we rarely have a clean break between a text, its origins and formation, and its later reception. As a number of recent studies have pointed out, the complicated history of the origins and formation of the Pentateuch is indeed part of its history of use and reception (Roskop Erisman 2012; Breed 2014; Bolin 2016). For example, Deuteronomy's reworking of laws from the Covenant Code can be seen as the use and reception of the laws from Exodus. Thus, we need to be careful in making too sharp a distinction between a text's formation and its later use and impact, especially given the complex nature of the Pentateuch's history. Nevertheless, it remains the case that the pentateuchal texts, traditions, and stories have had an immeasurable impact on religious traditions as well as culture and society over the past two millennia, and the study of this impact is an increasingly significant part of research on this collection. With this in mind, the present chapter explores some key issues in the reception of the Pentateuch, first investigating the role of the Pentateuch in the traditions of Judaism, Christianity, and Islam, followed by an exploration of the use and impact of these texts and traditions in wider social and cultural contexts.

Religious traditions

The Torah or Pentateuch has played a central role in Judaism, Christianity, and Islam, sometimes called the Abrahamic traditions or religions because they all claim Abraham as a patriarch (see Levenson 2012 and Hughes 2012, however, on some of the complexities of this label). As we have already seen in previous chapters, there are significant differences in how these traditions use and appropriate these texts; and yet, they point to important elements in all three religious traditions, and the complex relationship between them. A number of specific examples have already been noted in this volume; in what follows, we highlight some of the underlying perspectives of how and why these traditions engage with the Pentateuch/Torah.

Genesis to Deuteronomy within the Jewish tradition

The Torah occupies a central position in Jewish life and faith where it is, in many ways, a canon within the canon. It has been a common misconception, particularly in Christianity, that legalism is a central element of a Jewish understanding of Torah. This is, in fact, far from the truth. Although Jewish devotion to the Torah recognizes its legal element, it encompasses much more than this. While *torah* can be translated as law, as often happens in English and in the Christian tradition, the Hebrew term comes from the word 'to teach'. Indeed, *torah* has an expansive and positive range of meanings, including instruction and guidance. Thus, in the Jewish tradition, the Torah is much more than law – it is the teaching and instruction that God has revealed for his people that should guide and regulate all of life. An example of this broad-ranging understanding of the Torah can be seen in the work of the medieval Jewish philosopher Maimonides, who maintained that the Torah was concerned with the welfare of both the body and the soul (*Guide for the Perplexed* 3:27). This belief illustrates that, within Judaism, the Torah holds a central place because it guides the whole of human existence.

Various traditions grew up in Jewish thought about the Torah and its contents. One of these is that the Torah was pre-existent before the creation of the world, alongside wisdom. This tradition can be found both in the deutero-canonical book Ecclesiasticus (see, for example, 1.1-5; 34.8) and in later Jewish interpretation of the Torah (see, for example, *Genesis Rabbah* 1.4). Another tradition grew up around the account of creation in Gen. 1.1–2.3. The writings of the Mishnah indicate that certain portions of scripture became the subject of mystical speculation. This mystical speculation, known as Merkabah mysticism, was regarded as dangerous in some circles, especially to the uninitiated. Indeed, *Mishnah Hagigah* 2.1 forbids the exposition of the account of creation because of the danger which might befall an inexperienced person: 'The laws of forbidden sexual relations [Leviticus 18 and 20] may not be expounded by three persons, nor the account of creation [Gen. 1.1-2.3] by two, nor the merkabah [Ezekiel 1] by one, unless he is a scholar and has understood on his own.' The tradition associating Gen. 1.1–2.3 with mystical speculation became known as *ma'aseh bereshit*, or the workings of creation.

The Torah also has a central role within Jewish liturgy. Each year, it is read from beginning to end in the synagogue services. Each service contains a reading from the Torah and a reading from the Prophets. This coupling of the reading from the Prophets with the reading from the Torah is known as the *haftorah*, or completion of the Torah. This practice existed from an early stage in the history of worship in the synagogue, and references to it may be found in New Testament passages such as Lk. 4.17 and Acts 13.15.

The Torah also has significant practical implications for observant Jews. Issues such as appropriating clothing, dietary regulations (*kashrut*), use of phylacteries (*Tefillin*), and of course Sabbath observance (*Shabbat*) all trace their roots back to the Torah. These aspects of Torah observance are in many ways markers of identity, again pointing to the fundamental role of these books, not only in recounting the past but also in shaping identities in the present.

Finally, it is worth noting the physical significance of the Torah in Jewish tradition. The Torah in its physical form plays an important role in various aspects of Jewish life and culture. Every synagogue, for example, is to have its own Torah scroll, written by a trained scribe, and housed in what is known as a Torah ark. This scroll is used for reading portions of the Torah in weekly services as well as on holy days. The completion of the annual cycle of Torah readings is celebrated with a holiday known as *Simchat Torah*, and often includes dancing and singing with the scrolls. Torah scrolls are also used for significant rites of passage, such as the Bar Mitzvah, where a young person reads from the Torah as part of the rituals indicating that one is now obliged to follow the commandments. Thus, even the physical Torah has an iconic dimension in Jewish tradition, and is used in a number of ways that signify its symbolic importance in the tradition (Watts 2006).

Genesis to Deuteronomy in the Christian tradition

The writers of the New Testament also made extensive use of the Pentateuch in various ways (Moyise 2015). Like the Hebrew Bible, the books of the New Testament contain allusions to the Pentateuch's narratives. These include references to the themes of the Pentateuch such as creation (Mk 13.18; Rom. 1.19), Abraham (Gal. 4.22), and the appearance of God to Moses in the burning bush (Lk. 20.37). Another interesting phenomenon in the New Testament is the (sometimes-subtle) engagement with pentateuchal themes and traditions. For example, many scholars regard the prologue to the

Gospel of John (Jn 1.1-18) as a meditation upon, among other texts, Genesis 1. Quotations are also common, such as Mk 10.6-7, which brings Gen. 1.27 and 2.24 in one statement:

> But from the beginning of creation, 'God made them male and female.' 'For this reason a man shall leave his father and mother and be joined to his wife.'

This regular and wide-ranging use of the Pentateuch by the writers of the New Testament demonstrates the importance of these texts in the earliest Christian traditions.

In subsequent Christianity, however, the Pentateuch, as a collection, has been less central. Within Jewish tradition, the first section of the Hebrew Scriptures – Torah – has precedence over the other two sections. While these five books remain at the beginning of the Christian Old Testament, within the Christian tradition, all sections of the Hebrew Bible are regarded more or less equally. This diminished significance of the first five books may be attributed to numerous factors. One such factor is that, as a Jewish sect attempting to account for an increasingly Gentile (non-Jewish) base of adherents, the question of how the various laws of the Torah should be understood was a matter of great debate. This conundrum was not limited to the early church, but would recur throughout the history of the church; for example, during the Reformation period, M. Luther and other reformers juxtaposed law and grace in a way which left little doubt that the law was not helpful for Christians. This particular stance has played a role in the long and at times fraught relationship between Jews and Christians, though much has been done in recent decades to heal some of these wounds.

Another factor to consider is the canonical ordering of the Bible. The Vulgate is the Latin text of the Bible, traditionally attributed to St Jerome (fourth c. CE), and it was the major version of the Bible used within the Western church until the time of the Reformation. Although the Vulgate was based on both Greek and Hebrew texts, it followed the order of the Septuagint (the Greek translation of the Hebrew Bible) rather than that of the Hebrew texts. This order was Pentateuch, historical books, poetic and wisdom literature, and prophetic literature, and this order is still maintained in modern Christian translations of the Bible. One of the effects of this was the abandonment of the Jewish tripartite ordering of the books into Torah, Prophets, and Writings. While the Jewish canon concludes with the books of Chronicles, the Christian canon ends with the prophets, texts which became increasingly important as they were seen as pointing 'forward' to Jesus. Thus, although Genesis to Deuteronomy remained important within Christianity as books in their own right, the five books viewed together, as a collection, became less significant.

Nevertheless, the stories of the Pentateuch would play a foundational role in the early church, and have continued to play a vital role in Christian liturgy, theology, and spirituality. And, in spite of the ambivalence with which Christians have engaged with the 'law', recent years have witnessed a renewed interest in exploring how Christians can appropriately use and read these important texts, while remaining sensitive to their significance in Judaism (Wijk-Bos 2005; Briggs and Lohr 2012).

Genesis to Deuteronomy in the Islamic tradition

The Hebrew and Christian scriptures play an important yet complex role in the Qur'an and Islam, and this is certainly the case with the Pentateuch. As we have pointed out elsewhere in this volume, biblical characters, stories, and sayings can be found in the Qur'an and other Islamic literature, but this use is quite distinct from the Christian appropriation of the entire Hebrew Bible. In Islam it is recognized that there have been many prophets through the years who have spoken for God, including pentateuchal figures such as Adam, Noah, Abraham, and Moses. Indeed, the Islamic tradition recognizes the Torah (*Tawrat*) as having been given by God to Moses (Qur'an, Surah 5:44). In fact, the *Tawrat* is mentioned by name eighteen times in the Qur'an. However, from an Islamic perspective, aspects of these texts have been falsified and corrupted (*tahrif*) over time by Jews and Christians, so that the only revelation which can be trusted is that which has been received and passed down by the prophet Muhammed (Lambden 2006). Thus, there are many echoes of the Torah found in the Qur'an and other Islamic texts, and while some of these are quite close to that which is found in the Hebrew texts, others vary substantially from their form in the Hebrew Scriptures. Nevertheless, it is clear that elements of Islam can be traced back to the Pentateuch, even if the traditions, stories, and characters are taken up in new ways.

Social and cultural reception of the Pentateuch

The use and influence of the Pentateuch is not limited to religious traditions. Indeed, these texts and traditions have impacted societies and cultures well beyond what one would expect of a set of texts that emerged from a relatively small and insignificant group in the ancient world. We outline here just a few examples from law and ethics, politics and social movements, as well as arts and culture.

Law and ethics

As discussed in Chapter 12, the place of biblical law in civil life is one of both influence and controversy. The label 'Judeo-Christian' has been applied to many Western societies, and this is due in part to the formative role of Jewish and Christian traditions in the moral and ethical dimensions of these societies, including key elements such as the Ten Commandments. Indeed, the Ten Commandments have become an iconic representation of justice and law, to the point that replica tablets of Moses' law are displayed in courtrooms and other legal settings. While this close relationship was long assumed to be natural and appropriate, it has led to some conflict in recent years, as there is disagreement as to whether religiously based law should inform public and civil law in pluralistic societies. Other issues have also been front in centre in discussions of law and morality in recent years, including sexual ethics. For example, recent debates over homosexuality and same-sex marriage have included discussions on biblical material on these subjects, including the prohibitions of Leviticus (Lev. 18.22, 20.13). Various arguments have been made from people on all sides of these debates, both within and outside of religious traditions, in terms of how Leviticus should be interpreted and employed in the modern world (for an overview, see Brownson 2013). Taken together, it is clear that biblical law and ethics continue to exert a powerful influence over individuals and societies, even if the place of such influence is being debated in the contemporary world (Chancey, Meyers, and Meyers 2014).

Politics and social movements

In historical perspective, there are a number of ways in which the Pentateuch has shaped political and social movements. A few examples are worth noting. R. Hendel (2013) has pointed out the complex role which the Bible, and Genesis in particular, played in the debates concerning slavery and its abolition, particularly in the nineteenth-century United States. Many who held a pro-slavery position justified their beliefs using the story of Noah in Genesis 9, where Noah's grandson Canaan is cursed and will serve his brothers because of the actions of Canaan's father, Ham. Not only does this text seem to indicate servanthood or slavery among groups of people, but the descendants of Ham were associated with Africa (Gen. 10.6). Because of this, many felt the story advocated slavery, particularly of African peoples. There are numerous problems with this reading of the story, as many abolitionists pointed out. For example, it is Canaan that is cursed rather than Ham, and Canaan's line is all associated with Canaanite peoples in the biblical text, not African. Indeed, Abraham Lincoln, among others, drew from other texts from Genesis (such as Gen. 3.19) and beyond to make the case *against* slavery. In a sense, both sides were drawing from the same sacred text to bolster their own arguments, while disagreeing over issues of interpretation. In the end, the abolitionist reading of Genesis won out.

The same struggle can be seen in various labours for gender equality, issues which we have touched on elsewhere in this volume. Early feminist interpreters such as Elizabeth Cady Stanton in the late nineteenth century offered readings which pushed back against the patriarchal dominance in both religious and social contexts. Of great import here were the creation stories of Genesis 1–2, and the place of woman and man in these narratives. While many assumed these stories give dominion to men, interpreters such as Stanton used critical scholarship, such as source criticism, to suggest that there were different sources and traditions at work here, and that some of these, such as the account in Genesis 1, were more egalitarian than others (Hendel 2013). Again, issues of interpretation became vital, as people on both sides of a contentious issue drew on Scripture to back up their claims and ideas.

In Chapter 11, we outlined how the story of Moses and the exodus from Egypt has played a vital role in liberation theology, and in associated movements for social reform, particularly in South America. Martin Luther King Jr also used this notion of freedom and the exodus in his fight for American civil rights in the mid-twentieth century. This became a central motif not only in King's rhetoric but also for the movement as a whole, which saw itself in need of liberation. As J. Coffey (2014) has pointed out, King stands in a long line of those who have used the exodus in the quest for liberation.

Thus, in a variety of social and political realms, the Pentateuch has had a formative effect through the centuries, even if both sides of many such issues often used and laid claim to the biblical text. Such complex use of the Bible is a reminder of the importance of interpretation, and the sometimes-contested role of the Bible in the public sphere.

Arts and culture

Along with legal, ethical, political, and social usage, the Pentateuch has been used extensively in the arts and broader cultural contexts.

The stories and characters of the Pentateuch have been the subject of countless works of art, from representations in sacred contexts such as stained glass and statues in churches to classical and modern depictions in more recognized works of art. Certain stories and events from the Pentateuch have proven especially fruitful for such work; here it is worth mentioning the near sacrifice of Isaac by Abraham in Genesis 22, which was painted by Caravaggio (1598) and Rembrandt (1634), among countless others. Other scenes which have received extensive attention in art include Adam and Eve in the Garden of Eden (Genesis 2–3), the flood account (Genesis 6–9), Jacob's wrestling match at the Jabbok river (Genesis 32), the parting of the sea in the exodus (Exodus 14), and Moses receiving the law on Sinai (Exodus 20).

The stories and characters of the Pentateuch have also found their way into literature (Wright 2007). Mark Twain wrote *The Diaries of Adam and Eve* (1904), humorous accounts given from the vantage points of Adam and Eve. John Steinbeck's *East of Eden* (1952) draws from the book of Genesis in a number of ways, including the title, which refers to Gen. 4.16, which speaks of Cain dwelling 'east of Eden' following the murder of his brother. Meir Shalev has written a novel called *Esau* (1991), a complex tale of family life in modern Israel based on the prototypes of the biblical brothers Jacob and Esau, exploring issues such as family rivalry and loyalty. Poets have also found inspiration in the pages of the Pentateuch. The American Muslim poet Mohja Kahf has drawn on the story of Hagar in her poem 'The First Thing', giving voice to immigrants and those who find themselves expelled into an unknown world.

The world of music has also drawn on the Pentateuch for inspiration. S. Dowling Long (2013), for example, has recently demonstrated how the *Akedah* of Genesis 22 has been used in music across various genres, from classical oratorios to contemporary cantatas. Other uses of Genesis include the musical *Joseph and Amazing the Technicolor Dreamcoat* (1968), written by Andrew Lloyd Webber and Tim Rice, based on the story of Joseph in Genesis 37–50, and Bruce Springsteen's 'Adam Raised a Cain' from the album *Darkness on the Edge of Town* (1978). Exodus motifs have also proved popular in music. One notable example is Bob Marley and the Wailers' album *Exodus* (1977), with a title track of the same name.

It is also worth noting the widespread influence of the Pentateuch in film and television. Some of the earliest films – including silent films – used the Bible as their subject matter, including stories from the Pentateuch such as Cain and Abel, Noah and the flood, and Moses and the exodus (Shepherd 2013). Over time, the story of Moses would be told and retold countless times in some of the past century's most famous movies: from Cecil B. DeMille's *The Ten Commandments* (1956), to the DreamWorks production *The Prince of Egypt* (1998), to Ridley Scott's blockbuster *Exodus: Gods and Kings* (2014), the story of Moses has been a tremendous draw for filmmakers. Meanwhile, the popular television show Lost (2004–2010) featured recurring characters named Jacob and Esau. These characters, whose portrayal on the show was enigmatic, nevertheless had a sibling rivalry and were representative of good and evil, echoing the story of Genesis and the later reception of Isaac's sons. Themes and tropes from the Pentateuch continue to emerge in interesting and surprising places in cultures – particularly Western – which have been influenced by the biblical traditions. K.B. Edwards (2012), for example, has drawn attention to the use of the Bible in advertising, and in particular the way in which Eve has become a symbol of both sexuality and consumer power in the contemporary world. Thus, the stories and characters of the Pentateuch continue to have an impact in our contemporary culture in ways we might not expect.

Concluding remarks

While much of our attention in this volume has been given to understanding and interpreting the texts and traditions of the Pentateuch, it is also vitally important to recognize the way in which these books, characters, and stories have been used down through the years, and the impact they have had in various times and places.

Most obviously, the Pentateuch has been used in the three religious traditions that trace their roots back to Abraham: Judaism, Christianity, and Islam. In all of these traditions, the stories, laws, and themes of the Pentateuch have shaped the liturgical and theological trajectories of these communities. And yet, while they share this heritage, there are very real differences in how these traditions understand, use, and interpret these first five books of the Bible. It is also clear that the legacy of the Pentateuch stretches far beyond the religious traditions for which it is sacred. Whether in legal and ethical debates, political and social movements, or artistic and cultural representation, the stories, characters, and themes of the Pentateuch have woven their way into the very fabric of many societies and cultures. From early Jewish rabbis and church fathers to twenty-first-century Hollywood filmmakers, these ancient texts have produced – and continue to produce – an astounding legacy. Such reception is an increasingly important part of the critical study of the Pentateuch.

Further reading

Helpful introductions to how Jews and Christians read and use the Torah can be found in Kaminsky and Lohr (2011). The relationship of the Bible (including Torah) and Islam is explored by Lambden (2006). Studies on the reception of the Bible and various parts therein are increasing exponentially. For the present subject, one might note works such as Hendel's (2013) 'biography' of the book of Genesis, and the study of the reception history of Exodus offered by Langston (2006).

Bibliography

Abegg, M.G., P. Flint, and E. Ulrich (2002), *The Dead Sea Scrolls Bible*, New York: HarperOne.

Achenbach, R. (2003), *Die Vollendung der Tora: Studien zur Redaktionsgeschichte des Numeribuches im Kontext von Hexateuch und Pentateuch*, BZABR 3, Wiesbaden: Harrassowitz.

Albertz, R. (2014), 'Wilderness Material in Exodus (Exodus 15–18)', in T.B. Dozeman, C.A. Evans, and J.N. Lohr (eds), *The Book of Exodus: Composition, Reception, and Interpretation*, VTSup 164, 151–68, Leiden: Brill.

Alexander, P.S. (1990), 'Akedah', in R. Coggins and J.L. Houlden (eds), *A Dictionary of Biblical Interpretation*, 44–7, London: SCM.

Alexander, T.D. (2012), *From Paradise to the Promised Land: An Introduction to the Pentateuch*, 3rd edn, Grand Rapids, MI: Baker Academic.

Alt, A. ([1934] 1966), 'The Origins of Israelite Law', in A. Alt (ed.), *Essays on Old Testament History and Religion*, 101–71, Oxford: Basil Blackwell.

Alter, R. (1981), *The Art of Biblical Narrative*, New York: Basic Books.

Alter. R. (2004), *The Five Books of Moses: A Translation with Commentary*, New York: Norton.

Anderson, B.A. (2011), *Brotherhood and Inheritance: A Canonical Reading of the Esau and Edom Traditions*, LHBOTS 556, London: T&T Clark.

Anderson, B.A. (2012), 'Edom in the Book of Numbers: Some Literary Reflections', *ZAW*, 124(1): 38–51.

Anderson, R.T. and T. Giles (2012), *The Samaritan Pentateuch: An Introduction to Its Origins, History, and Significance for Biblical Studies*, Atlanta, GA: SBL.

Arnold, B.T. (2008), *Genesis*, NCBC, Cambridge, MA: Cambridge University Press.

Assmann, J. (1997), *Moses the Egyptian: The Memory of Egypt in Western Monotheism*, Cambridge, MA: Harvard University Press.

Auerbach, E. (1953), *Mimesis: The Representation of Reality in Western Literature*, Princeton, NJ: Princeton University Press.

Bach, A. (1993), 'Good to the Last Drop: Viewing the Sotah (Numbers 5:11–31) as the Glass Half Empty and Wondering How to View It Half Full', in J.C. Exum and D.J.A. Clines (eds), *The New Literary Criticism and the Hebrew Bible*, 26–54, Sheffield: JSOT Press.

Bach, A. (1999), 'With a Song in Her Heart. Listening to Scholars Listening for Miriam', in A. Bach (ed.), *Women in the Hebrew Bible*, 419–27, London: Routledge.

Baden, J.S. (2009), *J, E, and the Redaction of the Pentateuch*, FAT 68, Tübingen: Mohr Siebeck.

Baden, J.S. (2012), *The Composition of the Pentateuch: Renewing the Documentary Hypothesis*, New Haven, CT: Yale.

Baden, J.S. (2013), *The Promise to the Patriarchs*, Oxford: Oxford University Press.

Baker, D.W. and B.T. Arnold, eds (1999), *The Face of Old Testament Studies: A Survey of Contemporary Approaches*, Grand Rapids, MI: Baker Academic.

Bakhos, C. (2006), *Ishmael on the Border: Rabbinic Portrayals of the First Arab*, New York: State University of New York Press.

Bakhos, C. (2014), *The Family of Abraham: Jewish, Christian, and Muslim Interpretations*, Cambridge, MA: Harvard University Press.

Barr, J. (1993), *The Garden of Eden and the Hope of Immortality*, Minneapolis, MN: Fortress.

Barr, J. (2006), 'Is God a Liar (Genesis 2–3)–and Related Matters', *JTS*, 57: 1–22.

Barrett, R. (2012), 'The Book of Deuteronomy', in R.S. Briggs and J.N. Lohr (eds), *A Theological Introduction to the Pentateuch: Interpreting the Torah as Christian Scripture*, 145–76, Grand Rapids, MI: Baker Academic.

Barton, J. (1996), *Reading the Old Testament: Method in Biblical Study*, rev. edn, Louisville, KY: Westminster John Knox.

Barton, J. (2003), *Understanding Old Testament Ethics: Approaches and Explorations*, Louisville, KY: Westminster John Knox.

Barton, S.C. and D. Wilkinson, eds (2009), *Reading Genesis after Darwin*, Oxford: Oxford University Press.

Beal, J., ed. (2014), *Illuminating Moses: A History of Reception from Exodus to the Renaissance*, Leiden: Brill.

Berman, J. (2011), 'CTH 133 and the Hittite Provenance of Deuteronomy 13', *JBL*, 131: 25–44.

Berner, C. (2014), 'Exodus, Book of', in C.-L. Seow, et al (eds), *EBR*, 8: 428–36.

Berquist, J.L. and C.V. Camp, eds (2008), *Constructions of Space II: The Biblical City and Other Imagined Spaces*, LHBOTS 490, New York: T&T Clark.

Bibb, B.D. (2009), *Ritual Words and Narrative Worlds in the Book of Leviticus*, LHBOTS 480, New York: T&T Clark.

Bird, P. (1981), '"Male and Female He Created Them": Gen. 1:27b in the Context of the Priestly Account of Creation', *HTR*, 74: 129–59.

Bledstein, A.J. (1993), 'Binder, Trickster, Heel and Hairy-Man: Re-reading Genesis 27 as a Trickster Tale Told by a Woman', in A. Brenner (ed.), *A Feminist Companion to Genesis*, 282–95, Sheffield: Sheffield Academic Press.

Blenkinsopp, J. (1988), *Ezra-Nehemiah: A Commentary*, Louisville, KY: Westminster John Knox.

Blenkinsopp, J. (1992), *The Pentateuch: An Introduction to the First Five Books of the Bible*, New York: Doubleday.

Blenkinsopp, J. (2002), 'A Post-exilic Lay Source in Genesis 1–11', in J.C. Gertz, K. Schmid and M. Witte (eds), *Abschied vom Jahwisten. Die Komposition des Hexateuch in der jüngsten Diskussion*, BZAW 315, 49–61, Berlin: de Gruyter.

Blenkinsopp, J. (2011), *Creation, Uncreation, Re-creation: A Discursive Commentary on Genesis 1–11*, New York: Continuum T&T Clark.

Blenkinsopp, J. (2015), *Abraham: The Story of a Life*, Grand Rapids, MI: Eerdmans.

Blum, E. (1984), *Die Komposition der Vätergeschichte*, WMANT 57, Neukirchen-Vluyn: Neukirchener Verlag.

Blum, E. (1990), *Studien zur Komposition des Pentateuch*, BZAW 189, Berlin: de Gruyter.

Blum, E. (2012), 'The Jacob Tradition', in C.A. Evans, J.N. Lohr, and D.L. Petersen (eds), *The Book of Genesis: Composition, Reception, and Interpretation*, VTsup 152, 181–211, Leiden: Brill.

Bolin, T. (2016), 'Out of the Wilderness? Some Suggestions for the Future of Pentateuchal Research', in I. Hjelm and T.L. Thompson (eds), *History, Archaeology, and the Bible Forty Years after 'Historicity'*, 47–59, London: Routledge.

Breed, B.W. (2014), *Nomadic Text: A Theory of Biblical Reception History*, Bloomington: Indiana University Press.

Brenner, A., ed. (1993), *A Feminist Companion to Companion Genesis*, Sheffield: Sheffield Academic Press.

Brenner, A., ed. (2000), *A Feminist Companion to Exodus–Deuteronomy*, Sheffield: Sheffield Academic Press.

Briggs, R.S. (2009), 'Reading the Sotah text (Numbers 5:11–31): Holiness and a Hermeneutic Fit for Suspicion', *Biblical Interpretation*, 17: 288–319.

Briggs, R.S. (2012), 'The Book of Genesis', in R.S. Briggs and J.N. Lohr (eds), *A Theological Introduction to the Pentateuch: Interpreting the Torah as Christian Scripture*, 19–50, Grand Rapids, MI: Baker Academic.

Briggs, R.S. and J.N. Lohr, eds (2012), *A Theological Introduction to the Pentateuch: Interpreting the Torah as Christian Scripture*, Grand Rapids, MI: Baker Academic.

Bright, J. ([1960] 2000), *A History of Israel*, 4th edn, Louisville, KY: Westminster John Knox.

Britt, B. (2004), *Rewriting Moses: The Narrative Eclipse of the Text*, LHBOTS 402, London: T&T Clark.

Brooke, G.J. (2005), *The Dead Sea Scrolls and the New Testament*, Minneapolis, MN: Fortress.

Brownson, J.V. (2013), *Bible, Gender, Sexuality: Reframing the Church's Debate on Same-Sex Relationships*, Grand Rapids, MI: Eerdmans.

Brueggemann, W. (1982), *Genesis*, IBC, Atlanta, GA: John Knox.

Brueggemann, W. (1995), 'Pharaoh as Vassal: A Study of a Political Metaphor', *CBQ*, 57: 27–51.

Brueggemann, W. (1997), *Theology of the Old Testament: Testimony, Dispute, Advocacy*, Minneapolis, MN: Fortress.

Byron, J. (2012), 'Cain and Abel in Second Temple Literature and Beyond', in C.A. Evans, J.N. Lohr, and D.L. Petersen (eds), *The Book of Genesis: Composition, Reception, and Interpretation*, VTsup 152, 331–51, Leiden: Brill.

Callender, D.E., ed. (2014), *Myth and Scripture: Contemporary Perspectives on Religion, Language, and Imagination*, Atlanta, GA: SBL.

Calvin, J. ([1554] 1850), *Commentaries on the First Book of Moses Called Genesis, vol. 2*, Edinburgh: Calvin Translation Society.

Calvin, J. ([1536] 1960), *Institutes of the Christian Religion*, Philadelphia, PA: Westminster.

Campbell, A. and M. O'Brien, M. (1993), *Sources of the Pentateuch: Texts, Introductions, Annotations*, Minneapolis, MN: Augsburg.

Carr, D.M. (1996), *Reading the Fractures of Genesis: Historical and Literary Approaches*, Louisville, KY: Westminster John Knox.

Carr, D.M. (2010), *Introduction to the Old Testament: Sacred Texts and Imperial Contexts of the Hebrew Bible*, Oxford: Blackwell.

Carr, D.M. (2011), *The Formation of the Hebrew Bible: A New Reconstruction*, New York: Oxford University Press.

Carr, D.M. (2014), *Holy Resilience: The Bible's Traumatic Origins*, New Haven, CT: Yale University Press.

Carr, D.M. (2015), 'Changes in Pentateuchal Criticism', in M. Saebo (ed.), *Hebrew Bible/Old Testament: The History of Its Interpretation*, Vol. 3.2, *The Twentieth Century*, 433–66, Göttingen: Vandenhoeck & Ruprecht.

Chancey, M.A., C. Meyer, and E. Meyers, eds (2014), *The Bible in the Public Square: Its Enduring Influence in American Life*, Atlanta, GA: SBL.

Charlesworth, J.H., ed. (1983), *The Old Testament Pseudepigrapha*, 2 vols, New York: Doubleday.

Childs, B.S. (1974), *Exodus: A Critical, Theological Commentary*, OTL, Louisville, KY: Westminster John Knox.

Childs, B.S. (1985), *Old Testament Theology in a Canonical Context*, Philadelphia, PA: Fortress.

Clifford, R.J. (2012), 'Genesis 37–50: Joseph Story or Jacob Story?', in C.A. Evans, J.N. Lohr, and D.L. Petersen (eds), *The Book of Genesis: Composition, Reception, and Interpretation*, VTsup 152, 213–29, Leiden: Brill.

Clines, D.J.A. (1968), 'The Image of God in Man', *Tyndale Bulletin*, 19: 53–103.

Clines D.J.A. (1990), 'The Ancestor in Danger: But Not the Same Danger', in D.J.A. Clines (ed.), *What Does Eve Do to Help? and Other Readerly Questions to the Old Testament*, 67–84, Sheffield: Sheffield Academic Press.

Clines, D.J.A. (1995), 'The Ten Commandments. Reading from Left to Right', in D.J.A. Clines (ed.), *Interested Parties: The Ideology of Writers and Readers of the Hebrew Bible*, 26–45, Sheffield: Sheffield Academic Press.

Clines, D.J.A. (1997), *The Theme of the Pentateuch*, 2nd rev. edn, JSOTSup 10, Sheffield: Sheffield Academic Press.

Clines, D.J.A. (2015), 'Contemporary Methods in Hebrew Bible Criticism', in M. Saebo (ed.), *Hebrew Bible/Old Testament: The History of Its Interpretation*, Vol. 3.2, *The Twentieth Century*, 148–69, Göttingen: Vandenhoeck & Ruprecht.

Coats, G.W. (1968), *Rebellion in the Wilderness: The Murmuring Motif in the Wilderness Traditions of the Old Testament*, Nashville, TN: Abingdon.

Coats, G.W. (1988), *Moses: Heroic Man, Man of God*, JSOTSup 57, Sheffield: JSOT Press.

Coffey, J. (2014), *Exodus and Liberation: Deliverance Politics from John Calvin to Martin Luther King Jr*, New York: Oxford University Press.

Collins, J.J. (2014), *Introduction to the Hebrew Bible*, 2nd edn, Minneapolis, MN: Fortress.

Crawford, S.W. (2007), 'The Use of the Pentateuch in the Temple Scroll and the Damascus Document in the Second Century B.C.E', in G.N. Knoppers and B.M. Levinson (eds), *The Pentateuch as Torah: New Models for Understanding Its Promulgation and Acceptance*, 301–17, Winona Lake: Eisenbrauns.

Cross, F.M. (1973), *Canaanite Myth and Hebrew Epic: Essays in the History of the Religion of Israel*, Cambridge, MA: Harvard University Press.

Cross, F.M. (1981), 'The Priestly Tabernacle in the Light of Recent Research', in A. Biran (ed.), *Temples and High Places in Biblical Times: Proceedings of the Colloquium in Honor of the Centennial of Hebrew Union College – Jewish Institute of Religion, Jerusalem, 14–16 March 1977*, 169–80, Jerusalem: Nelson Glueck School of Biblical Archaeology of Hebrew Union College – Jewish Institute of Religion.

Crouch, C.L. (2014), *Israel and the Assyrians: Deuteronomy, the Succession Treaty of Esarhddon, and the Nature of Subversion*, Atlanta, GA: SBL.

Dalton, R.W. (2015), *Children's Bibles in America: A Reception History of the Story of Noah's Ark in US Children's Bibles*, Scriptural Traces, London: Bloomsbury T&T Clark.

Davies, G.I. (1979), *The Way of the Wilderness: A Geographical Study of the Wilderness Itineraries in the Old Testament*, Cambridge, MA: Cambridge University Press.

Davies, G.I. (1992a), 'Sinai, Mount', in D.N. Freedman (ed.), *ABD*, 6: 47–9.

Davies, G.I. (1992b), 'Wilderness Wanderings', in D.N. Freedman (ed.), *ABD*, 6: 912–4.

Davis, E.F. (2009), *Scripture, Culture, and Agriculture: An Agrarian Reading of the Bible*, New York: Cambridge University Press.

Dawkins, R. (2006), *The God Delusion*, Boston, MA: Houghton Mifflin.

Day, J. (2013), *From Creation to Babel: Studies in Genesis 1–11*, London: Bloomsbury T&T Clark.

Douglas, M. ([1966] 2002), *Purity and Danger: An Analysis of the Concepts of Pollution and Taboo*, London: Routledge.

Douglas, M. (1993a), 'The Forbidden Animals in Leviticus', *JSOT*, 59: 3–23.

Douglas, M. (1993b), *In the Wilderness: The Doctrine of Defilement in the Book of Numbers*, Oxford: Oxford University Press.

Douglas, M. (1999), *Leviticus as Literature*, Oxford: Oxford University Press.

Dowling Long, S. (2013), *The Sacrifice of Isaac: The Reception of a Biblical Story in Music*, Sheffield: Sheffield Phoenix.

Dozeman, T.B. (2009), *Exodus*, Eerdmans Critical Commentary, Grand Rapids, MI: Eerdmans.

Dozeman, T.B., ed. (2010), *Methods for Exodus*, New York: Cambridge University Press.

Dozeman, T.B. (2011), 'The Priestly Wilderness Itineraries and the Composition of the Pentateuch', in T.B. Dozeman, K. Schmid, and B.J. Schwartz (eds), *The Pentateuch: International Perspectives on Current Research*, FAT 78, 257–88, Tübingen: Mohr Siebeck.

Dozeman, T.B. and K. Schmid (2006), *A Farewell to the Yahwist? The Composition of the Pentateuch in Recent European Interpretation*, SBLSymS 34, Atlanta, GA: SBL.

Dozeman, T.B., T. Römer, and K. Schmid, eds (2011), *Pentateuch, Hexateuch, or Enneateuch? Identifying Literary Works in Genesis through Kings*, Atlanta, GA: SBL.

Dozeman, T.B., C.A. Evans, and J.N. Lohr, eds (2014), *The Book of Exodus: Composition, Reception, and Interpretation*, VTSup 164, Leiden: Brill.

Edelman, D. (2012), 'Exodus and Pesach-Massot as Evolving Social Memory', in C. Levin and E. Ben Zvi (eds), *Remembering (and Forgetting) in Judah's Early Second Temple Period*, FAT 85, 161–93 Tübingen: Mohr Siebeck.

Edelman, D., P.R. Davies, C. Nihan, and T. Römer (2012), *Opening the Books of Moses*, BibleWorld, Sheffield: Equinox.

Edwards, K.B. (2012), *Admen and Eve: The Bible in Contemporary Advertising*, Sheffield: Sheffield Phoenix.

England, E. and W.J. Lyons (2015), *Reception History and Biblical Studies: Theory and Practice*, Scriptural Traces, London: Bloomsbury T&T Clark.

Evans, C.A., J.N. Lohr, and D.L. Petersen, eds (2012), *The Book of Genesis: Composition, Reception, and Interpretation*, VTSup 152, Leiden: Brill.

Exum, J.C. (1999), 'Who's Afraid of the Endangered Ancestress?', in A. Bach (ed.), *Women in the Hebrew Bible*, 141–58, London: Routledge.

Exum, J.C. (2016), *Fragmented Women: Feminist (Sub)versions of Biblical Narratives*, 2nd edn, London: Bloomsbury T&T Clark.

Exum, J.C. and J.W. Whedbee (1990), 'On Humour and the Comic in the Hebrew Bible', in Y.T. Radday and A. Brenner (eds), *On Humour and the Comic in the Hebrew Bible*, JSOTSup 92, 125–41, Sheffield: Almond Press.

Fewell, D.N. (1998), 'Changing the Subject: Retelling the Story of Hagar the Egyptian', in A. Brenner (ed.), *Genesis: A Feminist Companion to the Bible* (Second Series), 182–94, Sheffield: Sheffield Academic Press.

Fischer, I. ([1995] 2005), *Women Who Wrestled with God: Biblical Stories of Israel's Beginning*, Collegeville: Liturgical.

Fishbane, M. (1975), 'Composition and Structure in the Jacob Cycle (Gen. 25:19–35:22)', *JJS*, 26: 15–38.

Fishbane, M. (2003), *Biblical Myth and Rabbinic Mythmaking*, Oxford: Oxford University Press.

Firestone, R. (1989), 'Abraham's Son as the Intended Sacrifice (al-dhabih [Qur'an 37:99–113]): Issues in Qur'anic Exegesis', *JSS*, 89: 95–131.

Fleming, D.E. (2012), *The Legacy of Israel in Judah's Bible: History, Politics, and the Reinscribing of Tradition*, New York: Cambridge University Press.

Fokkelman, J.P. (1975), *Narrative Art in Genesis: Specimens of Stylistic and Structural Analysis*, Assen: Van Gorcum.

Fox, M.V. (2012), 'Joseph and Wisdom', in C.E. Evans, J.N. Lohr, and D.L. Petersen (eds), *The Book of Genesis: Composition, Reception, and Interpretation*, VTSup 152, 231–62, Leiden: Brill.

Freedman, D.N. (1962), 'Pentateuch', in *The Interpreter's Dictionary of the Bible*, 3:711–27, Nashville, TN: Abingdon.

Frei, P. (1984), 'Zentralgewalt und Lokalautonomie im Achämenidenreich', in P. Frei and K. Koch (eds), *Reichsidee und Reichsorganisation im Perserreich*, OBO 55, 7–43, Fribourg: Universitätsverlag.

Fretheim, T.E. (1988), *Exodus*, IBC, Louisville, KY: Westminster John Knox.

Fretheim, T.E. (1991), 'The Plagues as Historical Signs of Ecological Disaster', *JBL*, 110: 385–96.

Fretheim, T.E. (1994a), 'The Book of Genesis', in *The New Interpreter's Bible*, 1:319–674, Nashville, TN: Abingdon.

Fretheim, T.E. (1994b), 'Is Genesis 3 a Fall Story?', *Word and World*, 14(2): 144–53.

Fretheim, T.E. (1996), *The Pentateuch*, Nashville, TN: Abingdon.

Fretheim, T.E. (2010), *Creation Untamed: The Bible, God, and Natural Disasters*, Grand Rapids, MI: Baker Academic.

Fretheim, T.E. (2012), 'Genesis and Ecology', in C.E. Evans, J.N. Lohr, and D.L. Petersen (eds), *The Book of Genesis: Composition, Reception, and Interpretation*, VTSup 152, 683–706, Leiden: Brill.

Freud, S. (1939), *Moses and Monotheism*, New York: Random House.

Frevel, C. and C. Nihan, eds (2013), *Purity and the Forming of Religious Traditions in the Ancient Mediterranean World and Ancient Judaism*, Leiden: Brill.

Frevel, C., T. Pola, and A. Schart, eds (2013), *Torah and the Book of Numbers*, FAT II/62, Tübingen: Mohr Siebeck.

Friedman, R.E. (2003), *The Bible with Sources Revealed*, San Francisco, GA: HarperOne.

Gennep, A. van (1960), *The Rites of Passage*, Chicago, IL: University of Chicago Press.

George, M.K. (2009), *Israel's Tabernacle as Social Space*, Atlanta, GA: SBL.

Geraty, L.T. (2015), 'Exodus Dates and Theories', in T.E. Levy, T. Schneider, and W.H.C. Propp (eds), *Israel's Exodus in Transdisciplinary Perspective: Text, Archaeology, Culture and Geoscience*, 55–64, New York: Springer.

Gertz, J.C. (2000), *Tradition und Redaktion in der Exoduserzählung. Untersuchungen zur Endredaktion des Pentateuch*, Göttingen: Vandenhoeck & Ruprecht.

Gertz, J.C. (2011), 'Source Criticism in the Primeval History of Genesis: An Outdated Paradigm for the Study of the Pentateuch?', in T. Dozeman, K.

Schmid, and B. Schwartz (eds), *The Pentateuch: International Perspectives on Current Research*, FAT 78, 169–80, Tübingen: Mohr Siebeck.

Gertz, J.C. (2012), 'The Formation of the Primeval History', in C.E. Evans, J.N. Lohr, and D.L. Petersen (eds), *The Book of Genesis: Composition, Reception, and Interpretation*, VTSup 152, 107–36, Leiden: Brill.

Gertz, J.C. (2014), 'Elohist (E)', in C.-L. Seow, et al (eds), *EBR*, 7: 777–81.

Gertz, J.C., K. Schmid, and M. Witte, eds (2002), *Abschied vom Jahwisten. Die Komposition des Hexateuch in der jüngsten Diskussion*, BZAW 315, Berlin: de Gruyter.

Gertz, J.C., A. Berlejung, K. Schmid, and M. Witte (2012), *T&T Clark Handbook of the Old Testament: An Introduction to the Literature, Religion and History of the Old Testament*. London: T&T Clark.

Gillingham, S.E. (1998), *One Bible, Many Voices: Different Approaches to Biblical Studies*, London: SPCK.

Giuntoli, F. and K. Schmid, eds (2015), *The Post-Priestly Pentateuch: New Perspectives on Its Redactional Development and Theological Profiles*, FAT 101, Tübingen: Mohr Siebeck.

Goodman, M., G.H. van Kooten, and T.A.G.M. van Ruiten, eds (2010), *Abraham, the Nations and the Hagarites: Jewish, Christian, and Islamic Perspectives on Kinship with Abraham*, Leiden: Brill.

Gottwald, N.K. (1979), *The Tribes of Yahweh: A Sociology of Religion of Liberated Israel 1250–1050 BCE*, Maryknoll: Orbis.

Grabbe, L.L. (2014), 'Exodus and History', in T.B. Dozeman, C.A. Evans, and J.N. Lohr (eds), *The Book of Exodus: Composition, Reception, and Interpretation*, VTSup 164, 61–87, Leiden: Brill.

Green, A.R.W. (1975), *The Role of Human Sacrifice in the Ancient Near East*. Atlanta: Scholars Press.

Greenspahn, F.E. (1994), *When Brothers Dwell Together: The Preeminence of Younger Siblings in the Hebrew Bible*, Oxford: Oxford University Press.

Gudme, A.K.H. (2013), 'A Kind of Magic? The Law of Jealousy in Numbers 5:11–31 as Magical Ritual and as Ritual Text', in H.R. Jacobus, A.K.H. Gudme, and P. Guillaume (eds), *Studies on Magic and Divination in the Biblical World*, 149–67, Piscataway: Gorgias.

Gunkel, H. ([1901] 1964), *The Legends of Genesis: The Biblical Saga and History*, 6th edn, New York: Schocken.

Gunkel, H. ([1910] 1997), *Genesis*, trans. Mark E. Biddle, Macon: Mercer University Press.

Gunn, D.M. and D.N. Fewell (1993), *Narrative in the Hebrew Bible*, Oxford: Oxford University Press.

Gutiérrez, G. (1974), *A Theology of Liberation*, London: SCM.

Habel, N.C. (2009), *An Inconvient Text: Is a Green Reading of the Bible Possible?*, Adelaide: ATF Press.

Habel, N.C. (2011), *The Birth, the Curse and the Greening of Earth: An Ecological Reading of Genesis 1–11*, Sheffield: Phoenix.

Hackett, J.A. (1984), *The Balaam Text from Deir 'Alla*, Chico: Scholars.

Hagedorn, A.C. and R.G. Kratz, eds (2013), *Law and Religion in the Eastern Mediterranean: From Antiquity to Early Islam*, Oxford: Oxford University Press.

Harris, M. (2013), *The Nature of Creation: Examining the Bible and Science*, Oxford: Routledge.

Hauser, A.J. and D.F. Watson (2003), *A History of Biblical Interpretation*, Vol. 1, *The Ancient Period*, Grand Rapids, MI: Eerdmans.

Hauser, A.J. and D.F. Watson (2009), *A History of Biblical Interpretation*, Vol. 2, *The Medieval through the Reformation Periods*, Grand Rapids, MI: Eerdmans.

Hawting G. (2010), 'The Religion of Abraham and Islam', in M. Goodman, G.H. van Kooten, and T.A.G.M. van Ruiten (eds), *Abraham, the Nations and the Hagarites: Jewish, Christian, and Islamic Perspectives on Kinship with Abraham*, 477–501, Leiden: Brill.

Hays, C.B. (2014), *Hidden Riches: A Sourcebook for the Comparative Study of the Hebrew Bible and the Ancient Near East*, Louisville, KY: Westminster John Knox.

Hayward, C.T.R. (2012), 'Genesis and Its Reception in Jubilees', in C.E. Evans, J.N. Lohr, and D.L. Petersen (eds), *The Book of Genesis: Composition, Reception, and Interpretation*, VTSup 152, 375–404, Leiden: Brill.

Heard, R.C. (2001), *Dynamics of Diselection: Ambiguity in Genesis 12–36 and Ethnic Boundaries in Post-Exilic Judah*, Atlanta, GA: SBL.

Hendel, R. (2005), *Remembering Abraham: Culture, Memory and History in the Bible*, Oxford: Oxford University Press.

Hendel, R., ed. (2010), *Reading Genesis: Ten Methods*, Cambridge, MA: Cambridge University Press.

Hendel, R. (2011), 'Is the "J" Primeval Narrative an Independent Composition? A Critique of Crüsemann's "Die Eigenständigkeit der Urgeschichte"', in T.B. Dozeman, K. Schmid, and B.J. Schwartz (eds), *The Pentateuch: International Perspectives on Current Research*, FAT 78, 181–205, Tübingen: Mohr Siebeck.

Hendel, R. (2013), *The Book of Genesis: A Biography*, Lives of Great Religious Books, Princeton, NJ: Princeton University Press.

Hendel, R. (2015), 'The Exodus as Cultural Memory: Egyptian Bondage and the Song of the Sea', in T.E. Levy, T. Schneider, and W.H.C. Propp (eds), *Israel's Exodus in Transdisciplinary Perspective: Text, Archaeology, Culture* and *Geoscience*, 65–77, New York: Springer.

Hoffmeier, J. (2005), *Ancient Israel in Sinai: The Evidence for the Authenticity of the Wilderness Tradition*, Oxford: Oxford University Press.

Hughes, A.W. (2012), *Abrahamic Religions: On the Uses and Abuses of History*, Oxford: Oxford University Press.

Humphreys, W.L. (2001), *The Character of God in the Book of Genesis: A Narrative Appraisal*, Louisville, KY: Westminster John Knox.

Hurwitz, A. (1982), *A Linguistic Study of the Relationship between the Priestly Source and the Book of Ezekiel: A New Approach to an Old Problem*, Paris: Cahiers de la Revue Biblique.

Jacobs, M.R. (2007), *Gender, Power, and Persuasion: The Genesis Narratives and Contemporary Portraits*, Grand Rapids, MI: Baker Academic.

Johnstone, W. (1990), *Exodus*, Sheffield: Sheffield Academic Press.

Johnstone, W. (2003), 'The Revision of Festivals in Exodus 1–24', in R. Albertz and B. Becking (eds), *Yahwism after the Exile: Perspectives on Israelite Religion in the Persian Period*, 99–114, Assen: Van Gorcum.

Johnstone, W. (2014), *Exodus 1–19*, Macon: Smyth & Helwys.

Kaminsky, J.S. (2007), *Yet I Loved Jacob: Reclaiming the Biblical Concept of Election*, Nashville, TN: Abingdon.

Kaminsky, J.S. (2008), 'Loving One's (Israelite) Neighbor: Election and Commandment in Leviticus 19', *Interpretation*, 62(2): 123–32.

Kaminsky, J.S. and J.N. Lohr (2011), *The Torah: A Beginner's Guide*, Oxford: OneWorld.

Kartveit, M. (2009), *The Origin of the Samaritans*, VTSup 128, Leiden: Brill.

Kazen, T. (forthcoming), 'The Role of Law in the Formation of the Pentateuch and the Canon', in P. Barmash (ed.), *The Oxford Handbook of Biblical Law*, New York: Oxford University Press.

Klawans, J. (2000), *Impurity and Sin in Ancient Judaism*, Oxford: Oxford University Press.

Klawans, J. (2006), *Purity, Sacrifice, and the Temple: Symbolism and Supersessionism in the Study of Ancient Judaism*, Oxford: Oxford University Press.

Klein, R.W. (1996), 'Back to the Future: The Tabernacle in the Book of Exodus', *Interpretation*, 50(3): 264–76.

Knauf, E.A. (2010), 'Exodus and Settlement', in L.L. Grabbe (ed.), *Israel in Transition: From Late Bronze II to Iron IIA (ca. 1250–850 BCE), Vol. 2, The Text*, LHBOTS 521, 241–50, London: T&T Clark.

Knoppers, G.N. (2011), 'Parallel Torahs and Inner-Scriptural Interpretation: The Jewish and Samaritan Pentateuchs in Historical Perspective', in T.B. Dozeman, K. Schmid, and B.J. Schwartz (eds), *The Pentateuch: International Perspectives on Current Research*, FAT 78, 507–31, Tübingen: Mohr Siebeck.

Knoppers, G.N. (2013), *Jews and Samaritans: The Origins and History of Their Early Relations*, Oxford: Oxford University Press.

Knoppers, G.N. and B.M. Levinson, eds (2007), *The Pentateuch as Torah: New Models for Understanding Its Promulgation and Acceptance*, Winona Lake: Eisenbrauns.

Kratz, R.G. ([2000] 2005), *The Composition of the Historical Books of the Old Testament*, London: T&T Clark.

Kratz, R.G. (2011), 'The Pentateuch in Current Research: Consensus and Debate', in T.B. Dozeman, K. Schmid, and B.J. Schwartz (eds), *The Pentateuch: International Perspectives on Current Research*, FAT 78, 31–61, Tübingen: Mohr Siebeck.

Laffey, A. (1998), *The Pentateuch: A Liberation-Critical Reading*, Minneapolis, MN: Fortress.

Lambden, S.N. (2006), 'Islam', in J.F.A. Sawyer (ed.), *The Blackwell Companion to the Bible and Culture*, Oxford: Blackwell.

Langston, S.M. (2006), *Exodus through the Centuries*, Blackwell Bible Commentaries, Oxford: Blackwell.

Lapsley, J.E. (1998), 'The Voice of Rachel. Resistance and Polyphony in Genesis 31:14–35', in A. Brenner (ed.), *Genesis: A Feminist Companion to the Bible* (Second Series), 233–48, Sheffield: Sheffield Academic Press.

Lemmelijn, B. (2009), *A Plague of Texts? A Text-Critical Study of the So-Called 'Plagues Narrative' in Exodus 7:14–11:10*, Leiden: Brill.

Levenson, J.D. (1985), *Sinai and Zion: An Entry into the Hebrew Bible*, New York: Harper and Row.

Levenson, J.D. (1993a), *The Death and Resurrection of the Beloved Son: The Transformation of Child Sacrifice in Judaism and Christianity*, New Haven, CT: Yale.

Levenson, J.D. (1993b), *The Hebrew Bible, The Old Testament, and Historical Criticism: Jews and Christians in Biblical Studies*, Louisville, KY: Westminster John Knox.

Levenson, J.D. (2012), *Inheriting Abraham: The Legacy of the Patriarch in Judaism, Christianity, and Islam*, Princeton, NJ: Princeton University Press.

Levin, C. (1993), *Der Jahwist*, Göttingen: Vandenhoeck und Ruprecht.

Levine, B.A. (1993), *Numbers 1–20*, AB, New York: Doubleday.

Levine, B.A. (2000), *Numbers 21–36*, AB, New Haven, CT: Yale University Press.

Levine, B.A. (2003), *Leviticus*, JPSTC, Philadelphia, PA: Jewish Publication Society, 2003.

Levinson, B.M. (1997), *Deuteronomy and the Hermeneutics of Legal Revision*, Oxford: Oxford University Press.

Levinson, B.M. and J. Stackert (2012), 'Between the Covenant Code and Esarhaddon's Succession Treaty: Deuteronomy 13 and the Composition of Deuteronomy', *JAJ*, 3: 133–6.

Levy, T.E., T. Schneider, and W.H.C. Propp, eds (2015), *Israel's Exodus in Transdisciplinary Perspective: Text, Archaeology, Culture* and *Geoscience*, New York: Springer.

Lohfink, N. (1994), *Theology of the Pentateuch: Themes of the Priestly Narrative and Deuteronomy*, Edinburgh: T&T Clark.

Lohr, J.N. (2009), *Chosen and Unchosen: Concepts of Election in the Pentateuch and Jewish-Christian Interpretation*, Siphrut 2, Winona Lake: Eisenbrauns.

Lohr, J.N. (2012), 'The Book of Leviticus', in R.S. Briggs and J.N. Lohr (eds), *A Theological Introduction to the Pentateuch: Interpreting the Torah as Christian Scripture*, 83–112, Grand Rapids, MI: Baker Academic.

Lohr, J.N. (2015), 'Theology of Law', in B.A. Strawn (ed.), *The Oxford Encyclopedia of the Bible and Law*, Vol. 2, 374–84, Oxford: Oxford University Press.

Lundbom, J.R. (2013), *Deuteronomy: A Commentary*. Grand Rapids, MI: Eerdmans.

MacDonald, N. (2012a), 'The Book of Numbers', in R.S. Briggs and J.N. Lohr (eds), *A Theological Introduction to the Pentateuch: Interpreting the Torah as Christian Scripture*, 113–44, Grand Rapids, MI: Baker Academic.

MacDonald, N. (2012b), 'The Hermeneutics and Genesis of the Red Cow Ritual in Numbers 19', *HTR*, 105: 35–71.

MacDonald, N. (2013), 'A Text in Search of Context: The Imago Dei in the First Chapters of Genesis', in D. Baer and R.P. Gordon (eds), *Leshon Limmudim: Essays in the Language and Literature of the Hebrew Bible in Honour of A.A. Macintosh*, LHBOTS 593, 3–16, London: T&T Clark.

Matthews, V.H. and D.C. Benjamin (2006), *Old Testament Parallels: Laws and Stories from the Ancient Near East*, 3rd edn, Mahwah: Paulist.

McCarthy, D.J. (1978), *Treaty and Covenant: A Study in Form in the Ancient Oriental Documents and in the Old Testament*, 2nd edn, Rome: Biblical Institute.

Mendenhall, G.E. and G.A. Herion (1992), 'Covenant', in D.N. Freedman (ed.), *ABD*, 1: 1179–202.

Meyers, C. (1988), *Discovering Eve: Ancient Israelite Women in Context*, Oxford: Oxford University Press.

Meyers, C. (2005), *Exodus*, NCBC, Cambridge, MA: Cambridge University Press.

Middleton, J.R. (2005), *The Liberating Image: The Imago Dei in Genesis 1*, Grand Rapids, MI: Brazos.

Milgrom, J. (1990), *Numbers*, JPSTC, Philadelphia, PA: Jewish Publication Society.

Milgrom, J. (1993), 'The Rationale for Biblical Impurity', *JANES*, 22: 107–11.

Milgrom, J. (1998), *Leviticus 1–16*, AB, New York: Doubleday.

Milgrom, J. (2000), *Leviticus 17–22*, AB, New Haven, CT: Yale University Press.

Milgrom, J. (2001), *Leviticus 23–27*, AB, New Haven, CT: Yale University Press.

Miller, P.D. (1978), *Genesis 1–11: Studies in Structure and Theme*, JSOTSup 8, Sheffield: University of Sheffield.

Miller, P.D. (1990), *Deuteronomy*, IBC, Louisville, KY: John Knox.

Miller, P.D. (2000), 'God's Other Stories: On the Margins of Deuteronomic Theology', in P.D. Miller, *Israelite Religion and Biblical Theology: Collected Essays*, JSOTSup 267, 593–602, Sheffield: Sheffield Academic Press.

Miller, P.D. (2009), *The Ten Commandments*, Louisville, KY: Westminster John Knox.

Mirza, Y.Y. (2013), 'Ishmael as Abraham's Sacrifice: Ibn Taymiyya and Ibn Kathīr on the Intended Victim', *Islam and Christian-Muslim Relations*, 24(3): 277–98.

Moberly, R.W.L. (1988), 'Did the Serpent Get it Right?', *JTS*, 39(1): 1–27.

Moberly, R.W.L. (1992a), *Genesis 12–50*, OTG, Sheffield: Sheffield Academic Press.

Moberly, R.W.L. (1992b), *The Old Testament of the Old Testament: Patriarchal Narratives and Mosaic Yahwism*, Minneapolis, MN: Fortress.

Moberly, R.W.L. (2000), *The Bible, Theology, and Faith: A Study of Abraham and Jesus*, Cambridge, MA: Cambridge University Press.

Moberly, R.W.L. (2009), *The Theology of the Book of Genesis*, Cambridge, MA: Cambridge University Press.

Moberly, R.W.L. (2013), *Old Testament Theology: Reading the Hebrew Bible as Christian Scripture*, Grand Rapids, MI: Baker Academic.

Moshier, S.O. and J.K. Hoffmeier (2015), 'Which Way Out of Egypt? Physical Geography Related to the Exodus Itinerary', in T.E. Levy, T. Schneider, and W.H.C. Propp (eds), *Israel's Exodus in Transdisciplinary Perspective: Text, Archaeology, Culture* and *Geoscience*, 101–8, New York: Springer.

Moyise, S. (2013), *An Introduction to Biblical Studies*, 3rd edn, T&T Clark Approaches to Biblical Studies, London: Bloomsbury T&T Clark.

Moyise, S. (2015), *The Old Testament in the New: An Introduction*, 2nd edn, T&T Clark Approaches to Biblical Studies, London: Bloomsbury T&T Clark.

Na'aman, N. (2011), 'The Exodus Story: Between Historical Memory and Historiographical Composition', *Journal of Ancient Near Eastern Religions*, 11: 39–69.

Nicholson, E.W. (1998), *The Pentateuch in the Twentieth Century: The Legacy of Julius Wellhausen*, Oxford: Clarendon.

Niditch, S. (1987), *Underdogs and Tricksters: A Prelude to Biblical Folklore*, San Francisco, GA: Harper & Row.

Nihan, C. (2007), *From Priestly Torah to Pentateuch: A Study in the Composition of the Book of Leviticus*, FAT II/25, Tübingen: Mohr Siebeck.

Noth, M. ([1954] 1960), *The History of Israel*, London: A.C. Black.

Noth, M. ([1966] 1968), *Numbers*, London: SCM.

Noth, M. ([1948] 1972), *A History of Pentateuchal Traditions*, Englewood Cliffs: Prentice-Hall.

Noth, M. ([1943] 1981), *The Deuteronomistic History*, Sheffield: Sheffield Academic Press.

Olson, D.T. (1985), *The Death of the Old and the Birth of the New: The Framework of the Book of Numbers and the Pentateuch*, Atlanta, GA: Scholars.

Olson, D.T. (1996), *Numbers*, IBC, Louisville, KY: Westminster John Knox.

Otto, E. (2000), *Das Deuteronomium in Pentateuch und Hexateuch: Studien zur Literaturgeschichte von Pentateuch und Hexateuch im Lichte des Deuteronomiumrahmens*, FAT 30, Tübingen: Mohr Siebeck.

Otto, E. (2013), 'The Books of Deuteronomy and Numbers in One Torah', in C. Frevel, T. Pola, and A. Schart (eds), *Torah and the Book of Numbers*, FAT II/62, 383–97, Tübingen: Mohr Siebeck.

Pakkala, J. (2011), 'The Quotations and References of the Pentateuchal Laws in Ezra-Nehemiah', in H. von Weissenberg, J. Pakkala, and M. Marttila (eds), *Changes in Scripture: Rewriting and Interpreting Authoritative Traditions in the Second Temple Period*, BZAW 419, 193–221, Berlin: De Gruyter.

Patrick, D. (1985), *Old Testament Law*, Atlanta, GA: John Knox.

Person, R.F. and K Schmid, eds (2012), *Deuteronomy in the Pentateuch, Hexateuch, and the Deuteronomistic History*, FAT 56, Tübingen: Mohr Siebeck.

Pixley, G.V. (1987), *On Exodus: A Liberation Perspective*, Maryknoll: Orbis Books.

Pleins, J.D. (2003), *When the Great Abyss Opened: Classic and Contemporary Readings of Noah's Flood*, Oxford: Oxford University Press.

Pola, T. (1995), *Die ursprüngliche Priesterschrift: Beobachtungen zur Literarkritik und Traditionsgeschichte von Pg*, WMANT 70, Neukirchen-Vluyn: Neukirchener Verlag.

Pritchard, J.B., ed. (1969), *Ancient Near Eastern Texts Relating to the Old Testament*, 3rd edn, Princeton, NJ: Princeton University Press.

Propp, W.H.C. (1999), *Exodus 1–18*, AB, New York: Doubleday.

Rad, G. von ([1938] 1966), 'The Form Critical Problem of the Hexateuch', in G. von Rad, *The Problem of the Hexateuch and Other Essays*, 1–78. New York: Oliver and Boyd.

Rad, G. von ([1956] 1972), *Genesis: A Commentary*, OTL, London: SCM.

Rad, G. von ([1957] 1975), *Old Testament Theology*, London: SCM.

Reed, R.W. (2010), *A Clash of Ideologies: Marxism, Liberation Theology and Apocalypticism in New Testament Studies*, Eugene: Pickwick.

Rendsburg, G.A. (1988), 'The Egyptian Sun-God Ra in the Pentateuch', *Henoch*, 10: 3–15.

Rendtorff, R. ([1977] 1990), *The Problem of the Process of Transmission in the Pentateuch*, JSOTSup 89, Sheffield: Sheffield Academic Press.

Rendtorff, R. and J.A. Kugler, eds (2006), *The Book of Leviticus: Composition and Reception*, VTSup 93, Leiden: Brill.

Rogerson, J. (1974), *Myth in Old Testament Interpretation*, BZAW 134, Berlin: de Gruyter.

Rogerson, J. (1991), *Genesis 1–11*, OTG, Sheffield: Sheffield Academic Press.

Römer, T. (1990), *Israels Vater: Untersuchungen zur Vaterthematik im Deuteronomium und in der deuteronomistischen Tradition*, OBO 99, Freiburg and Göttingen: Vandenhoeck & Ruprecht.

Römer, T., ed. (2000), *The Future of the Deuteronomistic History*, Leuven: Peeters.

Römer, T. (2005), *The So-Called Deuteronomistic History: A Sociological, Historical, and Literary Introduction*, London: T&T Clark.

Römer, T. (2006), 'The Elusive Yahwist: A Short History of Research', in T.B. Dozeman and K. Schmid (eds), *Farewell to the Yahwist? The Composition of the Pentateuch in Recent European Interpretation*, SBLSymS 34, 9–27, Atlanta, GA: SBL.

Römer, T., ed. (2008), *The Books of Leviticus and Numbers*, BETL 215, Leuven: Peeters.

Römer, T. (2011a), 'How Many Books (teuchs): Pentateuch, Hexateuch, Deuteronomistic History, or Enneateuch?', in T.B. Dozeman, T. Römer, and

K. Schmid (eds), *Pentateuch, Hexateuch, or Enneateuch? Identifying Literary Works in Genesis through Kings*, 25–42, Atlanta, GA: SBL.

Römer, T. (2011b), 'Extra-Pentateuchal Biblical Evidence for the Existence of a Pentateuch? The Case of the "Historical Summaries"', in T.B. Dozeman, K. Schmid, and B.J. Schwartz (eds), *The Pentateuch: International Perspectives on Current Research*, FAT 78, 471–88, Tübingen: Mohr Siebeck.

Römer, T. (2013), 'Zwischen Urkunden, Fragmenten und Ergänzungen: Zum Stand der Pentateuchforschung', *ZAW*, 125(1): 2–24.

Römer, T. (2015), 'Moses and the Women in Exodus 1–4', *Indian Theological Studies*, 52: 237–50.

Roskop, A.R. (2011), *The Wilderness Itineraries: Genre, Geography, and the Growth of Torah*, Winona Lake: Eisenbrauns.

Roskop Erisman, A. (2012), 'Literary Theory and Composition History of the Torah: The Sea Crossing (Exod 14:1–31) as a Test Case', in K. Smelik and K. Vermeulen (eds), *Approaches to Literary Readings of Ancient Jewish Writings*, 53–76, Leiden: Brill.

Roskop Erisman, A. (2014), 'New Historicism, Historical Criticism, and Reading the Pentateuch', *Religion Compass*, 8(3): 71–80.

Rossing, B.R. (2011), 'Fourth Sunday in Creation: River Sunday', in N.C. Habel, D. Rhoads and H.P. Santmire (eds), *The Season of Creation: A Preaching Commentary*, 112–22, Minneapolis, MN, Fortress.

Rowland, C.C., ed. (2007), *The Cambridge Companion to Liberation Theology*, 2nd edn, Cambridge, MA: Cambridge University Press.

Rowley, H.H. (1950), *From Joseph to Joshua: Biblical Traditions in the Light of Archaeology*, London: Published for the British Academy by Oxford University Press.

Sacks, J. (2011), 'Bemidbar: The Space Between', available at http://www.rabbisacks.org/covenant-conversation-5771-bamidbar-the-space-between/.

Sarna, N.M. (1966), *Understanding Genesis: The Heritage of Biblical Israel*, New York: Jewish Theological Seminary.

Sarna, N.M. (1986), *Exploring Exodus: The Heritage of Biblical Israel*, New York: Schocken.

Sarna, N.M. (1989), *Genesis*, JPSTC, Philadelphia, PA: The Jewish Publication Society.

Sarna, N.M. (1991), *Exodus*, JPSTC, Philadelphia, PA: The Jewish Publication Society.

Sasson, J.M. (1992), 'The Gilgamesh Epic', in D.N. Freedman, *ABD*, 2: 1024–7.

Savran, G. (1994), 'Beastly Speech: Intertextuality, Balaam's Ass and the Garden of Eden', *JSOT*, 64: 33–55.

Schearing, L.S. and S.L. McKenzie, eds (1999), *Those Elusive Deuteronomists: The Phenomenon of Pan-Deuteronomism*, Sheffield: Sheffield Academic Press.

Schmid, K. (2002), 'Die Josephsgeschichte im Pentateuch', in J.C. Gertz, K. Schmid, and M. Witte (eds), *Abschied vom Jahwisten. Die Komposition des Hexateuch in der jüngsten Diskussion*, BZAW 315, 83–118, Berlin: de Gruyter.

Schmid, K. (2007), 'The Persian Imperial Authorization as Historical Problem and as Biblical Construct: A Plea for Differentiations in the Current Debate', in G.N. Knoppers and B.M. Levinson (eds), *The Pentateuch as Torah: New Models for Understanding Its Promulgation and Acceptance*, 22–38, Winona Lake: Eisenbrauns.

Schmid, K. ([1999] 2010), *Genesis and the Moses Story: Israel's Dual Origins in the Hebrew Bible*, Siphrut 3, Winona Lake: Eisenbrauns.

Schmid, K. (2015), 'Distinguishing the World of the Exodus Narrative from the World of Its Narrators: The Question of the Priestly Exodus Account in Its Historical Setting', in T.E. Levy, T. Schneider and W.H.C. Propp (eds), *Israel's Exodus in Transdisciplinary Perspective: Text, Archaeology, Culture* and *Geoscience*, 331–44, New York: Springer.

Schneider, T.J. (2008), *Mothers of Promise: Women in the Book of Genesis*, Grand Rapids, MI: Baker.

Schneider, T. (2015), 'Modern Scholarship versus the Demon of Passover: An Outlook on Exodus Research and Egyptology through the Lens of Exodus 12', in T.E. Levy, T. Schneider, and W.H.C. Propp (eds), *Israel's Exodus in Transdisciplinary Perspective: Text, Archaeology, Culture* and *Geoscience*, 537–53, New York: Springer.

Scholz, S. (1998), 'Through Whose Eyes? A "Right" Reading of Genesis 34', in A. Brenner (ed.), *Genesis: A Feminist Companion to the Bible* (Second Series), 150–71, Sheffield: Sheffield Academic Press.

Schungel-Straumann, H. (1993), 'On the Creation of Man and Woman in Genesis 1–3: The History and Reception of the Texts Reconsidered', in A. Brenner (ed.), *A Feminist Companion to Genesis*, 53–76, Sheffield: Sheffield Academic Press.

Schwartz, R.M. (1997), *The Curse of Cain: The Violent Legacy of Monotheism*. Chicago: University of Chicago Press.

Schwartz, B.J., D.P. Wright, J. Stackert, and N.S. Meshel, eds (2008), *Perspectives on Purity and Purification in the Bible*, LHBOTS 474, London: T&T Clark.

Schwartz, B.J. (2011), 'Does Recent Scholarship's Critique of the Documentary Hypothesis Constitute Grounds for Its Rejection?', in T.B. Dozeman, K. Schmid, and B.J. Schwartz (eds), *The Pentateuch: International Perspectives on Current Research*, FAT 78, 3–16, Tübingen: Mohr Siebeck.

Shectman, S. (2010), 'Bearing Guilt in Numbers 5:12–31', in J. Stackert, B.N. Porter, and D. Wright (eds), *Gazing on the Deep: Ancient Near Eastern, Biblical, and Jewish Studies in Honor of Tzvi Abusch*, 479–93, Bethesda: CDL Press.

Shepherd, D. (2008), 'Prolonging "The Life of Moses": Spectacle and Story in the Early Cinema', in D. Shepherd (ed.), *Images of the Word: Hollywood's Bible and Beyond*, 11–38; Atlanta, GA: SBL.

Shepherd, D. (2013), 'The Life of Moses (1909–1910)', in A. Reinhartz (ed.), *Bible and Cinema: Fifty Key Films*, 182–6, New York: Routledge.

Sheridan, M. (2002), *Genesis 12–50*, Ancient Christian Commentary on Scripture, 2, Downers Grove: InterVarsity.

Simkins, R.A. and S.L. Cook, eds (1999), *The Social World of the Hebrew Bible: Twenty-Five Years of the Social Sciences in the Academy*, Semeia 87, Atlanta, GA: SBL.

Ska, J.-L. (2006), *Introduction to Reading the Pentateuch*, Winona Lake: Eisenbrauns.

Smith, J.Z. (1992), *To Take Place: Toward Theory in Ritual*, Chicago, IL: University of Chicago Press.

Smith, M.S. (1997), *The Pilgrimage Pattern in Exodus*, JSOTSup 239, Sheffield: JSOT Press.

Sommer, B.D. (2015), *Revelation & Authority: Sinai in Jewish Scripture and Tradition*, New Haven, CT: Yale University Press.

Soulen, R.N. (2009), *Sacred Scripture: A Short History of Interpretation*, Louisville, KY: Westminster John Knox.

Stackert, J. (2007), *Rewriting the Torah: Literary Revision in Deuteronomy and the Holiness Legislation*, FAT 52, Tübingen: Mohr Siebeck.

Stackert, J. (2014), *A Prophet Like Moses: Prophecy, Law and Israelite Religion*, Oxford: Oxford University Press.

Stanley, C.D. (2010), *The Hebrew Bible: A Comparative Approach*, Minneapolis, MN: Fortress.

Sugirtharajah, R.S., ed. (2006), *The Postcolonial Biblical Reader*, Oxford: Blackwell.

Thompson T.L. (1974), *The Historicity of the Patriarchal Narratives: The Quest for the Historical Abraham*, BZAW 133, Berlin: de Gruyter.

Tigay, J.H. (1996), *Deuteronomy*, JPSTC, Philadelphia, PA: Jewish Publication Society.

Tov, E. (2011), *Textual Criticism of the Hebrew Bible*, 3rd edn, Minneapolis, MN: Fortress.

Trible, P. (1978), *God and the Rhetoric of Sexuality*, Philadelphia, PA: Fortress.

Trible, P. (1984), *Texts of Terror: Literary-Feminist Readings of Biblical Narratives*, Minneapolis, MN: Fortress.

Trible, P. (1991), 'Genesis 22: The Sacrifice of Sarah', in J.P. Rosenblatt and J.C. Sitterson (eds), *Not in Heaven: Coherence and Complexity in Biblical Narrative*, 170–91, Bloomington: Indiana University Press.

Trible, P. (1994), 'Bringing Miriam Out of the Shadows', in A. Brenner (ed.), *A Feminist Companion to Exodus to Deuteronomy*, 166–86, Sheffield: Sheffield Academic Press.

Turner, V. (1969), *The Ritual Process: Structure and Anti-Structure*, Chicago, IL: Aldine.

Ulrich, E. (2010), *The Biblical Qumran Scrolls: Transcriptions and Textual Variants*, VTSup 134, Leiden: Brill.

Utzschneider, H. (2015), 'Tabernacle', in T.B. Dozeman, C.A. Evans, and J.N. Lohr (eds), *The Book of Exodus: Composition, Reception, and Interpretation*, VTSup 164, 267–301, Leiden: Brill.

Van Seters, J. (1975), *Abraham in History and Tradition*, New Haven, CT: Yale University Press.

Van Seters, J. (1992), *Prologue to History: The Yahwist as Historian in Genesis*, Louisville, KY: Westminster John Knox.

Van Seters, J. (1994), *The Life of Moses: The Yahwist as Historian in Exodus-Numbers*, Louisville, KY: Westminster John Knox.

Van Seters, J. (1999), *The Pentateuch: A Social-Science Commentary*, Sheffield: Sheffield Academic Press.

Van Seters, J. (2013), *The Yahwist: A Historian of Israelite Origins*, Winona Lake: Eisenbrauns.

Watts, J.W. (1999), *Reading Law: The Rhetorical Shaping of the Pentateuch*, Sheffield: Sheffield Academic Press.

Watts, J.W., ed. (2001), *Persia and Torah: The Theory of Imperial Authorization of the Pentateuch*, Atlanta, GA: SBL.

Watts, J.W. (2005), 'Ritual Legitimacy and Scriptural Authority', *JBL*, 124(3): 401–17.

Watts, J.W. (2006), 'The Three Dimensions of Scriptures', *Postscripts*, 2: 135–59.

Watts, J.W. (2007), *Ritual and Rhetoric in Leviticus: From Sacrifice to Scripture*, Cambridge, MA Cambridge University Press.

Watts, J.W. (2011), 'Aaron and the Golden Calf in the Rhetoric of the Pentateuch', *JBL*, 130(3): 417–30.

Watts, J.W. (2013), *Leviticus 1–10*, Historical Commentary on the Old Testament, Leuven: Peeters.

Weinfeld, M. (1991), *Deuteronomy 1–11*, AB, New York: Doubleday.

Wellhausen, J. ([1883] 1885), *Prolegomena to the History of Israel*, Atlanta, GA: Scholars.

Wellhausen, J. (1899), *Die Composition des Hexateuchs und der historischen Bücher des Alten Testaments*, 3rd edn, Berlin: Reimer.

Wenham, G.J. (1979), *The Book of Leviticus*, New International Commentary on the Old Testament, 3, Grand Rapids, MI: Eerdmans.

Wenham, G.J. (1981), *Numbers*, Tyndale Old Testament Commentaries, Downers Grove: InterVarsity.

Wenham, G.J. (1987), *Genesis 1–15*, WBC 1, Waco: Word.

Wenham, G.J. (1995), *Genesis 16–50*, WBC 2, Waco: Word.

Wenham, G.J. (1997), *Numbers*, OTG, Sheffield, JSOT Press.

Wénin, A. (2001), *Studies in the Book of Genesis: Literature, Redaction, and History*, BETL 155, Leuven: Peeters.

West, G. (1990), 'Reading "The Text" and Reading "Behind the Text": The Cain and Abel Story in a Context of Liberation', in D.J.A. Clines, S.E. Fowl and S.E. Porter (eds), *The Bible in Three Dimensions: Essays in Celebration of Forty Years of Biblical Studies in the University of Sheffield*, 299–320, Sheffield: Sheffield Academic Press.

Westbrook, R. (1988), *Studies in Biblical and Cuneiform Law*, Paris: Gabalda.

Westermann, C. ([1982] 1986), *Genesis 37–50*, CC, Minneapolis, MN: Fortress.

Westermann, C. (1988), *Genesis*, Edinburgh: T&T Clark.

Westermann, C. ([1981] 1995), *Genesis 12–36*, CC, Minneapolis, MN: Fortress.

Westermann ([1990] 1996), *Joseph: Studies on the Joseph Stories in Genesis*, Edinburgh: T&T Clark.

Whybray, R.N. (1987), *The Making of the Pentateuch: A Methodological Study*, JSOTSup 53, Sheffield: JSOT Press.

Wijk-Bos, J. (2005), *Making Wise the Simple: The Torah in Christian Faith and Practice*, Grand Rapids, MI: Eerdmans.

Wright, D.P. (1992), 'Clean and Unclean (OT)', in D.N. Freedman (ed.), *ABD*, 6: 729–41.

Wright, D.P. (2009), *Inventing God's Law: How the Covenant Code of the Bible Used and Revised the Law of Hammurabi*, Oxford: Oxford University Press.

Wright, T.R. (2007), *The Genesis of Fiction: Modern Novelists as Biblical Interpreters*, Aldershot: Ashgate.

Yee, G.A. (2010), 'Postcolonial Biblical Criticism', in T.B. Dozeman (ed.), *Methods for Exodus*, 193–233, Cambridge, MA: Cambridge University Press.

Index of Biblical Texts

Subject and Author Index

Other titles in the T&T Clark Approaches
to Biblical Studies series include

50 Bedford Square	1385 Broadway
London	New York
WC1B 3DP	NY 10018
UK	USA

Printed in the USA
CPSIA information can be obtained
at www.ICGtesting.com
LVHW010943141123
763890LV00001B/63